MANIFEST YOUR POTENTIAL *in the* BAHÁ'Í FAITH

How the beliefs, practices, and vision of the Bahá'í Faith can change your life

NATHAN THOMAS

Written by Nathan Thomas

Cover design by Andrew Johnson

First Printing, 2013
ISBN: 978-1-939174-01-7

Greysands Media, LLC
www.greysandsmedia.com

THE WHYUNITE? SERIES BOOKS AND VIDEOS

MANY PATHS TO THE BAHÁ'Í FAITH
How people from different faith experiences discover fulfillment in the Bahá'í Faith

QUOTATIONS FOR MANY PATHS TO THE BAHÁ'Í FAITH
Selected passages from the Bahá'í holy writings and other materials

FIRESIDE TALK FOR MANY PATHS TO THE BAHÁ'Í FAITH
A video presentation about the Bahá'í Faith by the author, Nathan Thomas

MANIFEST YOUR POTENTIAL IN THE BAHÁ'Í FAITH
How the beliefs, practices, and vision of the Bahá'í Faith can change your life

QUOTATIONS FOR MANIFESTING YOUR POTENTIAL IN THE BAHÁ'Í FAITH
Selected passages from the Bahá'í holy writings and other materials

FIRESIDE TALK FOR MANIFESTING YOUR POTENTIAL IN THE BAHÁ'Í FAITH
A video presentation about the Bahá'í Faith by the author, Nathan Thomas

MAKING A BETTER WORLD WITH THE BAHÁ'Í FAITH
How Bahá'ís are transforming our world into a more unified, prosperous, and spiritual home for all mankind

QUOTATIONS FOR MAKING A BETTER WORLD WITH THE BAHÁ'Í FAITH
Selected passages from the Bahá'í holy writings and other materials

FIRESIDE TALK FOR MAKING A BETTER WORLD WITH THE BAHÁ'Í FAITH
A video presentation about the Bahá'í Faith by the author, Nathan Thomas

PATHS TO THE BAHÁ'Í FAITH
A nine-part collection of video interviews of Bahá'ís from a variety of backgrounds

TABLE OF CONTENTS

PREFACE TO THE WHYUNITE? SERIES

A NEW WORLD RELIGION DEDICATED TO TRANSFORMING HUMANITY

The Bahá'í Faith is a world religion that brings teachings designed to help all of mankind while renewing the spiritual capacities of the human race. Founded by Bahá'u'lláh (meaning "the Glory of God" in Arabic) in the mid-nineteenth century, the goal of the Bahá'í Faith is to bring out the best in humanity. As Bahá'u'lláh wrote, through the teachings of this worldwide faith "every man will advance and develop until he attaineth the station at which he can manifest all the potential forces with which his inmost true self hath been endowed." (*Gleanings from the Writings of Bahá'u'lláh,* no. 27.5).

With practical teachings, a diverse global community, acceptance for of all the world's religions, and a message specifically designed to solve humanity's most pressing needs, the Bahá'í Faith brings a contemporary approach to religion that is unique among all the world's faiths. Bahá'u'lláh writes, "My object is none other than the betterment of the world and the tranquility of its peoples." (*Gleanings from the Writings of Bahá'u'lláh,* no. 131.2).

Today millions of people from every background have found this Faith through the individual investigation of truth. For them, it offers a compelling and fulfilling foundation for their spiritual experience. As 'Abdu'l-Bahá, the son and successor of Bahá'u'lláh said, "Man must walk in many paths and be subjected to various processes in his evolution upward." (*Promulgation of Universal Peace,* p. 295). Throughout all these paths we take in our lives, every person must judge for him or herself what is good and true for their own spiritual journey. For many, that process leads to the Bahá'í Faith.

AN INVITATION TO LEARN MORE WITH THE WHYUNITE? SERIES

The WhyUnite? Series is an individual initiative begun to produce compelling, unique, and practical content about the Bahá'í Faith. Our goal is to develop materials that educate, empower, and inspire people to follow their own path to the truth, to manifest their own potential as spiritual beings, and to make this world a better place in the process. To that end, we are dedicated to the continuous development of books, compilations, videos, and more to help people discover the spiritual richness, endless diversity, and wondrous wisdom offered to humanity through the Bahá'í Faith. Learn more about our work and get involved at www.whyunite.com.

INTRODUCTION

CHAPTER 1:

WELCOME TO MANIFESTING YOUR POTENTIAL

"From among all created things He hath singled out for His special favor the pure, the gem-like reality of man, and invested it with a unique capacity of knowing Him and of reflecting the greatness of His glory."

—Bahá'u'lláh, *Gleanings from the Writings of Bahá'u'lláh,* no. 34.1.

UNTAPPED POTENTIAL

Human beings are incredible creatures. We look around and see people doing amazing things all the time. We see ordinary people serving others in extraordinary ways through teaching, healing, counseling, protecting, and coaching. We see people painting, dancing, and signing in every society and culture in the world. We see people conceiving, designing, building, and transforming our world through a continuous stream of innovations affecting every aspect of our lives. We see families striving together to overcome adversity and to create a better reality for the next generation. And the most wonderful thing is that each of us has the capacity to contribute to this process when we work to manifest our potential to the best of our ability.

Each of us is special, important, and unique. But because we are all so distinct, no one person can tell us how to manifest our potential. We cannot follow the paths of our parents, friends, preachers, political leaders, or heroes in this process. Each of us comes to this world at a unique time, with unique qualities, facing unique challenges and opportunities. And it is up to us to make the best of whatever we are given in this life.

Making the most of our lives starts with our beliefs about who we are, why we are here, and where we are going. If we open ourselves to the possibilities that there are deeper meanings in this world, higher purposes for our lives, and unlimited potential available to us if we call upon it, then we become an unstoppable force for change.

As we discover a higher purpose for our lives, then comes the hard work of transforming ourselves into something new and better in alignment with that purpose. As any great pianist, painter, inventor, entrepreneur, educator, author, doctor will tell you; greatness is never accidental. This work of bettering ourselves requires every ounce of our energy and focus. To get there, we have to overcome laziness, attachments, addictions, and apathy. We have to exercise our muscles of will-power, self-discipline, restraint, focus, detachment, and spiritual awareness. Lasting change comes from channeling our energies in our lives, spending our time accomplishing things that add value, practicing every day, picking ourselves up when we fall, and learning how to live well on a daily basis.

Yet this transformation into a more capable person is not complete if it is limited to our own selves. Manifesting our true potential comes when we put our capacity to work through helping, serving, loving, protecting, caring-for, educating, healing, and sacrificing for others. Serving others is the true path to freedom and progress for our souls.

This book offers you a modern approach to manifesting your potential through the beliefs, practices, and spiritual power of the Bahá'í Faith. This new world religion, brought to the world by Bahá'u'lláh, offers a prescription not just for humanity today, but for the future of all people. *Manifest Your Potential in the Bahá'í Faith* is about how people from all backgrounds and walks of life are finding their true inborn capacity to change and grow as spiritual beings in this cause. I invite you to find out if there is something here for you.

OBJECTIVES OF THE BOOK

This book uses the lens of what we call "the spiritual seeker" to explore many of the concepts of the Bahá'í Faith. The spiritual seeker is anyone who wants to find truth, meaning, and purpose in life. Anyone who questions the world around him or herself in an open and honest way is a spiritual seeker. Using the term to describe someone on a journey of spiritual self-discovery is helpful because it removes labels that are divisive or exclusive. It helps us free ourselves from what we think we are, or how we think we should be. It opens up the mind to the possibility that any one of us can be a spiritual seeker.

There are three objectives of this book. The first objective is to inspire people to live a more fulfilling life by looking at how spiritual seekers make sense of the world around them. The second objective is to look at how people realize their potential by examining how spiritual seekers channel their energies into refining their characters. The third objective is to examine how helping people discover true spiritual potential can transform the world by exploring ways in which spiritual seekers devote themselves to the betterment of humanity.

The first question is, "what makes a fulfilling life?" Fulfillment is a little hard to describe. Fulfillment, for the purposes of this book, is feeling that we matter. It is feeling complete, whole, and part of something bigger than our own selves. It is feeling connected to the world. Fulfillment is feeling as though our lives are important, that we have a purpose, and that we have work to do. Lastly, fulfillment comes from feeling as though we have achieved something that will endure.

So, the next question is: Where does fulfillment come from? Does a fulfilling life come from the quest for material things? Is it found in consumerism, materialism, and self-absorption? Will a new car, a new house, a new outfit, a new job, or a new college degree bring fulfillment? When do we feel satisfied? When can we say we are fulfilled from such things?

Anyone who has researched this question knows that these material attainments do not bring people lasting fulfillment. Instead, people find fulfillment in intrinsic things. People find fulfillment from healthy and loving relationships, from connections to others and to our community, from meaningful work and service in the world. Fulfillment comes when we matter to others in deeper ways. That is, fulfillment comes when we become a true friend, a spiritual servant, a loving guide, a supportive helpmate, and an inspiring companion through all of life's ups and downs, trials and tribulations, victories and successes.

The Bahá'í Faith provides guidance for many millions of people around the globe from every conceivable background to find fulfillment. Free of much of the baggage of history and tradition, the Bahá'í Faith offers a new approach to religion. It offers a fresh perspective on faith, community, and spirituality. It fuses the good elements of all the world's religious traditions into something new, fresh, and different. At the same time, it leaves out many of the elements that have divided humanity over the ages. It is a religion that teaches peace, unity, justice, and individual spiritual accountability. It is familiar to any person of faith from any spiritual background, but it is also unique and new to many others at the same time.

Many people find fulfillment in the Bahá'í Faith because it helps them discover their true capacity as spiritual beings. Its beliefs, practices, and vision for a better world help bring out the best in people. These elements teach us, refine us, discipline us, improve us, focus us, and drive us to make a difference in the world. The Faith oftentimes asks people to change their lives. It asks the spiritual seeker to alter his perspectives, to give up his prejudices, to abandon his unhealthy habits, and to rise to a higher standard of service to humanity. It asks the spiritual seeker to be more, to achieve more, and to matter more in the world. Spiritual seekers see in the Bahá'í Faith not only a fit for the lives that they live today, but a goal for the life they want to live in the future.

That's where the beliefs, practices, and vision of the Bahá'í Faith come into play. The beliefs help us see the world with spiritual eyes. The practices help us refine our character with spiritual qualities. And the vision of Bahá'u'lláh, which is the heart of what the Bahá'ís are working for in the world, helps us see how we can serve something greater than ourselves.

Through this process of transforming hearts, the Bahá'í Faith is changing the world. It is spreading ideas of unity, moderation, and tolerance. It offers basic moral education for children, spiritual training and devotionals for adults, and active paths to service for all people. The Bahá'ís are at the forefront of important causes such as the equality of women and men, universal education, elimination of prejudice, economic justice, religious unity, world peace, sustainable development, and spiritual awareness for all people. Through these efforts Bahá'ís are pouring their faith into action, their belief into service, and their spirit into a lasting legacy for all of humanity.

In reality, Bahá'ís believe this transformation of the world into something better is the ultimate purpose of all religious and spiritual development. As the Bahá'í writings state, "The purpose underlying the revelation of every heavenly Book, nay, of every divinely revealed verse, is to endue all men with righteousness and understanding, so that peace and tranquility may be firmly established amongst them. Whatsoever instilleth assurance into the hearts of men, whatsoever exalteth their station or promoteth their contentment, is acceptable in the sight of God. How lofty is the station which man, if he but choose to fulfill his high destiny, can attain! To what depths of degradation he can sink, depths which the meanest of creatures have never reached! Seize, O friends, the chance which this Day offereth you, and deprive not yourselves of the liberal effusions of His grace. I beseech God that He may graciously enable every one of you to adorn himself, in this blessed Day, with the ornament of pure and holy deeds. He, verily, doeth whatsoever He willeth." (Bahá'u'lláh, *Gleanings from the Writings of Bahá'u'lláh,* no. 101.1)

WHAT IS THE BAHÁ'Í FAITH?

The Bahá'í Faith is a new world religion started in the Middle East in the mid-1800s by a man known as Bahá'u'lláh. Bahá'u'lláh brought a message of peace, unity, equality, and spiritual awareness to all men. For that He was persecuted, imprisoned, and banished by authorities who feared His magnetic influence. Despite constant persecution, Bahá'u'lláh founded a worldwide community that today has millions of followers, and has spread to nearly every corner of the globe.

The Bahá'í Faith teaches that all the religions of the world are part of one religion of God, and that all people find fulfillment when they live up to their true spiritual capacity. It provides a path for people to live up to their potential through leading a moral lifestyle, cultivating a spiritual perspective, and working for a better world.

There is not just one holy book for the Bahá'í Faith. Instead there are many books that offer guidance and instruction. For example, Bahá'u'lláh wrote about the faith's basic theology in *The Book of Certitude* (*Kitáb-i-Íqán*), He wrote a series of passages that offer life-teachings called *The Hidden Words*, a work of mystical instructions called *The Seven Valleys*, and many other tablets, letters, prayers, and epistles.

The Bahá'í Faith has no clergy. Every Bahá'í is responsible for his or her own spiritual development. The affairs of the community are managed by small councils of people who serve in a spirit of service, and who are chosen regularly by the body of believers in a completely non-partisan election process at local, regional, national, and international levels. The global Bahá'í community is led by the Universal House of Justice, which is a council based in Haifa, Israel.

Bahá'ís are guided in their work by the vision of Bahá'u'lláh. The vision of Bahá'u'lláh is a world where war is outlawed, where every child receives an education, where there is no extreme poverty, where all men and women are treated as equals, where governance is focused on solving problems rather than holding onto power, and where faith and spirituality are focused on what brings us together rather than on what tears us apart. Bahá'ís work to make this world a reality through individual, family, community, and global efforts.

BOOK OVERVIEW

This book covers the beliefs, practices, and vision of the Bahá'í Faith. It explores how these elements help change us into more spiritual beings. Through this process, the book shows how spirituality offers us more fulfillment in life. In addition, the book shows how becoming more spiritual and finding true fulfillment in life can help transform our world into a better place.

Chapters 1 and 2 set the stage for the book, with an introduction to its content and an introduction to the Bahá'í Faith in general.

Part One of the book is focused on the beliefs of the Bahá'í Faith. These beliefs help us find our place in the world. They help inform, guide, and empower us in our lives. They give us perspective and insight into why we are here, where we are going, and how the universe all fits together.

Chapter 3 starts with a discussion of what makes a fulfilling life. It asks what makes a purposeful life? How do we grow spiritually? How do we find meaning in this world? And how can we leave a legacy for the generations to come that will truly endure?

Next, we have two chapters about God and religion. In Chapter 4 we explore the Bahá'í concept of God and how we develop a relationship with Him. In Chapter 5 we look at religion and why we need it. We separate true religion from falsehood, and explore the Bahá'í concept of a healthy, dynamic, and adaptive religious community that lifts people up and inspires them to become better in all aspects of their lives.

In Chapter 6 we look at life and death. We explore the concept of death, why it scares us, how we can prepare for it, and how to deal with the loss of our loved ones. We also explore the Bahá'í concept of the afterlife and we try to understand how knowing where we are going after we die should affect how we live today.

Chapters 7 and 8 look at happiness and detachment. Chapter 7 looks at how true happiness is a spiritual reality that comes from selflessness, openness, and choice in life. We explore how living a spiritual life can help us find a state of true happiness where we radiate joy and wonderment in all aspects of life. Next, in Chapter 8, we look at detachment and explore how we can free ourselves from all the attachments that hold us back while aligning ourselves with enduring and spiritual values that lift us up.

Chapter 9 looks at accountability and the Bahá'í approach to sins and forgiveness. It asks what is sin, how can we find forgiveness, why should we try to live up to a higher standard, and what does it mean to take responsibility for our own spiritual development?

Chapter 10 examines how we deal with tests and difficulties in life. It asks why we struggle to live a good life, what are the sources of tests, what are we supposed to learn from our trials and tribulations, and how can we reduce the suffering that we cause ourselves and others?

This brings us to Part Two of the book, which introduces the practices of the Bahá'í Faith that help us achieve success in our spiritual development. These practices involve daily, annual, and even once-in-a-lifetime duties that all Bahá'ís are supposed to strive to fulfill. Some obligations and standards are easier than others to live up to, but they are all important to our proper development as spiritual beings in today's modern age.

Chapter 11 introduces the concept of moderation in all things. It lays out the different forces that threaten to disrupt our spiritual nature, and it explores the concepts of balance, simplicity, wealth, and poverty. It then looks at how spiritual meaning can be found in any situation.

In Chapter 12, we cover the laws of the Bahá'í Faith. The book explores what the laws are and how Bahá'ís see them in their path toward spiritual perfection. It explores the purposes behind the different laws in terms of the spiritual qualities we are developing when we follow them. This chapter also offers tips for how we can better live up to high standards on a daily basis.

Chapters 13 and 14 cover prayer and meditation in the Bahá'í Faith. We ask about what to pray for, how to pray, and what is happening in the universe when we pray? In terms of meditation, we ask what form of meditation to follow, how meditation affects us, and what kinds of topics we can choose to meditate on?

Chapters 15 and 16 describe fasting and obligatory prayer. These two laws are some of the most important laws in the Bahá'í Faith. We explore the role of fasting in the Bahá'í Faith and how the act of fasting helps us mature as spiritual beings. Chapter 15 also offers tips for making fasting one of the most intense spiritual experiences of our year. In addition, we explore the law of obligatory prayer in the Bahá'í Faith. We talk about what the law of obligatory prayer is, what the prayers themselves are about, and how saying them every day helps us develop spiritually.

Chapter 17 describes the role of Bahá'í Pilgrimage in our spiritual development. It talks about where Bahá'ís go for pilgrimage, and the impact it can have on the individual and the community.

In Chapter 18 we explore the Bahá'í concept of marriage and family life. We look at the role of the family in society, and we offer insight for helping Bahá'ís achieve lasting success in their marriages and in raising responsible, ethical, and service-minded children.

Chapter 19 offers the Bahá'í perspective on work and careers. We ask what careers are most spiritual, how can we succeed in work and service, what should we work for, what should motivate us in our professions, and how we can be of service to others in the workplace.

Chapter 20 describes the lifetime approach that Bahá'ís take to educating themselves in all aspects of life, including in the study of the Bahá'í Faith. We look at what books are important in the Bahá'í Faith, where we start, and what attitude we show in our study. We explore all these questions and offer some tips for improving the quality and effectiveness of our study of the Bahá'í faith.

Finally, we close out Part Two of the book with Chapter 21, which is a look at teaching the Bahá'í Faith. We ask what teaching is, how it works, and how we can prepare ourselves to be most effective at it. We explore the benefits of teaching, and we offer some advice for our approach and perspective when teaching.

Part Three of the book explores the vision of Bahá'u'lláh and how that vision is changing things around us for the better. It focuses on our outward expression of faith through service to the world of humanity. It offers the elements of the Bahá'í Faith that help people find healing, purpose, and connection to a wider global community.

Chapter 22 describes the basic vision of Bahá'u'lláh as the foundation for the entire mission of the Bahá'í Faith. It is a vision that encompasses all aspects of life, and it is a vision that every Bahá'í strives to realize. The vision outlines the purpose of the Bahá'í cause, the objectives it is trying to achieve, and the methods the Bahá'ís employ in achieving them.

Chapter 23 explores the healing power of the Bahá'í community. It explains that Bahá'ís are not expected to be perfect, but that it is a community that is trying to perfect itself every day. Some individuals are farther along than others, but all are on that road to a better world together. This chapter describes how every community offers bounties and tests that Bahá'ís can learn from and appreciate.

Chapter 24 explores the Bahá'í Administrative Order and its basic structure, principles, and objectives. It offers insights into how Bahá'ís approach their religious organization, and how their Administrative Order inspires confidence, service, and love from the community.

Chapter 25 offers the powerful tool of Bahá'í consultation. The

Bahá'í concept of consultation is one of the faith's most valuable assets, and this chapter explores how it works, what it achieves, how it improves decision-making, and how it can aid effectiveness in a community.

In Chapter 26 we look back at the story of the Bahá'í Faith in order to see where the faith is going. Bahá'ís believe that studying history helps us appreciate the sacrifices made to get us here, and it helps us put our own efforts into a wider context. In this chapter we briefly explore the history of the faith and ask what we can learn as a community from every stage of our growth and development.

Chapter 27 describes the Bahá'í concept of world citizenship, which is one of the most important teachings for bringing about a peaceful planet. The vision of Bahá'u'lláh describes a time when people will think of themselves as citizens of the world before any other nationalistic or political allegiance. This chapter explores how this will change the world at a fundamental level.

Chapter 28 offers advice on overcoming common doubts that people of all spiritual paths might encounter. These can range from doubting the existence of God to doubting our capacity to live up to a higher standard. This chapter offers a perspective on the role of doubts in our spiritual development, and provides answers to some of the more common questions that people have about the Bahá'í Faith.

Finally, Chapter 29 explores some next steps for anyone interested in investigating the Bahá'í Faith, its teachings, and its community.

WHO IS THE SPIRITUAL SEEKER?

Throughout this book we will introduce the idea of the spiritual seeker. The spiritual seeker is our companion. The spiritual seeker has the following qualities that help us to see the path to spiritual awareness from a personal perspective. The spiritual seeker can be from any race, religion, gender, or cultural background.

- The spiritual seeker is a rational, open-hearted soul who just wants to live a better life and make a better world.
- The spiritual seeker is open to new ideas, new interpreta-

tions, and new ways of seeing the world.

- The spiritual seeker sees the world with common sense and is willing to consider anything that works and makes life better for people.
- The spiritual seeker is not imprisoned by any dogmas, superstitions, or prejudices that would hinder him from finding spiritual awareness or from realizing his full potential.

Therefore, as you read this book, you might see the spiritual seeker as someone you aspire to be. He may challenge you. He may inspire you. And he may offer you things to think about. And that is the point. The spiritual seeker is a fellow-traveler who will be looking at the paths that people take in their lives with a detached and open perspective.

DISCLAIMERS

As you read this book, you should be aware of a few points. First, what you are reading is just one point of view. It is one perspective of why people become Bahá'ís, one interpretation of the elements of the Bahá'í Faith that drive people to accept it, and one understanding of the vast array of paths that people tread in the spiritual search. It does not represent an authoritative or official interpretation of the Bahá'í Faith.

The fact is, there are no clergy in the Bahá'í Faith. There are no spiritual gurus, guides, ministers, or shamans who can tell you what you need to believe and how you need to practice your faith. In the Bahá'í Faith, we are all on our own spiritual journey. Each of us needs to read, study, pray, and understand for ourselves. Each of us is responsible for our own soul. This is a fundamental truth of the faith—that no mortal man can tell us what to believe. Therefore, we all have to search our own hearts for what is true for us. If we fail to do this, we may miss an opportunity to discover our true potential and purpose in life.

So as you read this book, keep an open mind. Compare what you read with your own interpretations of the Bahá'í writings. Investigate what the Bahá'í Faith says about these issues for yourself so you can make up your own mind and heart. This book should be seen as a beginning for your own spiritual investigation of the Bahá'í Faith, and never as an end in itself.

You should also realize that the stories used in this book are not meant to be historical. There are no names, places, or faces on the stories. They are not meant to be testimonials. Instead they are meant to be allegories and examples of paths that people have taken. They are meant to provide guide rails for those who want to understand some of the common paths people have taken to find the Bahá'í Faith.

With that said, let's explore why so many people from so many different backgrounds have become Bahá'ís. Let's also look at how becoming a Bahá'í is changing the lives of these people and changing the whole world at the same time.

CHAPTER 2:

WHAT IS THE BAHÁ'Í FAITH?

"The betterment of the world hath been the sole aim of this Wronged One."

—Bahá'u'lláh, *Epistle to the Son of the Wolf,* p. 36.

Before we get too far into why people seek spiritual truth, and how they do it, it may help to know a bit more about the Bahá'í Faith and what it is all about.

FACTS AND FIGURES

Today, the Bahá'í Faith has over five million members. It has established itself in over 100,000 localities in nearly every country and territory of the world. It has over 10,000 Local Spiritual Assemblies, which are democratically elected councils that run the local affairs of a community. Almost all the nations of the world have their own National Spiritual Assembly, which administers the affairs of the Bahá'í community on a national level. Bahá'í literature has been translated into more than 800 languages. Over 2,100 different tribes, races, and ethnic groups are represented among its membership. It is truly a cross-section of humanity working together to build a new world civilization founded on justice, universal love, and spiritual awakening.

TEACHINGS

The teachings of the Bahá'í Faith are both practical and profound. They offer guidance related to the spiritual, social, theological, and personal aspects of life.

The spiritual teachings of the Bahá'í Faith are many. They include the concepts that we are all connected; that physical reality is a material reflection of spiritual truths; that we must live in balance with our world; that we must show moderation in all things; that there is an afterlife; and that our spirits are continually progressing, developing, learning, and growing toward God throughout an endless existence.

The social teachings of the Bahá'í Faith provide guidance on how to get along. They teach us about the fundamental unity of all mankind, that men and women are equal, and that justice is the foundation of all society. Bahá'ís are taught that education is critical to the spiritual and material development of humankind; that science and religion must be in harmony; and that all people must be treated with love, dignity, and respect.

The Bahá'í Faith offers a historical perspective that ties all the world's major religions together into one continuous and unified story of faith. The Bahá'í Faith teaches that all faiths are part of a single faith of God, and that divisions, disunity, and disharmony amongst peoples of different faiths are due to misunderstandings, misinterpretations, and the limitations of man. Bahá'ís believe Bahá'u'lláh—the faith's Founder—represents the fulfillment of every major religious prophecy of the past, and that the day in which we live is a glorious Day of Fulfillment that has long been awaited by mankind. The arrival of the Day signifies the fact that humanity has reached its collective age of maturity as a species and must decide if it is to become spiritual, or if it will not. If we chose wisely, we can become so much more as a human race. If we delay our spiritual awakening, we will drift further and further astray into war, disunity, and self-inflicted suffering.

It is a day of decision and of judgment for all of humanity. We have the tools to bring all mankind out of the darkness of ignorance and greed. But we also have the tools to destroy all life on our entire planet, pollute it beyond recognition, and reduce existence to the meaningless pursuit of dust through materialism. The decision is ours.

The Bahá'í writings state, "Great indeed is this Day! The allusions made to it in all the sacred Scriptures as the Day of God attest its greatness. The soul of every Prophet of God, of every Divine Messenger, hath thirsted for this wondrous Day. All the divers kindreds of the earth have, likewise, yearned to attain it." (Bahá'u'lláh, *Gleanings from the Writings of Bahá'u'lláh*, no. 7.2.)

BAHÁ'Í LAWS AND OBLIGATIONS

The Bahá'í Faith has many moral and personal teachings that apply on a unique level. The faith brings high standards for living that Bahá'ís strive to attain on a daily basis. These include laws against backbiting, stealing, showing prejudice, fornication, adultery, and consuming alcoholic and intoxicating substances that can hinder our spiritual development. There are also daily duties, which include prayer and meditation. In addition, there are annual duties such as fasting and the observance of holy days. There are other obligations such as attending the nineteen-day feast (a community gathering), contributing to the Bahá'í fund (note: only Bahá'ís can contribute to the Bahá'í fund), serving the poor and needy, and treating work as worship.

The Bahá'í standards are very high and many Bahá'ís spend a lifetime struggling to live up to them. The Bahá'í laws are not about avoiding fire and brimstone or eternal damnation. The laws are seen as providing protection, preservation, and assistance for us in our spiritual, personal, and material development.

Bahá'u'lláh wrote of His laws and ordinances that we should "obey them with joy and gladness, for this is best for you, did ye but know." (Bahá'u'lláh, The *Kitáb-i-Aqdas*, ¶148.)

LITERATURE

There are a number of books containing the writings of the central figures of the Bahá'í Faith that shed a great deal of light on the key elements of the faith. They include: *The Book of Certitude* by Bahá'u'lláh, *The Hidden Words* by Bahá'u'lláh, *Some Answered Questions* by 'Abdu'l-Bahá, and *Bahá'í Prayers*. More information about these books can be found online, including at www.whyunite.com.

HISTORY OF THE BAHÁ'Í FAITH

The Bahá'í Faith started in the mid-1800s in Iran. It essentially began in 1844 when a man Who called Himself The Báb (meaning "the Gate" in Arabic) announced Himself to be a Prophet Whose purpose was to prepare the world for the coming of the Promised One of All Ages. The Báb gathered a group of followers, who became known as Bábís, to spiritualize themselves so they could immediately recognize, accept, and follow the Promised One when He declared Himself. For daring to challenge the entrenched and powerful religious leaders of the age, the Bábís were ruthlessly persecuted, imprisoned, and murdered. The Báb Himself was martyred in 1850.

The Day of Fulfillment came in 1863 when Bahá'u'lláh (meaning "the Glory of God") declared that He was the Promised One that the world had been waiting for. Bahá'u'lláh claimed to bring a new religion to the world founded on equality, peace, justice, and spiritual development for all of humanity. While many souls accepted the Bahá'í Faith and devoted their lives to spreading its message throughout the world, most of the authorities of Persia and the Ottoman Empire felt threatened by the new religion and worked actively to oppress its adherents and inflict an endless amount of abuse and torment upon Bahá'u'lláh and His family. Bahá'u'lláh was banished from city to city throughout the Middle East. However, because Bahá'u'lláh became known widely for His wisdom, tolerance, and magnanimity, and because He touched the hearts and souls of all with whom He came in contact, His banishments ultimately served to bring more people into the Bahá'í Faith and spread its message farther than would have been possible had He remained in Persia.

After the passing of Bahá'u'lláh in 1892, He appointed His eldest son, 'Abdu'l-Bahá (meaning "Servant of the Glory") to lead the Bahá'í community. 'Abdu'l-Bahá then guided and led the development of the worldwide community until his own passing in 1921. 'Abdu'l-Bahá's example of kindness, charity, and wisdom were known far and wide. He wrote many tablets and books, and traveled to Europe and throughout America helping to educate, develop, and empower the growing Bahá'í communities of the West. Today, 'Abdu'l-Bahá's life is a continuing source of inspiration to Bahá'ís.

In his Will and Testament, 'Abdu'l-Bahá designated his grandson, Shoghi Effendi, as the Guardian of the faith. The purpose of the institution of the Guardianship was to help guide the Bahá'í community and interpret the word of God for humanity. Shoghi Effendi was the first and only Guardian of the Bahá'í Faith, and his writings continue to be a living source of inspiration, wisdom, and insight for the Bahá'ís of the world. He provided great insight into what the Bahá'í Faith means in the world, how it should operate, and how Bahá'ís can make a difference through service to the cause.

Today the Bahá'í world operates under the guidance of the Universal House of Justice—an institution that Bahá'u'lláh Himself ordained to be the governing body of His faith, and which 'Abdu'l-Bahá further elaborated upon in His Will and Testament. The Universal House of Justice was first elected in 1963 and has inspired, guided, and governed the affairs of the Bahá'í world ever since.

ORGANIZATION

In order to channel its efforts and resources and in an effort to build a new just global society, the Bahá'í Faith has a dynamic and adaptive system of organization. This unique system helps transfer knowledge, develop collective wisdom, harness the full capacities of its membership, mitigate individual weaknesses, divide up the work of building a new global society, and give everyone a lasting legacy for their efforts. The Bahá'í Faith is the only independent religion in the world that had its organization clearly laid out for it by its Founder. Because of this, the community has remained free of splits or schisms within its structure.

There is no clergy or professional religious class in the Bahá'í Faith. This is both a blessing and a challenge. It is a blessing in that the community is less likely to be taken over by charismatic figures who would use it to further their own personal agenda, divided by divisive politics that would sap its capacity to make a difference in the world, or constantly undermined by intrigue and conflict that could hinder it from moving forward.

The challenge of being an all-volunteer administrative order is that it is up to the general population to get things done. While staff is employed by some of the faith's institutions to take care of specific tasks and fulfill important technical, professional, and administrative functions at regional, national, and international levels, most of the day-to-day work of growing, deepening, and building this new world community is taken care of by volunteers at the local level. The fact is, Bahá'ís are simply a collection of diverse (and imperfect) individuals trying to figure things out one day at a time. It is a long process of spiritual maturation for any Bahá'í who is called to serve in the faith's administrative order.

As Bahá'u'lláh wrote of His Faith's organization, "Mankind's ordered life hath been revolutionized through the agency of this unique, this wondrous System—the like of which mortal eyes have never witnessed." (Bahá'u'lláh, *Gleanings from the Writings of Bahá'u'lláh,* no. 70.1.)

THE COVENANT

One interesting fact is that over the years, the Bahá'í Faith has never been successfully split into different sects or divisions. While a few have tried to break the unity of the Bahá'í Faith, Bahá'ís believe that their faith will never be successfully divided. As some people investigate the Bahá'í Faith, especially on the Internet, they may come across some small groups of people who are trying to divide the faith. The fact is, these groups have never been successful in dividing the faith into sects and schisms. This is not just because their arguments are inadequate and divisive in nature, but because safeguards against division were built into the very structure of the faith by its Founder.

Bahá'ís believe the faith is protected by what is termed the *Covenant of Bahá'u'lláh*. This Covenant is an agreement that unites the entire Bahá'í world under the guidance of its designated leadership. The succession of authority within the faith has been explicitly laid out in writing starting with the pen of Bahá'u'lláh Himself. The clear and unalterable Covenant established by Bahá'u'lláh is unique among all of the world's faiths. All other religions and communities have been broken into countless sects, schools, schisms, and divisions. These divisions, which have caused endless wars and suffering for humanity, have been safeguarded against by the farsighted vision of Bahá'u'lláh and the Covenant He established.

In this way, the Bahá'í Faith offers hope to a divided mankind that this religion will not be the cause of more disunity in the world, and will represent, as Baha'u'llah wrote, "the Day that shall not be followed by night ..." (Bahá'u'lláh, *The Summons of the Lord of Hosts,* p. 34.)

WHAT IS BAHÁ'Í COMMUNITY LIFE LIKE?

Whenever people investigate the Bahá'í Faith they want to know what they are signing up for. People are busy, and they want to know what kind of time commitment is expected. Bahá'ís have nineteen separate meetings a year when the local community comes together in what is called a Feast. There are nineteen of them because the Bahá'í calendar year is made up of nineteen months of nineteen days each. The Nineteen-Day Feast happens at the start of each Bahá'í month.

The Nineteen-Day Feast has three portions: devotional, administrative, and social. The devotional portion usually consists of some prayers, readings, and songs chosen by the host for that evening. The administrative portion usually has news, announcements, and consultation about issues the community is facing. And the social portion usually involves some refreshments and fellowship. Each portion is considered an integral part of the Feast.

There are also a number of Holy Days throughout the year when Bahá'ís gather for celebrations and commemorations associated with the lives of the central figures of the faith. While participating in community events is seen as an important source for inspiration and edification in our own spiritual development, Bahá'ís are free to choose what events to attend, initiatives to support, and activities to participate in based on their time and energy. Bahá'ís are encouraged to have study classes and introductory meetings in their homes and communities, as well as to hold children's classes, and devotional meetings. There are also various summer schools, weekend seminars, and training institutes on a variety of subjects that Bahá'ís are often engaged in.

Being a Bahá'í should not be a burden. Instead, it should be a foundational guide that underlies, directs, balances, and motivates people to be of service in all aspects of their lives.

As Baha'u'llah wrote, "We, verily, have come to unite and weld together all that dwell on earth." (Bahá'u'lláh, *Epistle to the Son of the Wolf*, p. 24)

WHAT IS THE VISION OF BAHÁ'U'LLÁH?

It is the vision of Bahá'u'lláh that truly binds the Bahá'í community together. This vision is the ultimate solution to the problems, the sufferings, and the divisions in humanity. At its core the vision of Bahá'u'lláh is very simple. It is essentially to build a better world that is united in love and compassion for all mankind—a world finally at peace with itself, where war is outlawed and it is everyone's collective responsibility to keep and enforce peace. It is a world that is balanced through principles of equality between the sexes and unity across all racial, social, and cultural boundaries. It is a world where no one is above anyone else in spirit. It is a world where every soul is dedicated to revealing its nobility by striving for high morals in all endeavors. It is a world devoted to providing an education and an opportunity to every child. It is a world of moral integrity and uprightness, where people act with dignity and treat others with respect at all times. It is a world where the family unit is the foundation of all society, and its preservation, unity, and strength are critically important to everyone. It is a world without extremes of poverty or wealth, where everyone gets a fair chance to make an honest living and contribute to the well-being of society. It is a world that is inspired by a deep sense of spirituality in all things and that appreciates and cares for our natural environment by harnessing the bonds of love that hold the universe together. It is a world full of justice for all, with a new global system founded on spiritual principles that is designed to solve problems, get things done, ensure fairness, dispense justice, avoid gridlock and corruption, and take care of the needs of all of humanity.

This is the vision of Bahá'u'lláh. This is the world Bahá'ís strive to create. To many, this vision sounds utopian and unrealistic. In an age of cynicism, corruption, and moral degeneracy, the vision of Bahá'u'lláh seems almost alien, impossible, and inconceivable.

But Bahá'ís are not afraid to dream or set high goals. The vision of Bahá'u'lláh is a goal. And yet, even though it is an expansive and wondrous goal, His vision provides a practical and realistic path to achieving that goal. Each of us can find a role to play in getting us there. Each of us can make a contribution that matters. It starts in our hearts, in our actions, and in our individual contribution to something bigger than our own selves.

As Baha'u'llah wrote, "The whole human race hath longed for this Day, that perchance it may fulfill that which well beseemeth its station, and is worthy of its destiny." (Bahá'u'lláh, *Gleanings from the Writings of Bahá'u'lláh,* no. 16.1.)

BECOMING A BAHÁ'Í

To become a Bahá'í a person accepts Bahá'u'lláh as the Manifestation of God for this Age. This acceptance comes with a recognition that all the religions of God come from the same source and that each faith brings guidance and wisdom for humanity that meet the needs of society. This acceptance does not negate religions of the past. Instead, it connects and fulfills them. Many people who become Bahá'ís, therefore, do not abandon their love for the faith they grew up with. Instead, they expand that love to encompass all the faiths of God. This is not a blind acceptance though. It is often the conclusion of a heartfelt examination of the teachings, beliefs, practices, and vision of this faith and its potential impact for society. It is a conclusion that people come to by examining the fruits of this faith. It is a realization that the guidance offered by Bahá'u'lláh to humanity offers the surest path to a fulfilling life in this day and age. They join this world community and contribute to this Cause that works for justice, peace, prosperity, and the unity of all mankind because they believe it is the mandate of God for this time.

As the Bahá'í writings state, "This is the Day in which God's most excellent favours have been poured out upon men, the Day in which His most mighty grace hath been infused into all created things. It is incumbent upon all the peoples of the world to reconcile their differences, and, with perfect unity and peace, abide beneath the shadow of the Tree of His care and loving-kindness. It behoveth them to cleave to whatsoever will, in this Day, be conducive to the exaltation of their stations, and to the promotion of their best interests." (Bahá'u'lláh, *The Proclamation of Bahá'u'lláh,* p. 120)

PART I: BELIEFS

CHAPTER 3:

ACCEPTING A PRACTICAL CONCEPT OF GOD

"The vitality of men's belief in God is dying out in every land; nothing short of His wholesome medicine can ever restore it. The corrosion of ungodliness is eating into the vitals of human society; what else but the Elixir of His potent Revelation can cleanse and revive it?"

—Bahá'u'lláh, *Gleanings from the Writings of Bahá'u'lláh,* no. 99.1

STARTING WITH GOD

Many of us find it hard to talk about God. This is because many people have had mixed experiences with religion, God, and spiritual matters. Some of us might be afraid to offend others with discussions of things that are deep or controversial. Others may be afraid of being preached at in response, and so they never raise their spiritual questions because they do not want people telling them what to believe. Some may be afraid to share their beliefs for fear of being branded a fanatic. Some may not want to be written off as a fool by people they respect. Others are not comfortable with talking about things they just do not understand. Many people are not even sure of what they believe in the first place.

The human experience provides a seemingly infinite variety of paths of faith and belief in the world. Some people come from a religious background that gives them strong morals and firm foundations of beliefs and understandings to live by. But others have been disenchanted with the concept of God or the idea of organized religion, and so they are not sure what to keep and what to leave behind when it comes to finding their own way in spiritual matters.

Some people have investigated various churches, communities, and faiths. They have asked the hard questions. They have given other paths a chance to convince them, to embrace them, and to inspire them. In this process, they have had varying degrees of success. Others have thrown out the whole idea of God and religion altogether. They have decided to go their own way and make their own path in life without any spiritual or religious insight. Still others have collected beliefs, ideas, and understandings that they like without committing to one path or another.

In the end, faith is an intensely personal matter. Most of us want to believe that whatever helps one get through life is probably good. Many of us do not want anyone else's faith pushed on us, and so we do not push the subject on anyone else. We may also know that some people of strong faith are often branded as extremists, fanatics, or otherwise "abnormal" people. So oftentimes we avoid any discussions that might make us appear strange.

For many, it is a lot easier to just do what everyone else does and avoid the whole subject. It is simpler to just believe what our parents and friends believe. The path of least resistance is often the path of acceptance of whatever people tell us about religion, faith, and God. Unfortunately, this path denies our ability to search, to discover, and to manifest our true capacity to grow, develop, and mature as spiritual beings in the world.

The spiritual seeker strives to overcome all these fears of being different. The spiritual seeker is someone who is not afraid to ask questions about God, religion, faith, history, science, living, and dying all in the same breath. The spiritual seeker has overcome his fear of not knowing all the answers all the time. The spiritual seeker is open to new questions, new challenges, and new experiences. The spiritual seeker is someone who is ready to have the conversation, no matter where it takes him. Once a person has become a spiritual seeker he is ready to ask the hard questions.

ARGUMENTS FOR THE EXISTENCE OF GOD

One of the first questions a spiritual seeker might ask is, "What is God?" Is believing in God a philosophical idea that our rational minds struggle to bring meaning and purpose to? Or is it more about believing in mystical forces beyond our comprehension? Is it an emotional feeling that cries out in our heart for fulfillment? Or is it a hope for something more than this material existence? Is it a trust in some higher authority that brings justice and love? Or is it a choice that some decide is worth the risk of giving their spirits over to, and others do not? The questions above are important to explore when investigating the question of God.

There are a few who believe in God strictly because of philosophical reasoning. They may go through long and detailed ontological, cosmological, teleological, and moral arguments. They may weigh all the pros and cons and come to the conclusion that there must be, might be, or could be a God.

That is, some may come to the conclusion that the universe needs a First Cause to get it going, as nothing comes from nothing. They may look at the intricate complexity of the universe and come to the conclusion that there must be a designer setting it all in motion, as one does not logically find order without something or someone to impose that order. They could come to the conclusion that because they can conceive of a Being beyond their existence that there must be one, otherwise people would have no need to conceive of it. In addition, they may analyze human history and come to the conclusion that the source of all morality, right and wrong, and all such universal truths in the world comes from some source of moral authority. They may conclude that humans on their own could not invent such concepts if they were mere animals. They might recognize that there must be a source for the universal truths that transcends all religions, cultures, and societies throughout history.

The spiritual seeker enjoys the philosophical arguments, but is often left wanting. He knows that belief is not something that can be proven 100% one way or another. Otherwise there would be no choice or free will in faith. The spiritual seeker believes that logic and reason is often just a tool we use to justify the things we want in our heart. Countless studies have proven that people bend reason to fit their desires. The fact is, logical reasoning can be twisted in any way we want. Even the most terrible person in the world can invent reasons why they need to oppress others. So for the spiritual seeker, logic alone is an imperfect solution. It is just one tool in the toolbox of the spiritual seeker to be balanced with other tools of the heart and spirit.

On the other hand, many other people find God through emotion. They find God when they fill their heart with love instead of hate, when they fill their mind with hope instead of discouragement, and when they fill their spirit with courage instead of fear. They find God when they fill up their lives with the power that comes from faith in the divine.

Emotion-based belief in God can power our hearts like no other feeling. It can fill us with a love that is perfect, unfailing, and ever-present. It can fill us with a hope that guides and inspires us to carry on no matter how hard the task. It can fill us with courage that gives us the strength to overcome our self-doubt. It can fill us with wisdom that helps us understand why things happen, and inspire us to find meaning and learn lessons from whatever life throws at us.

But the spiritual seeker believes the power of emotion is also imperfect on its own. Emotions can lead people to throw off reality. Emotion can lead people to superstition, dogma, and blind obedience. The spiritual seeker sees the need to balance those emotions in our lives. Without a logical center, a core to his emotional heart, he knows that he will drift from one feeling to another without any sense of up or down, right or wrong, or true or false.

Some people believe in God because they sense mystical forces in the universe. They may not be able to explain it or even describe it, but they have a sense that there is something more, something greater, something loving and abiding in all things. This mystical feeling comes from the spirit.

The spiritual seeker feels this mystical presence at various times in his life. He feels it when he stands atop a mountain and looks in awe over the majesty of the lands below. He feels it when he holds the tiny hands of a newborn baby. He feels it when he walks alone along the ocean beach with the sand between his toes and waves calling his soul back to the infinite source beyond the horizon. He feels it when surrounded by good-hearted people working together in service of mankind. He feels it when he hears a preciously moving song that stirs the inmost pangs of his heart. He feels it when he lives, breathes, and thinks at a higher level. But mysticism is also imperfect on its own. It can lead a person to make false connections and poor decisions if it is not informed with logic and reason, or is not powered by empathy and love for mankind.

In addition to those who take logical, emotional, and mystical paths to belief, there are those who come to believe in God because they sense worlds beyond this one. They come to believe that this material world of matter and substance is a reflection of something deeper. They recognize that this life is a transient existence. They realize that their material accomplishments and possessions do not last, and that all that endures is the spirit that transcends this material world. They may come to the realization that all things are momentary glimpses of divine truths, and that our job in this life is to transcend this world of changes and chances in order to find God inside our hearts.

In addition to the reasons above, some may believe in God because they need to know that there is justice in the world. They see the pain, loss, and suffering of mankind, and they believe that it must be set right. They have to believe that those who abuse, murder, and deceive their fellowman will be held accountable. They have to believe that those who live lives of sorrow and loss will be redeemed. They have to believe that there is a balance, a judge, and an ultimate standard by which all life is measured. It comes from an inborn need to see righteousness in the world, and this drives them to seek a God that can provide that order.

Toward that end, the spiritual seeker believes that he must work every day to bring as much goodness into the world as he can. But he also knows he cannot solve every problem, heal every wound, and warm every heart on his own. He knows that he cannot punish the sinners and redeem the suffering. The spiritual seeker leaves the ultimate balancing of the world to God. Without this belief in God he would be lost, hopeless, and cynical. He would be overwhelmed by the endless suffering and infinite capacity of mankind to inflict evil on others. Without a strong conviction that what he is doing is part of something bigger in the Universe, he would not be able to wake up in the morning and keep going.

The truth is, belief in God has taken many forms throughout human history. It is a phenomenon that crosses cultural, racial, gender, and geographic boundaries. It is something that people have always struggled to define. Many of the greatest thinkers, philosophers, scientists, politicians, humanitarians, theologians, mystics, and leaders of men throughout human history have grappled with this question.

A PRACTICAL APPROACH

The spiritual seeker takes a practical approach to belief in God. The question for the spiritual seeker is not what belief is, but rather what it does for us. If belief in God makes the world better, if it brings out the best in people, if it orders society, if it inspires greatness in even the meekest of persons, and if it results in powerful acts of sacrifice for our fellowman, then it is a choice to live a better life.

Some people see the superstitions, the blind obedience, the empty acceptance, and the collective subservience that has been called *belief in God* over the ages and they are rightly suspicious of the concept. They have seen how men of evil and corrupt inclinations have used this concept of belief to abuse, manipulate, and deceive people over the ages in the name of God. They see this misuse of the capacity to believe as a sign that belief in God itself is not good or healthy.

But the spiritual seeker thinks this is a false analysis. The spiritual seeker does not blame the teacher for the acts of the student. It is not the teacher's fault if the student chooses not to follow the guidance of the teacher. For the spiritual seeker, the divine teachers of humanity included Jesus, Moses, Muhammad, the Buddha, Krishna, and Zoroaster. They came into the world and told us to be truthful, kind, and righteous. They taught us to love one another, to respect one another, to tolerate one another, and to live well. If we choose not to follow that guidance, then whose fault is that?

Therefore, for belief in God to be healthy, it must result in something good. For the spiritual seeker, belief in God is belief in that which makes us better people. It is that which makes us truly happy, content, and stronger in our lives. It is that which inspires us to make up our own mind and not follow whatever we are told. It brings us fulfillment and peace of mind. It brings meaning and purpose to our existence. For the spiritual seeker, this kind of belief in God changes us, refines our character, and gives us a path of faith to follow that makes us better people.

Therefore, the spiritual seeker does not believe in a false god. He does not believe in a figment of his imagination that fits his desires, his needs, and his wishes. The spiritual seeker does not believe in a god that is like Santa Clause or the Tooth Fairy. It is not a petty god who is jealous, irrational, and unjust. The spiritual seeker does not believe in a god that does not make sense or who does things to spite people. He also does not believe in a god that never lets bad things happen or that does not let humanity have free will. He does not believe in a god that is detached from our world and that does not care about the fortunes of mankind.

This is because the spiritual seeker believes in a practical concept of God. The God the spiritual seeker believes in is a God that brings clarity and purpose. It is a God that is present in our lives and at home in our hearts. It is a wise, loving, powerful, and just concept of God. This is a concept of God that is restrained and lets us make choices and decide our own fate. It is a God that redeems and renews those who suffer and punishes those who inflict harm. It is a merciful God Who is forgiving, understanding, and caring. It is a God Who continuously revives our spirits through His love for all mankind.

The spiritual seeker believes in a concept of God that brings peace to his heart. He has a personal connection to this source. He believes he was created to have a relationship with God. For the spiritual seeker, belief in God is the beginning of understanding his own self. When he finds God, he find his own center, out of which all created things find their proper balance and orbit in his life. He discovers the connections between all things. He finds the unity of creation that ties and binds all of humanity together in a rich tapestry of meaning and purpose.

Lastly, the spiritual seeker believes in God because it brings accountability for his actions. It provides a measure for his life by which he can hold his actions, his thoughts, and his desires to a higher authority. For the spiritual seeker, there is final accountability for everything he is. Without God, the spiritual seeker can find no contentment. He cannot see a bigger picture for why he exists, what his purpose is in life, and where he is going as a spiritual being.

THE BAHÁ'Í CONCEPT OF GOD

Many spiritual seekers have found the Bahá'í concept of God to be a refreshing and fulfilling clarification of what it means to believe in God. Bahá'ís believe in God as an unknowable essence, and that if a creation could ever truly know the essence of its Creator it would be equal to it.

Just as a table can never comprehend its craftsman, a painting can never truly appreciate its painter, and a clock can never understand its watchmaker, humanity can never really *know* the essence of its Creator. But we can know of the existence of God through His creation. We can learn about God through His qualities. His qualities are revealed to us in all aspects of creation and through the revelation revealed by the Manifestations, or Prophets, of God Who came into the world to tell us about Him and to provide guidance for human advancement.

Bahá'ís believe in a God that can be discovered through His qualities—qualities that include all the virtues and capacities that make humanity noble. These include love, kindness, mercy, forgiveness, wisdom, tolerance, understanding, and reverence, and so on. When we know these qualities, we know God. When we exhibit these qualities, we become more like God, we fashion ourselves in His image, and we manifest our true potential as spiritual beings. One important point to mention is that God's qualities can also be discovered through scientific discovery of His Universe. That is, science and religion are considered to be in total agreement in the Bahá'í Faith. And so when we only follow science without religion, we fall into materialism and selfishness. And when we follow religion without science, we can fall into superstition and dogma. Therefore, from the Bahá'í perspective, science and religion balance each other and are both necessary.

In reality, both science and religion are necessary for our proper development. As the Bahá'í writings state, "Out of the wastes of nothingness, with the clay of My command I made thee to appear, and have ordained for thy training every atom in existence and the essence of all created things." (Bahá'u'lláh, *The Hidden Words*, Persian, no. 29)

The problem of interpretations arises when we start to ask whose miracles were best? Was Jesus healing the sick and feeding the multitude greater than Moses' parting the sea or the Buddha taming the elephant?

From a spiritual perspective, many of the stories of miracles from the religions of the world can be interpreted in a way that that illustrates spiritual concepts. While Bahá'ís believe that God is capable of anything, many of us interpret those stories as figurative in order to find more relevant meanings. For example, perhaps Jesus healed spiritual sicknesses and fed people with spiritual food? Perhaps Moses split the two great communities between the faithful and the faithless? And perhaps the Buddha tamed the animal instincts of his followers and brought them inner peace? These are spiritual interpretations that do not ask followers to believe in magic to make sense of them.

The interpretation of religious stories can be critical in giving us direction in our lives. Otherwise, miracles are only good for people who see them. But even then, not everyone who supposedly saw the miracles of Jesus, Moses, and the Buddha went on to believe in their faiths. So it is not clear what benefit such magical interpretations of miracles would have for the faith of men. In the end, believing in God is healthier for us when we focus on the spiritual qualities revealed in the world through the stories and instructions offered by the Manifestations of God. When we do this, we are not imprisoned by superstition and dogma, and we can develop a balanced and rational belief in God.

FINDING DIVINE LOVE

The spiritual seeker finds that this concept of God is like a love story. It starts differently in every heart. For some it hits us like a thunderbolt. For others, it creeps up and surprises us. In any event, such love challenges us. It transforms us. It pulls us out of our comfort zone and forces us to be more than we were before. It helps us discover new levels of awareness and understandings. It inspires us to appreciate the world around us when we stand in awe of creation. Through this process, we feel close to God when we worship His beauty, His majesty, and the wondrous universe that He has created for us to explore and understand.

But the spiritual seeker believes that any relationship takes effort to develop, cultivate, and maintain. Love requires something of us in order to become real. It requires that time and energy be invested in communing, meditating, and manifesting our devotion through acts of service for our Beloved. It requires renewal and change as we grow and develop as spiritual beings. That is, as we learn new things, discover new capacities, and master new talents and abilities, we need to keep our relationship with our Beloved balanced and constant. We need to take God with us throughout our journey in this life.

The spiritual seeker believes that this love is at the core of all existence. He recognizes that the entire universe was created to enable this relationship between Creator and created. Everything exists for this love story to play itself out in our hearts. God has hidden Himself in the inmost reality of all things, and the spiritual seeker spends his life discovering and manifesting each quality of God in his life in order to fulfill his destiny and reflect God's light.

Finally, the spiritual seeker believes that love only becomes real when it becomes action. Love for God becomes real when we serve God's creatures. Otherwise, this love is just words. And words without action are meaningless. Of course, service takes many forms. For many, serving the efforts of the Bahá'í Faith is an effective path to showing the love for God that they feel in their hearts. They see realizing the goals of peace, justice, love, unity, and equality as paths of realizing love for God.

As the Bahá'í writings state, "I loved thy creation, hence I created thee. Wherefore, do thou love Me, that I may name thy name and fill thy soul with the spirit of life." (Bahá'u'lláh, *The Hidden Words*, Arabic, no. 4)

THE LOGICAL MAN AWAKENED BY LOVE

There was a logical young man who did not believe in God. His parents were engineers, and he grew up with a very practical and scientific outlook on life. His parents were also humanitarians, however. His father was a man of deep conviction who treated everyone with respect. And his mother was a woman of great tenderness who taught him to show compassion and care for all people.

As the young man grew up, he investigated some aspects of religion but found them simplistic and superstitious. He did not think he needed to believe in God to be a good person. He did not need hope of getting into heaven to make him do the right things in life. Reason and logic taught him that he had to do his best to make the world a better place. For him, that was enough. He became involved in many causes of social justice and environmental preservation, and he did not need any concept of God to tell him to be of service to those causes.

Yet, in college, the young man had a classmate in one of his science classes who was a Bahá'í. The man was intrigued by the fact that such a rational, clear-headed, and good-hearted person could be deluded by the superstitious belief in a deity. He took it upon himself to free his Bahá'í friend of his delusions. In the process, the two young men had many long, involved, and profound debates about the existence of God.

To the logical young man's surprise, the Bahá'í did not try to defend the fantastical stories of religions to make his case. Instead, the Bahá'í was reasonable, logical, and rational. The young man left those conversations impressed with his Bahá'í friend's conviction and approach, but it did not change his mind. He still did not believe in God. He did, however admit that if he ever did believe in God, he would want to know more about this Bahá'í Faith.

Many years later, the logical man had a successful career as an engineer. He raised a family of his own and traveled to many places in the world. He supported many causes over his lifetime and was of service to many people. In the process, the man's mind opened to new ideas and new ways of thinking. He developed an appreciation for art, music, and nature that he fostered in his children. He became less dogmatic in his belief that science could solve all of mankind's problems. He had seen its limitations to inspire people.

Instead, the man came to believe that the human spirit could achieve amazing things and that there had to be some kind of power that transcended nature. He realized that life was not always as black and white as he had thought when he was younger. He recognized that some coincidences could not be explained by chance, that some of the wonders of the universe were too improbable to be random occurrences, and that the love that he felt for his family was something that he could not quantify or measure. He came to believe that there was something more to this world than what the senses could perceive.

One day the man ran into his old Bahá'í friend at a conference. This time the logical man was less skeptical. He was more open. He wanted to hear the Bahá'í explanations again. And this time those explanations made more sense to him. He was open to the idea that science and religion could balance one another. He was open to the guidance that we can set aside superstitions and traditions and instead focus on the spiritual truths at the heart of scripture. And he was open to the concept that our Universe has underlying mystical purposes and meanings that we can discover with a logical, balanced, and moderate approach. He told his friend that now he was ready to believe in something more in this world, and that he might want to become a Bahá'í.

Once he opened his spiritual eyes he saw God in all things. His realized that his scientific approach had been a spiritual expression of an inner longing to find meaning and purpose in the universe. As he grew in his faith, his belief in God grew and evolved as well. He still supported his causes and worked to make a difference in the world. Now, however, it was for a bigger cause. He started to see himself as a spiritual being trying to make a spiritual contribution to the world through science and service.

Of course, accepting God was not easy for the man. He still had many questions. But as his personal faith grew, his new belief in God eventually became something that grounded him. He never felt as though he *needed* God. Instead, he *wanted* God. He wanted to be a part of something bigger than himself. He wanted to pass something good and enduring on to his children that gave them standards to strive for, beliefs to ground them, and a vision to realize in the world. He wanted to know that his consciousness, his reality, and his very soul were transcendent above and beyond the material senses. To him, this helped him bring his artistic, creative, and spiritual self together with his rational, logical, and scientific self. When fused together he found they reinforced each other, they inspired each other, and they balanced each other as light upon light.

ANALOGY OF GRAVITY

One way to think about the existence of God is to think about the existence of gravity. The fact is, we know gravity exists. We see its effects. We can test it. We can drop an apple and see it hit the ground, time and again. But we do not know what causes two objects in the universe to be drawn together. There seems to be a force that binds the planets, the stars, and the galaxies together that is beyond our comprehension. We can see its signs and explain its effects, but we cannot fully define it with today's limited tools, understandings, and capacities.

The same is true of God. We see the concept of God in all cultures, all faiths, and all nations. It endures no matter how hard we try to get rid of it. It transcends everything. It binds people together. When properly balanced with the laws of nature, faith in God helps people achieve greatness in all fields. It consoles them during times of test and tribulation. It guides them and protects them during times of confusion and distraction. It holds them to account to a higher standard when the world is not watching. It proves its power to bring people together time and again by inspiring all of the greatest civilizations in history.

But like gravity, we cannot explain the underlying force behind the ever-present reality of God in all human endeavors. We cannot point to it and say, "this is where our idea of God comes from." Of course, there may come a time when we understand what causes gravity, just as there may come a time when we better understand the existence of God. It is just a matter of growing up as a species and developing our capacity to understand. Just as we recognize gravity by its effects, we can recognize the power of God by the results of a logical and balanced approach to faith. Once we see the effects of the force of belief in our lives to transform us, inspire us, and compel us to become better people, we can begin to realize that this force is real, it is important, and it is worth aligning with, even if we cannot fully comprehend its essence.

CHAPTER 4:

RENEWING THE ROLE OF RELIGION IN MODERN LIFE

"Religion is verily the chief instrument for the establishment of order in the world and of tranquility amongst its peoples. The weakening of the pillars of religion hath strengthened the foolish and emboldened them and made them more arrogant. Verily I say: The greater the decline of religion, the more grievous the waywardness of the ungodly. This cannot but lead in the end to chaos and confusion."

—Bahá'u'lláh, *Tablets of Bahá'u'lláh*, p. 63

REINTRODUCING RELIGION

The whole concept of religion has changed dramatically in the past couple of hundred years. For most of human history, religion was an essential part of life. Religion was a daily part of every civilization, nation, society, and culture that has ever existed in recorded history. Religion was used to define who we are, why we are here, how we should live, and how we understand our universe. Religions inspired people to track the stars, create calendars, monitor seasons, and investigate the world. Religions were often founded on strong moral codes that ensured all people were held accountable to a higher standard. And religions had their ebb and flow—some would rise to great heights of influence and enlightenment only to become corrupted and slide into superstition and oppression.

It is undeniable that religion has been an essential ingredient for identity, understanding, and living for most of human history. Religions have identified people with who and what they are. In the past, there was no shopping for religions. There was no exploring different faiths of the world and picking and choosing what was and wasn't appealing. Few people could choose not to be a part of religion, because it meant choosing not be part of society. Occasionally the community religion might fracture into different sects or schools, but generally the majority of a community held to one religious tradition or another. You were either part of the community, or not.

Religions, in this context, set out the foundations for society. They guided, inspired, encouraged, and tended to the emotional, material, physical, and spiritual needs of a community. They were the sources of learning and understanding. Oftentimes the only people who could read and write in a community were the religious people. The only books were the religious books. Science, philosophy, politics, and family were all informed by the teachings, guidance, and moral boundaries established by the local religion.

At times in history there have been one or two religious minority communities living amongst a larger majority community. The degree of civilization and moral integrity of the majority community was often tested by this in how they treated those minorities. Sadly, too often, communities would fail miserably to uphold their spiritual traditions and turn instead to persecution of those in the minority. Occasionally, an entirely new religion would arise in a community. When this happened it might challenge or upset an established way of doing things, and offer a new way forward that helped people grow and develop. Generally speaking, each community had its own religious structure, and most people were either part of the fold or were not.

In the past couple of hundred years this model has broken down. Today, the world's religions live side-by-side together in an ever-changing, ever-unifying, ever-advancing global culture. In the past, a spiritual seeker might never have encountered a single person from another religion. Today, that same spiritual seeker might work in an office with people from every conceivable spiritual tradition in the world, from Hindu, to Buddhist, to Christian, to Jew, to Muslim, to agnostic, to any number of native faiths. That spiritual seeker might even have people in their own family from different faiths.

This has changed the way people find spiritual meaning and fulfillment in their lives. Today we have access to the holy books of every faith translated into almost every language. We have ancient spiritual teachings and concepts available to us that were once reserved for monks who had spent decades in monasteries in the remotest corners of the land. Today, in order to find spiritual truth, anyone who can read can truly shop through the entire spiritual experience of mankind and find what fits their needs, desires, lifestyles, hopes, and aspirations.

But what any person who has engaged in a vigorous search soon discovers is that all of the world's religions have very similar teachings at their cores. While the forms, laws, practices, names, myths, and rituals may differ from faith to faith, the core of religious faith remains consistent. That is, at their center all religions teach us to be good people. Every religion teaches some variation of the Golden Rule. They all teach us to be honest, generous, charitable, faithful, wise, chaste, trustworthy, and true to our spiritual natures.

On the other hand, any student of history also knows that terrible things have been done to our fellowman in the name of religion. This has given the concept of organized religion a bad reputation in many circles. Whether it is fanatical terrorism, oppressive inquisitions, genocidal crusades, brutal colonization, or religious wars fought between sects of the same faith, religion has been at the center of mankind's most shameful episodes. In fact, many people today are turned off by the whole concept of organized religion because of this history. Some may believe in God and spiritual things, but they do not want to join one religion or another because they do not want to be associated with such acts.

For the spiritual seeker, abandoning religion altogether is like throwing the baby out with the bathwater. The spiritual seeker believes that we are social creatures. We need each other to inspire us, guide us, test us, improve us, hold us to a high standard, and provide endless chances to serve and help those in need as a community. We were not meant to be isolated. We were not meant to be divided and distant from one another in spiritual matters. Without such opportunities to grow and develop socially, the spiritual seeker believes that he can never reach his full potential as a spiritual being. The question for the spiritual seeker is not whether or not to join a faith community based on what he can or cannot obtain from material or social perspective. The question is rather, "What do I truly believe?"

WHAT IS RELIGION?

For the spiritual seeker, joining a religion is about more than just a name on a membership card. It is more than just a list of esoteric points that we say we say we believe in. It is more than a community that looks like us and talks like us. It is more than a cultural or social group. It is more than the holidays we celebrate, the rituals we participate in, and the laws we try to follow. For the spiritual seeker, religion is a force for change in the world. It is a unifying force, an ennobling force, a restraining force, and a force for progress and advancement.

The fact is, religion is the most powerful unifying force in the history of the world. No other movement, cause, philosophy, or ideology has ever been able to unite so many people from so many different backgrounds across so many geographic areas over so many centuries and millennia. When used for good, this unifying force can bring warring, diverse, and distant peoples together in peace and understanding. It can unify people of faith so much that they are willing to sacrifice, serve, and even die for each other in the name of the love of God.

Religion is also a powerful ennobling force in human lives. It teaches us right from wrong from the earliest days of our lives. We are given examples of service, mercy, and uprightness to follow through the stories of martyrs, heroes, and poets and artists in all of our faiths. Religion provides a moral compass that guides people to live true to each other under all circumstances. Religion provides tools to improve our emotional, social, and spiritual lives through prayer, fasting, meditation, and acts of charity and sacrifice.

In addition, religion provides a restraining force. It provides laws to follow and standards to live up to. It protects us from our own baser natures. Religions give us boundaries that keep us safe from our animal instincts. Spiritual laws provide a divine standard to live up to in every aspect of life. We know that God sees everything. Therefore, if we break a spiritual law, we are going to face consequences, whether we are caught or not. In this way, religion provides a civilizing force for keeping humanity safe and healthy at all times.

Religion has traditionally been a source of knowledge and wisdom. The reality is that many of the earliest universities were founded by religions. Throughout much of history religious institutions and schools have been the centers of learning, knowledge, and understanding in society. Whether it is the ancient monasteries of Ireland or mountain communities of Tibet, the schools of theology in Egypt or the shaman orders of the Native Americans, it has often been religious institutions that have held on to the stories, experiences, and acquired wisdom of a community throughout history.

Lastly, religion provides an inspiring force for moral development of the human race. In addition to being a foundation of knowledge and ancient wisdom in a community, the religious and spiritual leaders throughout history have also offered mankind basic foundational principles in how to interpret reality and live a good life. That is, religion has taught us that there are consequences to our actions, there is an accounting for our deeds, and that we must all treat one another kindly. In fact, the major religions of history all offer similar basic moral teachings at their core. That is, they all offer some variations of the Golden Rule. They all tell their followers not to lie, steal, commit adultery, commit murder, and the like. In fact, the basic forms of many legal codes today have their origin in religious standards of the past.

All these benefits of religion are not by accident. This is the legacy of a powerful, effective, and lasting element of society that has always been a part of the human experience.

DISTINGUISHING TRUE RELIGION

The spiritual seeker also recognizes that this force of religion in society is just a tool. This means that, like any tool, it can be used for good or for evil. The reality is that while religion has often been used to unify, ennoble, restrain, and advance society throughout the ages, it has also been used as justification by those who would divide, debase, restrict, and retard the advancement of society for selfish aims.

A helpful analogy is found if we look at the purpose of ironworking. Ironworking can be used to make farming equipment or weapons of war. The same is true of religion in that it can be used to make the world a better place or a deadly place depending on what it is applied to. The spiritual seeker realizes that the fact that you can bend iron into a sword does not mean you should never use ironworking in the first place. The same logic holds true for the value of religion. The spiritual seeker realizes that the plow and the shovel can be used to farm and build a better world for everyone. It would be foolish not to use such important tools for improving our lives simply because the same process that made them can also potentially be used to make weapons and tools of destruction.

The spiritual seeker recognizes that true religion must be distinguished from false religion. For him, true religion is that which leads to goodness in the world. As the Bible says, "Every tree that bringeth not forth good fruit is hewn down, and cast into the fire." (Matthew 7:19). Therefore, the spiritual seeker wants to distinguish the fruit-bearing trees from the unproductive ones—that is, true religion from false religion.

Religion could be described as false when it is used for selfish and divisive purposes. False religion plays to the baser nature of men in order to demand uncompromising loyalty. It feeds on fear and hatred in order to keep its flock obedient. It is powered by greed and resentment in order to grow its material influence. It is full of uncompromising dogma, unquenchable fanaticism, and illogical superstition that cannot be reasoned with or challenged. It calls people to give up their free will and their individual capacity to decide for themselves. It demands that followers blindly accept whatever they are told. It convinces people that questioning those in authority is the same as blasphemy against God. While it may engage in some charity at the edges, such false religion is fundamentally an instrument of preserving the power and influence of those in authority at any costs.

For the spiritual seeker, true religion is different. True religion is focused on uniting people, teaching them spiritual qualities, improving their lives, and protecting the innocent. It uplifts, ennobles, and educates them. It is a source of wisdom, tolerance, and justice in the world. It leads people to paths of service to mankind. It brings out the best in all of us. Its goals are a better life, a better community, and a better world.

The spiritual seeker is looking for true religion. He seeks a religion that is open, reasonable, practical, and adaptable. He is looking for a religion that has a high standard to live up to, that inspires him to be his best no matter what, and that provides him the tools he needs to pass through the trials and tribulations of life.

The spiritual seeker recognizes that many religions often start out as true religions, but become corrupted over time. In the beginning they bring a fresh perspective, a new spirit, and a revived spiritual vision for humanity. They spread, grow, and mature into forces of learning, development, and discovery. They are focused on the future, united in spirit and faith across every barrier of race, culture, and age.

But as time goes on, these true religions start to change. Over the course of history, true religions sink into false religions. Their hierarchies are infiltrated with people who lust for power and influence. Empty rituals and traditions end up replacing inspired acts of service and worship. The message becomes simpler and simpler as leaders look for quick ways to motivate and intimidate people. As the religion sinks into superstition and dogma, the people become sedated, apathetic, and tired of the same thing over and over again.

For the uncreative and uninspired leaders of the community, the only way to wake the people up seems to be to fire up the fear and damnation rhetoric. They look for outside threats to rally people against. Sometimes this turns communities against minorities or foreigners, but whatever the form it always ends badly. Anyone who challenges the status quo is seen as a threat to the established flow of things. As the moral authority is lost, the religious community begins to fracture and then divides into endless sects. This weakens the spirit, creates separate camps, and inspires more suspicion and hatred between people. What started as true religion has then become false not through the fault of the religion itself, but rather through the weakness and frailty of mankind.

In the end, the spiritual seeker recognizes that society needs a healthy spirit of true religion. It needs the civilizing forces of unity, ennoblement, restraint, and progress in order to develop properly. Without true religion, society languishes. Without a spiritual nature to focus on, people turn to satisfying their baser nature at any cost. People start worshiping idols of their own imaginations. They lose their moral compass. Right and wrong are confused. Good and evil are seen as relative. There is no higher order between men. No universal authority tells people that we are all equal, we are all noble, and we are all deserving of justice and peace. We focus on each others' faults. We fail to find common ground. And we stop caring for one another as spiritual brothers and sisters. Without true religion, we sink back into the depths of our animal instincts full of fear, cynicism, resentment, and ignorance.

INTRODUCING THE BAHÁ'Í CONCEPT OF RELIGION

Many spiritual seekers find the Bahá'í concept of religion to be fulfilling, uplifting, and inspiring. It is fulfilling because it provides teachings and practices that align with our modern understandings of the world. Bahá'ís have clear explanations for many of the most profound spiritual questions. The Bahá'í Faith is uplifting because it calls people to a higher standard of living that makes us healthier, happier, and more content with our lives. The Bahá'í Faith is inspiring because it offers a vision for a better world for every man, woman, and child, no matter what background they come from.

Bahá'ís believe that religion is a core element of human society, but that it must be guided by its moral foundation. If it ever leaves that moral foundation and becomes infected with manmade dogma, superstition, and useless power structures, then that core sprit of religion needs cleansing and renewal.

As the Bahá'í writings state, "Our purpose is to show how true religion promotes the civilization and honor, the prosperity and prestige, the learning and advancement of a people once abject, enslaved and ignorant, and how, when it falls into the hands of religious leaders who are foolish and fanatical, it is diverted to the wrong ends, until this greatest of splendors turns into blackest night." ('Abdu'l-Bahá, *The Secret of Divine Civilization,* p. 79)

Unfortunately, over time people tend to add their own interpretations, rituals, institutions, and practices to religions. These additions may have been well-meaning when they were introduced, but the effects are nearly always the same. All these additions threaten to become more important than the spirit and teachings at the core of the faith. They threaten to become tools of manipulation and division amongst men. They end up degrading the moral integrity of the faith, sewing disunity, bringing out the baser instincts of men, lessening the authority to restrain people from evil, and weakening the capacity of the community to progress and develop.

All these manmade additions to religion become baggage that weighs down, confuses, and clouds the spirit of religion in society. Bahá'ís believe that religion must be cleansed of all this baggage from age to age. This cleansing takes the form of a new religion coming without any of the manmade traditions, dogmas, and superstitions that have infected the existing community's spiritual paths.

When a new religion comes, it is often filled with new teachings that are relevant to the needs of the age in which it appears. Those who believe in their religion for the spirit and faith that it offers will recognize the new spirit renewed, revived, and remade through the new religion. Those who were attached to their manmade structures, rituals, interpretations, traditions, practices, and institutions will stay behind clinging to the idols of their own imaginations. As the Bahá'í writings say, "God verily will test them and sift them." (Bahá'u'lláh, *Kitáb-i-Íqán*, p. 255).

Bahá'ís believe that today's world requires a fresh measure of divine inspiration. They believe that the world has changed, mankind has matured, and that we are ready for a renewed faith that is accessible to all people from all backgrounds. The Bahá'í Faith is a religion that offers teachings, laws, and a vision specifically targeted to today's modern, global, educated, diverse, and connected world culture.

The Bahá'í Faith is a force for unity in today's world because it teaches the oneness of all religions and the oneness of all mankind. It teaches that all the world's great religions bring the same core sprit of faith, and that this core sprit of faith has been renewed for today's world in the form of the Bahá'í Faith. It teaches that all people are created equal regardless of race, gender, nationality, religion, education, or class. It teaches that we must treat one another with utmost kindness and respect, and it provides tools such as consultation and the concept of world citizenship for helping us interact with each other in ways that increase our capacity to solve problems and improve our world collectively.

The Bahá'í Faith is also a force for ennoblement in today's world because it teaches us about our fundamental purpose in life. It teaches us how to find happiness, detachment, fulfillment, and spiritual awareness. It provides us help in dealing with the trials and tribulations of life, it shows us how to live our lives in balance with nature, it inspires us to work and contribute to society as a form of worship, and it calls us to build families that are spiritually healthy.

The Bahá'í Faith is also a force for restraint in the world because it provides laws that help us live in alignment with the will of God. It provides laws that protect us from our lower nature, that call us to be accountable for our actions, and that set a high standard for righteousness, service, sacrifice, and clean-mindedness. The Bahá'í Faith has laws against anything that lessens our mental and physical capacity, weakens our bonds of marriage and family life, poisons our relations with others, and throws off our balance with nature. These laws help us to become the people we want to be and to build the world we want to see.

Finally, the Bahá'í Faith is a force for progress in the world because it is guided by the vision of Bahá'u'lláh. The vision of Bahá'u'lláh is to create a world of peace, justice, equality, education, moderation, and unity. To realize this vision Bahá'ís have individual, community, and global obligations. Individually, Bahá'ís strive to refine their characters, hold themselves to account each day, and try to be better people in everything they do. At the community level Bahá'ís serve others, build the institutions of the faith's administrative order, and strive to add value to the lives of others. In the world at large Bahá'ís cultivate new understandings, spread new perspectives, and support the progress of humanity toward achieving the vision of Bahá'u'lláh in every respect.

Bahá'ís are actively involved in social and economic development projects in every corner of the globe, often at a neighborhood level. These efforts often revolve around empowering individuals to change their own lives by discovering their own path to fulfillment, to awareness, and to developing their capacity in their own lives. Bahá'ís do this work through educating, training, and inspiring communities to realize their collective potential regardless of their background.

Every Bahá'í has a role to play in this process. In this reality, religion is a foundation upon which civilizations are built and sustained. As the Bahá'í writings state, "The purpose of religion as revealed from the heaven of God's holy Will is to establish unity and concord amongst the peoples of the world; make it not the cause of dissension and strife. The religion of God and His divine law are the most potent instruments and the surest of all means for the dawning of the light of unity amongst men. The progress of the world, the development of nations, the tranquility of peoples, and the peace of all who dwell on earth are among the principles and ordinances of God. Religion bestoweth upon man the most precious of all gifts, offereth the cup of prosperity, imparteth eternal life, and showereth imperishable benefits upon mankind." (Bahá'u'lláh, *Tablets of Bahá'u'lláh,* p. 129)

THE FREE-SPIRITED WOMAN WHO FINALLY FOUND A HOME

There was a free-spirited woman who considered herself very spiritual, but who did not want to be a part of any organized religion. This was because the woman had had some bad experiences in her childhood with religion. These experiences had led her to believe that religion was a corruption of spirituality, and that it became a barrier between people and God.

The free-spirited woman spent much of her adulthood exploring different faiths and traditions in the world. She took some spiritual teachings from all of them and combined them into her own belief-system. She felt her search was empowering and liberating. It gave her the ability to decide for herself what was true and false. She did not need any dogma or theology to tell her what to believe. She followed her own heart.

She did feel one thing was lacking in her spiritual search, however. She missed having a community of like-minded people around her. She felt alone in her search. She felt as though she was an observer of the world, and that she was distant from the movement of things. She wanted to feel a connection with her fellow-human beings that transcended every barrier, but she was not sure how to achieve that. She would try to discuss spiritual things with people, but she had difficulty getting others to accept her personal understandings. Because she had created her own path, she had little common ground with people of other faiths. They wanted her to join their cause, and she wanted them to be free thinkers like she was. The woman looked and looked, but could not find a cause where her free spirit could be appreciated, and where her heart could feel at home.

Then one day she came across a book about the Bahá'í Faith. As she read about it, she instantly felt that it was what she had believed her whole life. It was a religion that put the individual investigation of truth at the core of everything. It was a community dedicated to making the world a better place by making humanity into a better people. It was a cause with a vision for a new world of peace, unity, education, equality, and spirituality. And it was a cause of action that was doing something tangible to make its vision into a reality.

The woman began to seek out the Bahá'ís to learn more. As she did, she realized that the Bahá'ís were just like her. They were not perfect people. They were fellow-travelers in the spiritual search. They were all imperfect beings working to perfect themselves through learning, discovery, and personal development. The only difference was that they had the guidance of the Bahá'í writings to help them. They had a common language, a common standard, and a common foundation to build on. It was a community of volunteers working together in unity to realize a common vision for humanity.

To her, this was what religion should be. It should be a vehicle for making people better. It should be a force for organizing the capacities, ideas, and resources of mankind into making the world into a heavenly place. It should be a tool for channeling the spirituality of humanity into collective spiritual awareness. The free-spirited woman joined the Bahá'í Faith and became an active and devoted believer in its cause.

ANALOGY OF THE TREE

We can look to the life of a tree and see how it relates to the life of a religion. First, a seed falls to the ground as something small, weak, and tiny. It is soon embedded in the earth and starts to spring roots and a shoot. It requires much water, sunlight, and nutrients to grow and develop. Soon the small sapling branches off and grows toward the sky. Finally it matures and begins to bloom and give fruit. Eventually, it grows old and begins to die. It stops giving fruit, is prone to decay and disease, and falls to the ground in order to return to the earth and fertilize the next generation of trees.

A religion goes through the same process. While all divine religions are born from an emanation from the Divine, the process of physically spreading the message throughout the world is similar. Often born in obscurity, the world's great religions usually spread roots among family and friends of their Founders in the very beginning. As Christianity started with just a few disciples, as Judaism was born amongst a lost and enslaved tribe of Israel, as Islam began with Muhammad's wife and a tribe of abandoned people, as Buddhism started with a tiny band of monks who wandered with their Master, as the Bábí Faith started with the Báb and His first follower Mullah Husayn, so every religion begins with only a few hearts.

Soon enough, however, a new religion spreads its spiritual influence deep into the soil of the human world. The first sapling of a new religion is fed by the enthusiasm and hope of the first believers, it is watered by the divine forces of the Holy Spirit, and it is guided upward by the vision of the Founder through His teachings and organization.

As a new religion grows upward, it finally bears fruits in the form of a new race of men and women who are wise, compassionate, noble, and virtuous. These souls produce a revolution in the arts and sciences. They discover new powers and capacities, they explore the deepest mysteries and furthest reaches of the land, and they strive to experience more from life and from themselves.

After a while, however, many of the followers of religion catch the disease of complacency and apathy. Those seeking power and influence seep into leadership in the community. Rituals, dogmas, superstitions, and divisive practices begin to infect the pure spirit of the faith. This disease eventually overtakes the religion and it falls to the storms of this world. As it begins to die and decay, its nutrients are reformed, renewed, and remade into a new tree, and the process repeats itself.

CHAPTER 5:

FINDING HAPPINESS THAT ENDURES

"The Great Being saith: Blessed and happy is he that ariseth to promote the best interests of the peoples and kindreds of the earth."

—Bahá'u'lláh, *Gleanings from the Writings of Bahá'u'lláh*, no. 117.1

WE ALL WANT TO BE HAPPY

We all want to feel joy. We want to laugh and feel free to live our lives any way we please. We want to feel connected, inspired, and hopeful. We want to feel loved. These are all human needs. They are fundamental to all of us. They are all part of feeling happy in one way or another.

There are many types of happiness, but generally speaking, we can use two main categories of happiness: temporary and enduring. Temporary happiness can be found in the things that come and go. Sometimes we are up; sometimes we are down. Sometimes things work out for us; sometimes they do not seem to go our way. Sometimes we win; sometimes we lose. When we are up, when things work out of us, when we win, we find this temporary happiness.

Temporary happiness can come from many things in life. It can come from material possessions. We can find a bit of happiness in a new car that smells great and looks good. We can find it in a new outfit that makes us look stylish. We can find it in a great meal cooked to perfection. We can find it in a vacation that leaves all our cares behind. We can find it in a party where we are surrounded by friends and family having a good time. We can find it in a sports game where our team wins and the crowd around us fills us with collective euphoria. We can find it in a new relationship with a new person who is interesting and exciting. Or we can find it in a new house, a new job, an elite degree, or a special award.

All these things bring a bit of happiness. But this bit of happiness does not last. The fact is, the car gets old and eventually breaks down. The clothes go out of style or they get holes and fall apart. The meal is consumed and we are left with a pile of dirty dishes (or a big bill to pay). The vacation ends and we have to go home to our mundane lives. The party is over and everyone leaves. Our favorite sports team can lose the next big game. The new relationship can become routine or the person's flaws come out and the passion and excitement fades. The new house will need a new roof, the new job can get stressful or boring, the degree might not pay off the way we expect, and the award might sit on the mantle and be forgotten. The fact is, life goes on, momentary happiness passes, and we end up waiting for the next experience to fill us up again.

On the other hand, *enduring happiness* is the happiness that lasts throughout all the ups and downs of life. This comes from the things we cannot buy, rent, or make. It is a happiness that wells up in our soul and brings peace to our heart. It is an inner joy that shines into the world without regard for who we are, where we live, how we look, or what we have.

The spiritual seeker sees the difference between momentary happiness and long-term, deep, and profound happiness as a result of choices in how we live and what we care about. The spiritual seeker seeks enduring happiness, what he calls spiritual happiness, before all else. This is happiness of the soul. It transcends all the accidents of life including age, wealth, education, race, class, gender, and religion. It is a happiness that lasts. It is a happiness that emanates out from us like a beacon shedding light on all those who encounter us. It is manifested in many ways, but most of all it is manifested in joy. This joy is a feeling that comes from being fully aware of one's spiritual condition and endlessly engaged in worship, love, and service to mankind.

Being fully aware of one's spiritual condition means we understand why we exist, what we are supposed to be learning, and how we are supposed to be living. The spiritual seeker believes that he exists to realize his potential in life. He does this by discovering God in all aspects of His Creation, through revelation, nature, and the passage of time. Therefore, the spiritual seeker sees meaning and purpose in everything that happens to him. Whether things are working out for him or not, whether he is winning or losing in the daily ups and downs of life, he is continuously seeking lessons to learn and grow from. The spiritual seeker is seeking the path to enlightenment, understanding, and wisdom at every stage. He is refining his character, developing new capacity, and becoming the person he was meant to become. Nothing that happens in life can deflect him from this higher purpose. He is full of joy in every victory over himself, in every triumph over his ego, in every test sent his way that he passes. But he is also full of joy when he learns from a mistake, when he changes his behavior, and when he grows close to God by asking for forgiveness, mercy, and strength to live better tomorrow. All these elements of spiritual living make him more aware of who he is, why he is here, and what he is here to accomplish.

Being endlessly engaged in love and service to mankind means that we always have a role to play in the world. We always have a place in the work of creating a better life for the people around us. The spiritual seeker finds meaning for his life when he adds value to the lives of others. More than just smiling all the time or just putting on a happy face to merely appear as though he is joyous, the spiritual seeker believes that spiritual happiness comes from a deeper place in the heart. It is manifested through his outlook, which is focused on learning and developing spiritual values. It is manifested in the hope, confidence, and wondrous appreciation he has for life and all of its complexities, intricacies, and wonders.

The spiritual seeker also manifests joy in all of his relationships. He is not content with superficial friendships, self-centered loves, or meaningless encounters. He is interested in understanding peoples' souls. He wants to know what people care about in their hearts, and how he can be of service to them. He finds joy in helping, caring for, understanding, and listening to others. He knows that the secret to happiness is to bring joy to the souls of others. Therefore, he strives to be a fountain of joy for all who cross his path. Some days it is easier than others, but he always comes back to this fundamental truth. Life is better when it is spent in service to humanity.

RECOGNIZING FALSE PROMISES

If one part of making oneself happy is by focusing on service to others and awakening spiritual awareness in our lives, another part is being aware of the false promises of happiness that surround us. We face false promises from many things in life including material, chemical, social, and physical enticements in life. And while these false promises of happiness may offer temporary distractions from the deeper questions of life, they offer no lasting satisfaction for the spiritual seeker. The fact is, we can never acquire enough of them. Indeed, the more we take, the more we need to sustain that initial euphoric feeling.

Material things offer false promises by encouraging us to buy things, own things, even just shop for things. In the end, however, there is always something better, something newer, or something flashier around the corner to desire. While the craving pretends to offer happiness if we buy the flashy new thing, actually buying it makes us feel unhappy soon afterward when we realize something better will come along.

Chemicals also pretend to offer happiness, but in fact often end up hurting us far more than we can ever imagine. Drugs, alcohol, and abuse of medicines can lead to destruction of brain cells, strong addictions that are difficult to overcome, poor decision-making that can lead to lasting consequences in our relationships, and the loss of many of the things we hold dear, including our money, our jobs, our friendships, and even our families.

The fact is, many people dealing with traumatic experiences, attention problems, or social anxieties end up self-medicating with chemicals. These chemicals become the means by which such people believe they can function in the world. They become crutches that these people truly believe they need in order to get through life. The spiritual seeker knows that many of our problems come from spiritual imbalances in our lives. If he has trouble with a spiritual imbalance, the spiritual seeker will use all the tools available to help him overcome his problems including doctors, therapy, exercise, prayer, and meditation. But most of all he will turn to service to humanity because he knows that only by focusing on truly caring for others, loving them for their spiritual capacities, and opening hearts to all that is good in the world do we align our own inner condition with its rightful direction. Only then do we begin to manifest our full potential in this world.

Some social elements of life also offer false promises of happiness. These social elements call us to fit in, to conform, to fall in line, and to look and act like everyone else. These are pressures to do what everyone else is doing and live how everyone else is living. These social pressures make it seem that by giving up our individuality, we will find happiness.

But the spiritual seeker believes this is also a false promise. He knows that giving up our individual capacity to discover, embrace, and live a meaningful life in our own unique way is the same as giving up the most rewarding, empowering, and truly remarkable parts of being human. He knows that he needs to be free of the way things have always been in order to make his own way. He knows that conforming to everyone else's standard of beauty and normalcy will make him feel fake, empty, and phony. The spiritual seeker believes that true liberty is liberty from the limitations imposed by others over our spiritual and personal development.

Finally, the physical elements of life also offer us false promises. People may think that the euphoric highs of casual sex, adrenaline rushes, exercise highs, fighting and combat, self-immolation, and even looking at pornography will make them feel happy. Unfortunately, the euphoria that some may experience from these activities quickly wears off. Once the feelings leave, we quickly find that we need another shot of it to keep the party going. In fact, too often we discover that we need greater and greater quantities of the feelings of euphoria to reach the same levels of satisfaction that we received from the initial experience. This path is an endless quest to nowhere that can only lead to emptiness and a sense of lost time and potential.

Now, all these things including the material, social, chemical, and physical distractions of life may have their place. It is OK to have physical pleasure in life. It is fine to have basic social norms in society that keep us civilized. Material things are not bad in themselves. And chemicals may be OK when they treat our diseases or protect us from viruses. But these elements must be kept in balance. We cannot wrap up our inner happiness in their acquisition or usage. True happiness must come from living up to our potential as spiritual beings. It must be firmly grounded in the things that endure. Once we find this deep happiness, all other joys and pleasures find their proper place in our lives.

It is not the distractions that test us, it is the way we interact with those elements. It is the voice we listen to when we decide how we are going to live. If it is the voice of the ego and the self, then we turn to selfishness, greed, envy, lust, hatred, superiority, numbness, ignorance, fear, anger, and resentment as ways to escape pain in the world.

The spiritual seeker believes that listening to the voice of the ego leads only to self-delusion. He believes that negative qualities are really just the lack of true spiritual qualities. He believes that the best way to overcome the voice of selfishness is with the voice of the spirit, which calls us to selflessness and benevolence. The best way to deal with envy is to replace it with a sincere desire to see others succeed and to be happy in fulfilling their unique paths. The best way to deal with lust is to see the nobility and spiritual reality of every soul. The best way to deal with ignorance and numbness in life is to replace it with knowledge, wisdom, and a commitment to spiritual awareness. Through this process, the spiritual seeker replaces resentment with forgiveness, fear with courage, and anger with love. He knows it is a life-long process to develop these spiritual qualities, but he considers refining his character to be the most important work of his life and the beginning of all of his services to humanity. And so he makes it a priority everyday.

ELEMENTS OF SPIRITUAL HAPPINESS

So how do we know spiritual happiness when we find it? How can we tell the difference between things that only bring us artificial happiness, and those things that offer deep spiritual happiness that is healthy and that will endure? One useful lens with which to examine different elements of life is the posing of certain pertinent questions. First, does the element lead to a happiness that transcends any stage of our lives? Second, does the element lead to a happiness that endures beyond momentary life? And third, does this element expand and reflect to other people? Finding out if the thing we are looking at is transcendent, if it endures, and if we can reflect it to others is then one way we can use to examine any element of life to see if it is something we want to invest our spiritual happiness in. But let us look a little more at these three concepts before we move on.

Transcendence offers independence from time and place. No matter who you are, no matter your age, race, gender, location, background, education, you must have access to this type of happiness. Like light it should shine in dark spaces and in bright places, that shines in lanterns as well as candles. It is independent of the instrument that calls it into being. It is pure, unfiltered, and distinguished. Transcendent happiness is available anywhere, anytime, to anyone. You do not need money to buy them. You do not need an extensive education to appreciate them. And you do not need someone else to give them to you.

Endurance is happiness that lasts. It creates a memory that makes you more complete and fulfilled in your life. Like bricks in the foundation of your beings, these moments of joy are the spiritual form that makes you who you are. They create the bedrock of your life upon which you build a home for your heart that is free of the shifting sands of daily life. Enduring joy is available forever. No one can steal them from you. No one can take them, destroy them, or use them up.

Reflectance is happiness that radiates from us. It is a joy that wells up in our souls and pours out upon all those around us. The recipient of this joy can then transfer it to yet another. The transference of spiritual happiness from your heart to another can be likened to passing the reflection of the sun from mirror to mirror. Reflective happiness exist to be shared. The more you manifest it, the brighter it shines, and the more you are able to shower it to the people around you.

These three qualities of *transcendence, endurance,* and *reflectance* can be found in many elements of a happy life including selfless love, connections to the universe, spiritual empowerment, and boundless optimism. Wherever we find these elements (or wherever we create them) in our lives, we can trust that they will lead us to deep, abiding, and spiritual happiness.

Selfless love is a love that asks nothing in return. It is a love that sees the eternity in another's heart and worships that everlasting reality rather than the person. Selfless love is a choice. A parent can choose to show selfless love for his or her child and give that child comfort, kindness, discipline, and both a material and spiritual education. A lover can choose to show selfless love for their beloved by loving them for all that they are as a spiritual being, or they can chose to love them for the way they make them feel. It is a choice.

Selfless love gives everything but expects nothing. It is pure. It is wondrous. It empties us of ego and pride, and in return fills our hearts with pure light. Selfless love is transcendent—anyone can show it in the world no matter who they are and what their background. Selfless love will endure. Once we have received selfless love from another our lives are changed forever. We are affected whether we realize it or not. The one we love becomes a part of us, connected to us on a deep level. When we pass on selfless love, it infects the heart of the recipient. Those receiving selfless love have seen an example of purity that they can follow. Like ripples in a pond, the drops of selfless love we let fall into the pool of humanity can spring waves of love throughout the body of mankind.

Connections to positive causes greater than oursleves can also lead to happiness. These connections can take many forms. We can be connected to faith groups, missions, philosophies, social movements, and any number of an endless array of communities of people working to do something good in the world. Depending on the kind of work these entities are involved in, these connections can give us a sense of accomplishment. They can bring us together in unity around a higher calling. This unity is electrifying. It is energizing. It is inspiring.

Spiritual empowerment also leads to true happiness by giving us a sense of mastery over our destiny. Spiritual empowerment means we believe we exist not for material development, but rather for spiritual empowerment. When we find spiritual empowerment, we find the power to make up our own mind on the most important decisions of our lives based on spiritual principles—on what is right for our souls and not necessarily for our immediate material reality. That is, spiritual empowerment gives us standards, faith, and a higher calling in our lives to live for something more. It provides the strength to stand for something true and right, even when it is difficult.

Spiritual empowerment can take many forms. It can happen when we choose a faith to belong to that offers us a path of higher awareness and deeper wisdom. But it can also happen when we choose a path in the arts or in the sciences that inspires our souls to make a unique contribution in the world. It can come when we choose to stand by our family and those we love no matter what the cost. It can come when we do the right thing, no matter what the cost. The reality is that we all face ethical choices every day. And each day, spiritual empowerment endures as long as people do the right thing. Finally it reflects to others who see us doing the right thing and they are strengthened in their own paths.

Boundless optimism is a final element of happiness that brings out the best in human beings. It comes from seeing a happy ending for the fortunes of mankind as not only possible, but inevitable. It comes from seeing the forces of our time working together to forge a new creation and bring us to a place of peace and world unity. It calls us to be the best we can, knowing that our children will take up the torch when we are done. It transcends the darkness and cynicism of our age and it offers a better path for a better day. It endures as long as people keep hope alive in their hearts. And it is reflected in the hearts of all those who carry on the work of bettering themselves, their families, their communities, and the world.

THE BAHÁ'Í FAITH AND THE PATH TO LASTING HAPPINESS

Many spiritual seekers have found that the Bahá'í Faith offers all the elements required for a spiritually happy life. First, Bahá'ís abound in selfless love. Bahá'ís are called to possess a love for all the peoples of the world, and to work for universal education, world peace, race unity, and the equality of women and men. The writings of the faith inspire a love for God and place high importance on prayer and meditation and working to align ones character with noble principles. The strong sense of community found in the faith engenders a genuine love among the members as they work to build the institutions, communities, and the global administrative framework envisioned by Bahá'u'lláh.

As the Bahá'í writings state, "Happy is the man that pondereth in his heart that which hath been revealed in the Books of God, the Help in Peril, the Self-Subsisting." (Bahá'u'lláh, *Gleanings from the Writings of Bahá'u'lláh,* no. 10.1).

In addition, Bahá'ís offer spiritual empowerment to all people with important teachings about the independent investigation of the truth. The fact is, every Bahá'ís most important task is refining his or her own character. It is a lifelong struggle that is undertaken through study, prayer, meditation, service, fasting, and worship. Bahá'ís work at perfecting themselves everyday and strive to live according to the teachings and principles of their faith.

Finally, Bahá'ís believe that a glorious, wondrous, and enlightened Age awaits humanity just beyond the horizon. They are optimistic that whatever they do, however they sacrifice, and wherever they render their service, their work is part of a greater cause bringing lasting goodness in the world.

As the Bahá'í writings state, "Behold, how the divers peoples and kindreds of the earth have been waiting for the coming of the Promised One. No sooner had He, Who is the Sun of Truth, been made manifest, than, lo, all turned away from Him, except them whom God was pleased to guide. We dare not, in this Day, lift the veil that concealeth the exalted station which every true believer can attain, for the joy which such a revelation must provoke might well cause a few to faint away and die." (Bahá'u'lláh, *Gleanings from the Writings of Bahá'u'lláh,* no. 6.1).

THE BUSINESSMAN WHO DISCOVERED HAPPINESS THROUGH SERVICE

There was a businessman who was very unhappy in his life. He had spent a long time acquiring an education and working to build a successful career, but these things did not make him happy. His work was not what he thought it would be. He had hard days and challenging tests to deal with. There was a lot of stress involved, and overall, he felt that his job was not very fulfilling.

The businessman married a wonderful woman and started a family. At first it was a happy time. He enjoyed his children and spending time with his wife. But as the years went by, he saw those happy moments fade away into the drudgery of life. There was a lot of stress and responsibility in the work of providing for a family and raising children, and it did not always make him happy.

The businessman eventually began to turn to his hobbies and interests to find happiness. He made a lot of money so he began to spend it on himself. He began to buy things. He bought gadgets, devices, and tools. But the happiness he found from these material things never lasted. There was always something newer to buy, something better to acquire, and something more to want.

As the man grew older, though, he realized that none of these things brought deep and abiding happiness. There was still an emptiness at the core of his heart that could not be filled with professional success, family, or hobbies. He had realized that work could bring a sense of temporary accomplishment, but it never lasted. Family could bring temporary satisfaction, but it never lasted. Hobbies could bring temporary diversions, but they were not enduring. There was something missing. There was still a voice in his heart that needed to answer the question of why he was alive, why all things existed, and what he was here to do.

The businessman embarked on a spiritual journey to answer these questions. He looked into religion. He investigated many of the world's faiths and explored their various teachings, beliefs, and practices. He found most of them did not meet his iner needs. This was because these religions of the world seemed focused on maintaining the past. They promised contentment and salvation, but in reality seemed ill-equipped to deal with the problems of this world. The man wanted to be part of something that was looking to the future, something that directly addressed the problems of our time, and something where he felt that his skills, abilities, and capacities would be useful for building something better for the world. True and abiding happiness, the man decided, would come when he felt truly engaged in service, truly connected to the efforts to solve problems, and truly inspired by a vision for the future that he believed in.

One day the man met a Bahá'í who worked in his office building. The man asked the Bahá'í about the religion and its beliefs and practices. The businessman immediately found the Bahá'í beliefs and practices sensible, rational, and practical.

The businessman then asked the Bahá'í about the future. He wanted to know what kind of world the people of the Bahá'í Faith envisioned. The Bahá'í told the man about the vision of Bahá'u'lláh of a world with a just and fair grassroots organization working for the betterment of every community, dedicated to reverence for the natural world, working for the elimination of extremes of wealth and poverty, striving to achieve universal education, and powering the spiritual renewal of every heart. This was something the businessman could believe in.

The businessman quickly became a Bahá'í and started trying to live the Bahá'í life. He worked to change his character, and through that effort worked to serve mankind. He strove to improve himself in all aspects of his life including in his work, his family, and his peripheral interests. In his work he strove to be more considerate, trustworthy, and encouraging. In his family life he strove to be more loving, understanding, and patient. In his hobbies he worked to be less materialistic and more focused on learning, discovering, and appreciating the wonders of this world. And as a Bahá'í he had a whole new community of diverse and open-minded people to befriend and work alongside in his efforts.

To his surprise, the businessman found that when he aspired to be a better person, this made him happier than he had ever been in his lifetime. He found that through striving to live up to his spiritual potential in all aspects of life, through engaging with the world and serving people at every level, and through finding ways to learn and improve himself in every pursuit, that he had found the ultimate source of lasting happiness. No one could take this kind of happiness away from him. This was true living and enduring happiness.

ANALOGY OF THE SCULPTURE

Like a set of sculpting tools, the Bahá'í beliefs, practices, and vision provide the equipment we need to become spiritually happy. The problem is, the work is all up to us. It is our duty to pick up the chisel and hammer and work away on ourselves until we become the spiritual beings we aspire to be. No one will do this work for us. We, alone, are responsible for becoming better people.

In the end, we hold ourselves to our own standards in the sculpting work. Each of us has our own sculpture to offer in the garden of mankind. Each of our sculptures must be unique, special, and interesting. Therefore, we must craft our contribution with all the care, dedication, and perseverance that is required for displaying it in God's everlasting garden.

CHAPTER 6:

ACHIEVING CONTENTMENT THROUGH DETACHMENT

"Free thyself from the fetters of this world, and loose thy soul from the prison of self."

—Bahá'u'lláh, *The Hidden Words*, Persian, no. 40

WHAT IS CONTENTMENT?

Today's world is busy. It is full of motion, information, and noise. People are constantly coming and going, constantly connected, constantly interacting, constantly working, and constantly consuming. We barely have time to share moments with the ones we love, let alone take the time to ask deep spiritual questions about who we are, why we are here, and what we are doing with our lives.

This is where contentment comes in. Spiritual contentment is a requirement for a spiritual life. Our souls are constantly seeking it, yearning for it, and crying out for it. Unfortunately, we do not always know what we are looking for. We are not even sure what spiritual contentment is. In reality, finding spiritual contentment is not about having everything we want in our lives. It is not about becoming complacent and bored with the world. It is not about fulfilling all our dreams and desires. It is not about having a life without any cares or stress. It is not about never worrying or caring about anything. It is not about never striving for anything, never risking anything, or never trying for more. Contentment is not about giving up and separating ourselves from the world around us. If these things were required for spiritual contentment, then no one could ever achieve it.

Instead, true spiritual contentment is about what we set our heart on. True spiritual contentment is a way of connecting to the things that really matter in life and holding on to those things, while letting all the distractions and noise of life pass us by. It is about not being affected by the changes and chances of this world in a way that weakens our spirit and confounds our souls.

Having spiritual contentment means having enough to be happy, full, and complete in our life. It is a feeling of sublime resignation that comes from trusting that we have tried our best, made the most of what we had, and done what we could in any situation. It is a feeling that things will work out as long as we do our part. The contented person does his best to serve others and improve his character, and then he leaves the rest to God. He is not burdened by the fate of the universe.

He believes in a God that will make things right, either in this world or the next.

The spiritual seeker believes he is here for a purpose, to learn and to love. He is here to learn about the world and its peoples. He is here to experience all the trials and tribulations of life. He is here to be tested, refined, and improved by everything that happens to him. If he is out of balance, he knows he has some lesson to learn. If he yearns to make a contribution, he knows he has to make a plan to do something to be of service. If he feels disconnected from others, he knows he has to go out of his way to make connections with people and find ways to care for, nurture, encourage, and inspire others.

The spiritual seeker believes that true spiritual contentment leads to living life more aware, more awake, and more alive than ever before. It is about being connected to the universe in ways that transcend the material world. It is about taking whatever life gives us and making the best of it. It is about actively creating opportunities to serve mankind and better ourselves. It is a knowingness of the heart that offers a deep and profound wisdom to help guide us in our decisions toward whatever provides balance in our lives and betterment to our world.

The contented person finds life is complete, no matter what he has, where he is, or how much he has to offer. As long as he has free will and the capacity to appreciate God, the spiritual seeker can find contentment. He is not waiting until he gets that new job, finds a spouse, changes careers, earns a degree, moves to a new city, or discovers a new solution. He can find contentment in any situation because he creates it with any means at his disposal.

SEEKING SOURCES OF SPIRITUAL CONTENTMENT

Spiritual contentment comes from freedom. That is, it comes from freedom from want and desire. Contentment is about liberation from material things, liberation from heavenly promises, liberation from specific outcomes, and liberation from our own egos. Once we understand the limitations of these elements, then we can learn to let go of them and move forward in our spiritual lives.

The spiritual seeker recognizes that material things can bring no lasting spiritual contentment. While having a basic ability to feed and clothe ourselves is important for laying the foundation for our spiritual success, it does not lead to spiritual contentment. Money can never satisfy our souls. We can never have enough money. In fact, having more money can lead to more cares and worries and attachments than if we had little to start with and little to lose. So it can actually lesson our spiritual contentment if we let it.

To the spiritual seeker, material treasures are illusions. They are idols of our imaginations that we use to distract us from our spirits. Only when we use material wealth to be of service does it bring us spiritual contentment. When we use it to take care of others, then it becomes a blessing to our lives. The spiritual seeker does not flee from wealth. He sees it as just another instrument that, if he has access to it, he can use to benefit the world.

On the other hand, some think that having physical health and fitness will lead to contentment. Yet even the most handicapped or physically challenged person can feel spiritually contented, so this is not enough. Some think that having a relationship, getting married, and starting a family will make them content. Yet the spiritual seeker believes that those things are just conditions of life. Spiritual contentment does not come from receiving love from another person. It comes from giving love to the world. It comes from giving of oneself to others. It does not take marriage and children to reach this state. Marriage and children can lead to contentment inasmuch as we use those elements of life to learn selflessness and compassion. But a person can learn those lessons under any condition. Just starting a family is by no means a recipe for contentment. Quite the contrary, a family can lead to more stress, more tests, and difficulties if a person is not focused on the spiritual aspects of life. Therefore, spiritual contentment is about making the most of whatever we are given in life.

Some have imagined that spiritual contentment comes from the idea of heavenly salvation. They think they will be content when they know they are going to get into heaven. But the spiritual seeker believes that being a member of one sect or another of a religion does not lead to true spiritual contentment. Having a membership card means nothing for the spiritual seeker. The spiritual seeker sees heaven in all things. He can find it here on earth inasmuch as he can find it in the love, compassion, forgiveness, mercy, and dignity that he shows in his life. Spiritual contentment is not just reserved for the next world. It is something we can find in this life as well.

Some imagine that they will find spiritual contentment when they achieve some goal, reach some milestone, or complete some task. But the spiritual seeker believes that spiritual contentment is not about outcomes. Instead, it is about the process of doing our best. The fact is, we do not always get what we want. The world does not always work out the way we plan. In fact, sometimes not getting what we want ends up being a blessing in disguise. Life is messy. Being attached to specific outcomes leads to loss and disappointment, so it is better to do our best and let go of the results.

The spiritual seeker does not focus on the end of things. Instead he focuses on the process. He focuses on the things he can control. When opportunities present themselves, he takes them and makes the most of them. When opportunities do not present themselves and he reaches a dead-end in life, then he looks for the lessons he is supposed to learn and he moves on. Contentment is a way of living, not a destination.

Finally, some believe that contentment comes when we fulfill our own desires. People who are trapped in the prison of self think they are entitled to have whatever they want, whenever they want it, especially if they think other people like them are getting what they desire. They think the universe owes them something. They go through life expecting others to satisfy their needs and desires. But the spiritual seeker believes that the selfish ego can never be satisfied. The spiritual seeker believes that the real trick is to focus on helping others reach their potential, achieve their spiritual goals, and become true to themselves in their lives. The real goal is to be of service to others, to forget our own selves, and to put others first. This does not mean that we give people anything they want. People do not always want what is good for them, and the spiritual seeker recognizes that. Instead of focusing on giving people what they think they want, the spiritual seeker helps people to see truth in the world, to see what matters, and to focus on the things that matter.

HOW BAHÁ'ÍS OFFER A PATH TO SPIRITUAL CONTENTMENT

Once we recognize the things that do not lead to spiritual contentment, it is time to focus on the things that do. This is because it can be hard to let go of something without having something to replace it. The spiritual seeker believes that it is not enough just to let go of attachments to the material world. One needs to grab hold of something else in the process. Otherwise, if we just let go of the desire for material things for a while, those desires will return sooner or later. In addition, if we let go of the drive for specific material outcomes without replacing it with a drive for spiritual outcomes, then we risk drifting onto a path that goes nowhere. If we try to forget ourselves and our own desires but we do not replace them with heavenly and spiritual objectives, then our selfish ego will come back ready to fill the vacuum in our heart.

Many spiritual seekers have found it useful to align themselves with a cause such as the Bahá'í Faith in their paths to spiritual contentment because the Bahá'í teachings offer clear and consistent steps to finding peace in our hearts. This is because the Bahá'í Faith teaches simplicity in daily life. As the Bahá'í writings state, "Say: Deliver your souls, O people, from the bondage of self, and purify them from all attachment to anything besides Me. Remembrance of Me cleanseth all things from defilement, could ye but perceive it." (Bahá'u'lláh, *Gleanings from the Writings of Bahá'u'lláh,* no. 136.1).

The spiritual seeker appreciates the example set by 'Abdu'l-Bahá, the son of Bahá'u'lláh, when it comes to detachment and being content with life. 'Abdu'l-Bahá is considered by Bahá'ís to be the perfect exemplar of the faith's teachings. That means that all Bahá'ís turn to 'Abdu'l-Bahá's life as a guide for their own lives.

Everywhere 'Abdu'l-Bahá went he showed charity, kindness, and mercy. He was kind to everyone. He healed hearts. He showered people with love, and he fed the spirits of those seeking divine inspiration. 'Abdu'l-Bahá gave everything he had to others, at times even giving the coat on his back. He worked tirelessly to serve mankind, yet he lived a simple life, ate simple foods, and approached problems with a simple and profound perspective. Whatever led to goodness was good. He did not get caught up in politics and intrigue. He was above it. He wanted only what led to a better world. This is the example that Bahá'ís and people of all spiritual backgrounds can turn to in order to see simplicity lived in service to humanity.

In addition to the example of 'Abdu'l-Bahá, the Bahá'í Faith offers countless outlets for selfless service. The cause of Bahá'u'lláh provides an endless array of opportunities to contribute to something bigger than ourselves. This work starts with refining our own characters, improving ourselves every day, calling ourselves to account, and engaging in daily prayer and meditation as well as the study of the holy writings. This internal work then begins to bear fruit when we turn to service and sacrifice for the greater good. It becomes real when we give our time, our energy to a cause that will endure long after we are dead and gone. The spiritual seeker finds spiritual contentment in the work of the Bahá'í Faith because he believes it is work that truly matters to mankind, no matter how small the task.

In addition to paths of service, the Bahá'í Faith calls people to strive for excellence in all things. Bahá'ís are taught to do their best in whatever endeavor they embark upon. In this way our work, when done in a spirit of service, becomes worship of our Creator. The spiritual seeker appreciates this perspective and how it changes even the most mundane jobs into paths to contentment. The spiritual seeker understands that sometimes all we need to do is adjust our attitude in order to find a whole new reality waiting to lift us up.

As the Bahá'í writings state, "Let nothing grieve thee, and be thou angered at none. It behooveth thee to be content with the Will of God, and a true and loving and trusted friend to all the peoples of the earth, without any exceptions whatever. This is the quality of the sincere, the way of the saints, the emblem of those who believe in the unity of God, and the raiment of the people of Bahá." ('Abdu'l-Bahá, *Selections from the Writings of 'Abdu'l-Bahá,* no. 9.3).

THE WEALTHY WOMAN WHO FOUND CONTENTMENT

There was a wealthy woman who spent much of her time managing her possessions and properties. For her there was always something to worry about, clean, check-on, restore, and upgrade. Her days were spent shuttling between homes making sure various rooms and possessions were cleaned properly and ensuring various ongoing improvements were on schedule.

But even with so many material possessions, the woman was not satisfied. She wanted to be part of something more. She wanted to help humanity and to add value in the world. She considered herself a very spiritual person. She loved God and believed that people were essentially spiritual beings making their own way toward the Creator. But beyond that, her belief did not inform her daily life or affect her many cares and concerns.

One day, one of the woman's friends came over to her home and seemed to be full of joy. The wealthy woman asked her what had changed, and what could make her so light and relaxed in life. Her friend told her that she had discovered a new faith called the Bahá'í Faith, and it had been something she was looking for her whole life. She said that she had been on a long spiritual journey looking for answers to questions that had plagued her since childhood. These questions included why God would create so many religions, how people from all faiths and backgrounds could get along, and how to interpret many scriptural prophesies and stories that she did not understand. Only when she found the Bahá'í Faith did she feel she was beginning to understand these things.

The wealthy woman listened to her friend describe her long spiritual journey and began to realize that she too had wondered all these things. She began to realize that these were the important questions of life, and that all her worries, cares, and concerns about her material existence were just a distraction from this core search that could be made to understand our world and our place in the Universe.

The wealthy woman began to spend more time studying, reading, meditating, praying, and consulting with her friends about spiritual questions. In the process, she found a new enthusiasm for life. She found a new zest to learn, grow, and develop in her understandings. She became a Bahá'í and joined a community of people from every walk of life who were on similar journeys. She found herself a part of something bigger than herself, a global project to transform the world into a more peaceful, hopeful, and fair place for all of humanity.

In the end, the woman created a new reality for herself around discovering her purpose in her life and rendering service to humanity as part of a global community of equals. In the process, all her material cares, concerns, and worries began to fade into the background of her life. If she had wealth, she would use it to serve others and care for her family. But beyond that, it was not the focus of her life. Instead, her spiritual development was her focus. This gave her a new sense of contentment that could never be owned, that could never be exhausted, and that would never end.

ANALOGY OF FINDING FLOW IN BASEBALL

In baseball, as in many sports, the great players have discovered the secret of what they call "flow." Reaching flow is about reaching a stage of ability where one does not have to think about what to do next. Action becomes all instinct. It becomes programmed reaction deep in our body. This kind of instinctual response is necessary for success in professional baseball, where the pitcher can throw the ball at over ninety miles an hour. A batter does not have time to think. He must react purely on instinct. He must know in his bones if he is going to swing, how hard, and to where. He must have the entire act preprogrammed in his mind so that his body reacts with pure efficiency.

The spiritual seeker strives to reach this state in his spiritual life if he is to achieve spiritual contentment. This kind of contentment comes when we do not need to consider, weigh, deliberate, and debate everything that comes at us in life. Spiritual contentment is then written in our countenance. Our countenance is how we carry ourselves in life, and it is shown in the way we treat people, the way we approach life, and the way we approach challenges. If we are confident, wise, patient, loving, empathetic, and adaptable, our countenance reflects that. People just know it when they meet us.

When we achieve spiritual contentment, our countenance is affected. We react purely on spiritual instinct to all the changes and chances that life throws at us. When bad things happen, we are not troubled in our core beliefs. When good things happen, we do not forget ourselves or our responsibilities. In every situation we react with spiritual efficiency. It can take a lifetime to master this skill. Some of us will get farther along than others. But the point is, we have to try. If we never try, then we never receive any portion of the bounties that come from a life of spiritual contentment.

CHAPTER 7:

APPRECIATING THE ROLE OF SINS AND FORGIVENESS IN FAITH

"... man's knowledge of God cannot develop fully and adequately save by observing whatever hath been ordained by Him and is set forth in His heavenly Book."

—Bahá'u'lláh, *Tablets of Bahá'u'lláh,* p. 268

WHEN RELIGION MAKES US FEEL BAD

We live in a society where feeling good is the order of the day. People are told by the media, as well as political leaders, that they deserve to get what they want, when they want it, and how they want it. Rules for morality or personal accountability are seen as old fashioned, unrealistic, impossible, a waste of time, or (worse yet) a hindrance to fully experiencing all that life has to offer. People today want to be free to do whatever makes them feel good in the moment. As long as we aren't hurting anyone else, we believe we should be able to do anything, anytime, anywhere.

Many believe that religions impose arbitrary or impossible rules on their followers in order to make them feel indebted to their faith. Some believe these rules are meant to restrict, inhibit, and restrain people from living full lives. They believe religions put too much emphasis on guilt and shame for doing things that are just human nature.

The fact is, most of us do not want to follow rules of morality. We do not like being told what we can and cannot do. We do not want to be judged by anyone. We do not want to feel guilty and ashamed for not living up to some religious standard of purity. At the same time, however, we see our world spinning out of control. We see the family unit, the basic building block of civilization, breaking down. We see divorce wreaking havoc in communities. We see people disconnected from one another in all aspects of life. We see economic inequality between the haves and have-nots getting worse everyday. We see the poor with access to fewer opportunities, less education, poorer health, and lower standards of living, all while the rich acquire greater and greater wealth, convenience, and opportunity.

People are busier than ever but they do not seem to be getting anywhere. The media is focused on divisions, crime, and sensationalism. Wars, terrorism, and disease seem to threaten us at all times. The environment is suffering from pollution in the air, water, and earth. Economies are broken from corruption and a global race to the bottom where factories move from country to country in order to find the lowest wages, poorest working conditions, fewest safeguards, and most permissive pollution policies, all in the name of endlessly increasing profits.

And yet, few see a connection between a breakdown in civilized life and a breakdown in morality. Few people stop to ask why people are more divided, more fearful, and less happy. Many people today have lost faith in government, politics, nonprofits, technology, and existing institutions of the world to solve our problems. Many are looking for something new, but they do not know what that is.

Few people would imagine that religion might be the solution they are looking for. People have many justifiable reasons to be suspicious of religion in the world. While the world's religious people have offered incredible amounts of charity and selfless sacrifice for their fellowman, some of the world's religious leaders have corrupted the messages of their faith's Founders.

Some religious leaders have turned to fear and guilt to motivate people. It is easy to understand why. Fear is the easiest way to motivate. If leaders can keep people afraid, they can keep people coming back on Sunday. These religious leaders tell the people that they are sinful and in need of religious services to free them from eternal damnation. These leaders have created manmade rituals, rights, and ideologies that they claim are the only paths to salvation.

Unfortunately, this is a short-sighted solution. Fear-mongering and guilt-inducing rhetoric only go so far. People want to feel good and hopeful in their faith and spirituality. They want to feel empowered and inspired. Making people feel weak and powerless does not change them. It does not help them solve the problems of society or of the world, let alone help them in their own personal lives. People are left in a state of collective helplessness where nothing ever seems to change.

SEEKING A BETTER WAY

The spiritual seeker believes that there must be a better way. He knows that true religion has the power to lift people up, bring people together, and inspire the best in them. He knows that intrinsic rewards are better than extrinsic fears. People do not change their lives in any lasting ways because they fear hell or damnation. Hell and damnation are too remote, too figurative, and not real to people. Intrinsic rewards, however, are within us all the time. Intrinsic rewards come into play when we do things because they make us better people, when we feel more complete, more helpful, more alive from living in alignment with a greater cause. Intrinsic rewards come from a life of service to humanity. These rewards come when we feel as though we are making a contribution and adding value.

Many spiritual seekers find the Bahá'í perspective on sin and forgiveness to be empowering and inspiring. Bahá'ís do not live in alignment with spiritual laws because they fear some remote concept of hell and damnation. On one hand, obeying the spiritual laws for the age in which we live makes Bahá'ís better people who are more capable of doing good in the world. But on the other hand, living in alignment with the Will of God for the age is also a protection from suffering. That is, living in alignment protects us from the negative consequences of our actions. We do not believe that a loving God wants to see us suffer. Instead, He wants us to succeed. And so God provides us with instructions on how to live well. It is our choice to follow those instructions or not to.

The concept of sinning in the Bahá'í Faith, therefore, is not about going into spiritual debt that then must be redeemed. It is more nuanced and personal. Sinning, for Bahá'ís, is about falling away from our own unique path toward God, and falling prey to our lower nature. Bahá'ís believe that spiritual laws are an essential tool for refining our characters and learning to grow into mature spiritual beings. They protect us from self-inflicted suffering that comes from following our baser instincts. Bahá'ís believe that humanity has two natures. One is the animal nature. The other is the heavenly nature. Our animal, or lower, nature is continuously calling us to be selfish, egomaniacal, and short-sighted. Our heavenly, or higher, nature, on the other hand, inspires us to be selfless, centered on the betterment of others, and with a view for the big picture of society. Therefore, Bahá'ís believe that spiritual laws ennoble us by empowering our heavenly natures and restraining our animal natures.

These laws give us protection from our lower natures and they help us see the world with clarity and purpose as spiritual beings in the process.

As darkness is the absence of light, in the Bahá'í view, evil is the absence of divine and spiritual refinement in our own lives. The Devil is figurative in the Bahá'í Faith. Satan is representative of our lower nature. He is personified as the voice that calls us to be selfish, greedy, and small-minded. To follow evil, for a Bahá'í, simply means following anything that leads us astray. To exist in hell means to live in a state of imperfection, distance, and disconnection from our true source. As the Bahá'í writings state, "The Evil One is he that hindereth the rise and obstructeth the spiritual progress of the children of men." (Bahá'u'lláh, *Gleanings from the Writings of Bahá'u'lláh*, no. 43.5)

The Bahá'í Faith offers a very high standard to live up to. No Bahá'í believes he or she can ever reach perfection. This is not because God wants us to continuously live in a state of guilt and shame for whatever we cannot achieve. Rather, it is because God wants us to never stop striving to improve ourselves. Bahá'ís believe in a God that is merciful and forgiving. If we feel guilt or shame, it is the result of our own choices not to live up to our spiritual nature. It is not something we should blame on anyone but ourselves. Ideally, it should inspire us to try harder, realign our lives, and make the necessary adjustments to refine our characters. It should inspire us to ask for forgiveness and then keep trying. We should not wallow in our guilt. We should not obsess over our shame. Instead, we should use it to recognize when we have fallen away from the true path, to motivate us to change our lives, and to become better people everyday. As the Bahá'í writings state, "Indeed, there existeth in man a faculty which deterreth him from, and guardeth him against, whatever is unworthy and unseemly, and which is known as his sense of shame." (Bahá'u'lláh, *Epistle to the Son of the Wolf*, p. 27).

UNDERSTANDING ACCOUNTABILITY

The spiritual seeker believes he has his own unique spiritual path toward God. No one can tell him what to believe, what is true, and how to live. He must decide in his own heart what is right and what is wrong. He is accountable for his own actions before God. This is the power of true faith. No government, no laws, no priests or clergy can hold him to a higher standard than the standard to which he can hold himself. Only he knows what is in his own heart. Only he knows his own thoughts and actions. He is the one who suffers the most if he does not live up to the standards of a healthy and balanced spiritual life. Therefore, only he is responsible for his life.

The spiritual seeker finds that the Bahá'í Faith offers a model for empowering his spiritual quest. There are no priests or clergy in the Bahá'í Faith. Bahá'ís have to figure out their own individual paths. They have to read the guidance in the writings of their faith, and strive to align their actions with what is ordained. Individuals are responsible not just for their actions, but also for their words and thoughts. Bahá'ís strive to avoid idle speech and conversations that lead to division and disunity. They are prohibited from backbiting and strive at all times to keep their minds focused on the betterment of humanity.

Bahá'ís are told to hold themselves to account for their own actions everyday. As the Bahá'í writings state, "O SON OF BEING! Bring thyself to account each day ere thou art summoned to a reckoning; for death, unheralded, shall come upon thee and thou shalt be called to give account for thy deeds." (Bahá'u'lláh, *The Hidden Words*, Arabic, no. 31).

The process of holding ourselves to account each day provides us the opportunity to meditate on our actions. Life is full of shades of gray. Right and wrong are not always easy to distinguish. The fact is, most humans can justify just about anything in their minds. Few think that they are really bad people—even the most hardened criminal makes up excuses for his actions. We are capable of explaining away or rationalizing just about any thought or action in life. We can choose to sin and make up reasons why it was OK this time, or why we deserved whatever we took, or why we could not do the right thing because of some outside force. We can blame society, our parents, our friends, or anything else that might influence us to do one thing or another. But in the end, it does us no good. The spiritual seeker believes that each of us is accountable for our own lives, and so to blame anyone else for our decisions is to fail to take responsibility for our actions.

Once we realize we have fallen away from the true path, the question is not "why did we fall short?" We often fail because we follow our lower nature. We fail because we give into fear or desire, lust or greed, or selfishness or short-sightedness. The question should instead be, "what can we learn from this, and how can we change?"

Sadly, some people convince themselves that they are destined to fail. They think they have to "learn the hard way" no matter what law or standard they are given. These people think they have to do the forbidden thing in order to experiment, see the results, and learn from them. From a Bahá'í perspective, no one has to learn the lessons of the universe the hard way. Instead, we can trust that the laws of God were revealed for our own good, and that we can benefit from living in alignment with the will of God.

Another important point is that while the spiritual seeker is responsible for his actions, he is also responsible for his inactions. We only pass through this world one time. If we fail to take advantage of the chances presented to us to live a kindly, generous, forgiving, and more spiritual life, then we miss those chances forever. Unfortunately, so many of us spend our lives trying to acquire material gain that we miss our opportunities to serve God by serving humanity. And once that time is passed, it is gone forever. As the Bahá'í writings state, "What advantage is there in the earthly things which men possess? That which shall profit them, they have utterly neglected. Erelong, they will awake from their slumber, and find themselves unable to obtain that which hath escaped them in the days of their Lord, the Almighty, the All-Praised." (Bahá'u'lláh, *Gleanings from the Writings of Bahá'u'lláh*, p. 138)

One important issue to consider is that of forgiveness. Bahá'ís are taught that asking forgiveness does not make us weak. Instead, it is an act of accountability. It is a sign of maturity and nobility. Asking for forgiveness leads to understanding and wisdom. It helps us understand our nature and our place in the world. When we ask for forgiveness from God, we also learn to forgive others who sin against us. As the Bahá'í writings state, "Wherefore, hearken ye unto My speech, and return ye to God and repent, that He, through His grace, may have mercy upon you, may wash away your sins, and forgive your trespasses. The greatness of His mercy surpasseth the fury of His wrath, and His grace encompasseth all who have been called into being and been clothed with the robe of life, be they of the past or of the future." (Bahá'u'lláh, *Gleanings from the Writings of Bahá'u'lláh,* no. 1136.1).

The truth is, asking for forgiveness from God might be one of the easier tasks. For many of us the hardest task is to forgive ourselves. Sometimes we do things that shock even us. We discover that we are all capable of falling short and that we all have moments of weakness. Even the most spiritual being may wake up some days ashamed and depressed by his own actions, thoughts, and words. The temptation is always there to beat up on ourselves, to lower our self-esteem, and to believe we are broken and incapable of doing anything right. It is the utmost height of humility and wisdom to realize that we are imperfect and we will always be imperfect.

Realizing that seeking forgiveness is important does not mean we should stop trying to perfect ourselves. It does not mean higher standards are not worth striving for. It just means the job is never done. We are never complete in our path to spiritual development, and we should never exalt ourselves or think we are better than anyone else. This is what it means for us to live humbly. We admit we are weak, and then we turn to God, ask for forgiveness, and get on with the work of building a better world for our children. The spiritual seeker realizes that a person can become paralyzed if he spends too much time dwelling on his own imperfections. It is better to ask for forgiveness, put it in God's hands, and try again the next day. Bahá'ís have many wonderful prayers for forgiveness that they can use to help them do this.

Finally, Bahá'ís are also encouraged to seek help and assistance whenever possible. Consultation within the community, among trusted friends and family can help us find ways to overcome our weaknesses and faults. If problems are very deep and psychological, we can also seek the help of mental health professionals, which is more powerful if those professionals take into account the spiritual aspects that guide our life. None of us are alone in our paths.

As the Bahá'í writings state, "O MOVING FORM OF DUST!

I desire communion with thee, but thou wouldst put no trust in Me. The sword of thy rebellion hath felled the tree of thy hope. At all times I am near unto thee, but thou art ever far from Me. Imperishable glory I have chosen for thee, yet boundless shame thou hast chosen for thyself. While there is yet time, return, and lose not thy chance." (Bahá'u'lláh, *The Hidden Words*, Persian, no. 21).

THAT VIRTUOUS MAN WHO LEARNED TO FORGIVE HIMSELF

There were two men who were good friends. One was very virtuous, and strived to always do the right thing. The virtuous man had a strong character. He had strong morals and he rarely broke any rules. The other man struggled with doing the right thing and often made poor choices. He did not have strong morals, guidelines, or very good self-control. He broke many rules and lived a much more difficult life as a result.

The virtuous man cared deeply for his misguided friend, and it saddened him to see how often his friend made a mess of his life. The fact was, the errant man was just very impulsive. He did not think through the consequences of his decisions. He always wanted things to be easy. He wanted to feel good all the time. He could never see the end in things, he could never be patient, and he could never restrain his desires. And because of his impulsiveness, the errant man made many poor choices and endured much self-inflicted suffering in his life.

The virtuous man tried not to pass judgment on his friend. He knew his friend had a good heart. He tried to help him with advice, example, and encouragement, but it never seemed to work. In the end, the errant man had to find his own way through life.

Later in life, though, the virtuous man failed a big moral test. It was a test that hit him when he was not expecting it. It snuck up on him and seduced him. His confidence and pride had blinded him to the idea that he too might be vulnerable to tests in life. In the beginning of failing the test, the virtuous man told himself that he was different, that he could control the situation, and that he would be OK even if he did the wrong thing. But things did not work out that way. The virtuous man ended up creating painful sadness for his family and hurting his reputation in the community.

Sad and depressed, the virtuous man did not know where to turn for help. He was so ashamed of himself. To his surprise, the first person to offer help and advice was his errant friend. His friend showed him the deepest understanding and compassion.

The virtuous man told his errant friend how he had thought that he was different and that he could control the situation. The errant man shook his head and said, "Yes, I understand completely. That's exactly what I tell myself, every time I mess things up."

The errant man went on to comfort his virtuous friend and explain that it was going to be OK. He offered the virtuous man tips on how he could make things right.

The virtuous man realized that through all of his friend's poor choices in life, his friend had developed a deep capacity to show compassion for his fellowman. The virtuous man found a new respect for his friend through this experience, and a new humility in himself.

ANALOGY OF PREPARING A MEAL

As we live out our lives and make choices about how we live, how we treat others, and how we treat ourselves, we can use the analogy of preparing a meal to share with our Lord. If we work hard at it, the meal will be delicious. If we try to get things right, to follow the recipes provided, and to use the best ingredients we have at hand, then the meal will be a delightful feast that we are happy to share with our Lord.

If we do not, then the meal will not be so good. If we cut corners, forget ingredients of the recipe, make mistakes in measurement and baking times, then we will be embarrassed to present this meal to our Lord.

In the same way, if we do not follow the instructions given to us by our Creator about how to live our lives in a healthy and productive path, then we risk dissipating our efforts and failing to fulfill our capacity. In addition, we recognize that failing to live up to the high standards of our Faith causes suffering for us, our family members, and for those who rely on us to be our best. We believe that to accept Bahá'u'lláh as the Manifestation of God for the Age means, in part, that we believe that His guidance, instructions, and laws are the medicine for our time perfectly attuned to the needs of society. This is something promised to humanity by God throughout history. Religion provides this bulwark to help us protect ourselves from our lower natures and find a path to a nobler life.

In the end, Bahá'ís do not fear God because of a fear of His wrath and anger. Instead they fear God because they fear disappointing God by failing to develop the spiritual potential that He has instilled in them. They fear being ashamed of their actions, words, or thoughts in this life. This fear of disappointing God can be inspirational. And they fear the consequences that come from living out of alignment with the instructions for the age. This, we consider, is a healthy balance that can help motivate us to do our best, to work hard, and to live up to our potential as best we can.

CHAPTER 8:

OVERCOMING TESTS AND DIFFICULTIES

"The winds of tests are powerless to hold back them that enjoy near access to Thee from setting their faces towards the horizon of Thy glory, and the tempests of trials must fail to draw away and hinder such as are wholly devoted to Thy will from approaching Thy court."

—Bahá'u'lláh, *Prayers and Meditations,* p. 3

NO LIFE IS FREE OF CHALLENGES

There is no getting around the fact that life is messy. No life is without tests and difficulties. No matter how much money we have, no matter who our parents are, no matter where we are born, and no matter how much we may plan, prepare, and work at things, sometimes things do not go how we want them to.

No one can remove all tests from life. No religion, no policy, no organization can remove all the factors that lead to suffering in the world. What they *can* do is help us mitigate the effects of events that are often out of our control. They can also help us reduce the amount of self-inflicted pain we bring upon ourselves.

For example, look at the tests we face when finding work and making a living. In today's world, most of humanity struggles just to survive. Billions of people work to keep a roof over their head, food on the table, and have enough for transportation to get around. For all of these people, suffering takes the form of constant fear and insecurity about the future. These people are acutely aware that they are one tragedy, one mistake, or one unlucky event away from homelessness, sickness, and starvation.

On the other hand, even among those who today live in countries where they can choose an education, pick a career, and make their own living, life is not without suffering. People in developed countries may find a job, but they still may struggle to find work that fulfills them. They may struggle to pay for childcare, to get out of debt, to save for retirement, or to take care of extended family. They may work hard to keep their skills up-to-date in the face of ever-changing technologies and business models. Some may fear economic changes that can cause the factory in town to move or shutdown, the software development that they specialize in to be outsourced, the big company they work for to drop benefits, or their family-run business being overwhelmed by a national chain-store. The fact is, people in developed countries are often one accident, one mistake, or one unlucky event away from being on the street or in a shelter.

Yet even those who appear to reach the pinnacle of career-success in life have challenges. For example, often wealthy people can be some of the most unhappy, unsatisfied, and stressed people we will ever meet. Their personal lives are often full of the burden of caring about all the possessions that they have. They often become overly accustomed to their wealth and become incapable of dealing with life outside of their bubble. They live in fear of losing all their privilege and superficial status.

Besides issues with making a living, many people have tests and difficulties with their health. Diseases strike rich and poor alike. Bad eating practices, poor exercise habits, and stressful personal lives are perpetuated by a materialistic society that is often working against us. Diseases can strike us at any moment. Risk for certain diseases can be affected by lifestyle, heredity, and what we eat to some extent, but in the end anyone can be stricken with cancer, heart disease, or the even the common cold. And these diseases cause us suffering.

In addition to physical diseases, there are countless mental illnesses that can bring us suffering. Addictions often creep into our lives without warning. We can become addicted to drugs, alcohol, gambling, shopping, pornography, cigarettes, and more. These addictions affect our moods, our physiology, our mental state, our ability to cope with life, our independence, our financial situation, our families, and our physical state. In the end such addictions can leave us depressed, weak, dependent, and endlessly suffering from anxiety that upsets everything in our lives.

If work and challenges from wealth or poverty do not strike us, and diseases or mental illnesses do not get to us, we will still face the tests and difficulties that come from aging. We are all getting older. Our bodies break down. No one who lives a long time on this earth is immune to the effects of aging.

People also have problems in their families. Divorce, dislocation, abuse, and lack of opportunity have ravaged the modern family's security. Today's families often do not have a healthy community-support network around them to help with childcare and with just dealing with the ups and downs of life. Many parents are disconnected from each other, many families are fearful of outsiders, and there are few effective models to follow.

Many couples struggle to remain faithful to each other in a society obsessed with sexual gratification at every turn. They strain to remain true to one another when unrealistic expectations are set. They expect marriage to make them happy, full, and complete in life. They believe that they deserve the excitement of a romantic love affair at any cost. Infidelity often appears to be a fresh start, but it ends up destroying everything they have worked to build, and in the process it hurts the ones they love most in life.

Finally, some of the most difficult tests and difficulties can come from larger factors in the world. People from all backgrounds face wars, terrorism, crime, and corruption. Entire communities can be impacted for generations by such events. These cause tragic trials and tribulations for people of all ages. Besides the manmade events listed, there are also the natural disasters and catastrophes that can turn our world upside-down. Under such conditions, no one is free of tests and difficulties.

SOURCES OF TESTS VS. THE SOURCES SUFFERING

One thing the spirial seeker realizes is that while we may all have tests and difficulties in our lives, we do not all have to suffer from them. Suffering comes when we let the tests and difficulties of life affect our inner spiritual condition. Those who have reached the heights of spiritual awareness and developed spiritual qualities of resilience and detachment do not let the rains, winds, and waves that come from the storms of life affect their inner spiritual condition. They are calm in the storm, steady in the quake, and cool in the fire. This does not mean that the spiritually aware person does not have tests, but rather that he is just not overly distressed by them.

The question for the spiritual seeker is not how to rid himself of tests and difficulties. He knows that, while he can mitigate them by living a spiritual life and making good choices, he cannot ensure a life without challenges. The first step for the spiritual seeker, then, is to realize where the suffering comes from, and how suffering itself is different from the challenges that it can create.

Many tests and difficulties in life come from the "changes and chances" of this world. That is, we live in a world of constant motion. The weather changes. The seasons change. The earth we stand on is even changing. Sometimes changes come fast, other times they take a long time to play out.

Besides the world itself changing, we are changing in ourselves. We are constantly aging, growing up, and going through different stages of development. With all these changes comes an element of chance. Chance comes from randomness and spiritual forces beyond our comprehension. Chance may be seen as luck. That is, sometimes we are lucky and things happen that we like. Other times we are not so lucky, and things happen that we do not like. But no matter what, we face an element of chance in everything we do. That is, outcomes and results are often outside our control, and we have to learn to deal with this fact.

The changes and chances of the world teach us to live between the ups and downs and to find the middle way in life. This constant motion in the universe teaches us to focus on the things that do not change in order to find that which is stable, constant, and reliable in life. Those unchanging things include spiritual truths, which represent the lifelines that we can hold onto during the tests and difficulties of life.

These changes and chances constitute a mighty barrier between people and their Lord. As the Bahá'í writings state, "Build ye for yourselves such houses as the rain and floods can never destroy, which shall protect you from the changes and chances of this life." (Bahá'u'lláh, *Gleanings from the Writings of Bahá'u'lláh,* no. 123.4).

Another source of suffering comes from tests and difficulties caused by other people. The spiritual seeker recognizes that everyone is at a different stage of development. Each of us has our own path to tread, our own lessons to learn, our own capacity to develop, and our own potential to manifest in the world. Some of us have worked hard on our character, and are doing so everyday. Others are trapped in the self, blind to the spiritual realities of life, and oblivious of the need to adapt, grow, and improve to meet the needs of a changing world.

The spiritual seeker must deal with all people openly, lovingly, and willingly no matter what stage of development they are in. While he treasures the companionship of people who inspire and uplift him, he knows he cannot shy away from caring for all people regardless of their spiritual condition. He knows that he cannot pass judgment, but he can and should protect himself. In this way he can look out for his loved ones by not giving them what is not good for them. Sometimes he must show wisdom and love through manifesting the qualities of caution and restraint.

Another source of suffering comes from tests and difficulties caused by our own choices in life. Many of us have high standards for ourselves, and we strive and struggle to reach those standards without ever seeming to succeed. Sometimes we face a test that confounds us and brings us back to the starting point. In fact, there are times we face the same test over and over, and keep failing it. This can be terribly discouraging, disappointing, and frustrating. Such an experience can be a great source of suffering in our lives. If tests and difficulties come from the changes and chances of life, from other people, and from our own choices, the suffering we endure actually comes from the manner in which we deal with those challenges. The spiritual seeker recognizes that suffering does not necessarily come from all of these factors in themselves. Instead, suffering comes from attachments. That is, if we have attachments to the way we think the world should work, then the changes and chances of life will constantly upset us. If we have attachments to how we think other people should behave, we will be terribly disappointed when people do not live up to our expectations. And if we have attachments to certain notions of personal success, then we are endlessly frustrated by our inability to overcome our own selves.

Attachments are the enemy of contentment, and contentment is the key to manifesting spiritual qualities in times of tests and difficulties. If we can find a state of contentment that endures, then we can deal with anything that life has to throw at us. Attachments come in many forms that include attachments to what we have, what we want, what we expect, and who we think we are. When things happen in life to take away what we have, deny us what we want, and alter the perception we have of ourselves, we feel suffering. These attachments are the real sources of suffering in our lives.

Bahá'u'lláh writes, "Help Thou Thy loved ones, O my Lord, them that have forsaken their all, that they may obtain the things Thou dost possess, whom trials and tribulations have encompassed for having renounced the world and set their affections on Thy realm of glory. Shield them, I entreat Thee, O my Lord, from the assaults of their evil passions and desires, and aid them to obtain the things that shall profit them in this present world and in the next." (Bahá'u'lláh, *Gleanings from the Writings of Bahá'u'lláh,* no. 138.3).

HOW TO REDUCE SUFFERING FROM LIFE'S TESTS AND DIFFICULTIES

Again, the spiritual seeker believes that he cannot rid himself of all of life's trials and tribulations. In fact, he believes that he needs such events (to a certain extent) in order to grow spiritually in the world. The fact is, life itself requires a certain amount of tests as we grow to maturity. We have to face challenges, overcome difficulties, and develop capacities throughout our lives. Therefore, the spiritual seeker is not looking for a religion or cause that promises to remove all bad things from life. That is not possible and it is not even healthy. What he can do is find a faith that reduces the suffering that comes from such tests and difficulties, and teaches us to appreciate the lessons that can be learned from such experiences.

The spiritual seeker recognizes that there are two types of tests in the world. The first type of test comes from the universe outside ourselves. These are tests we cannot avoid. They come in the form of actions from people, institutions, natural forces, and the environment in general. All we can do to mitigate the effects of these outside forces is to prepare ourselves spiritually, mentally, and physically to deal with whatever life hands us.

The second type of test comes from our own actions. These are the self-inflicted tests. We create them by not living up to a truly spiritual standard. That is, these are tests that come from making immoral, selfish, greedy, and ignorant choices. We can reduce such tests by following the laws of the divine religions.

In reality, for many spiritual seekers the laws of the Bahá'í Faith might seem too strict. But they offer a practical and modern approach to spiritual living. They provide a reasonable path for development in today's world. But no one is perfect. We will always be inflicting a certain amount of tests on our self no matter how good a person we are. Therefore, here too we need to prepare ourselves spiritually, mentally, and physically to deal with tests that come from our own actions. One of the best ways to build capacity for dealing with life's tests and difficulties is to develop spiritual qualities that can help us mitigate their effects. Such important qualities include detachment, obedience, moderation, selflessness, and forgiveness.

For example, detachment comes to mind as a very important quality to manifest when dealing with tests and difficulties. We can work on becoming detached from specific outcomes, specific goals, and specific achievements that may be out of our hands. We should only let ourselves be attached to the things we can control. In addition, we can learn to detach ourselves from desires for things that we do not need as spiritual beings. We can let go of the things that just add to the complexity of life, like materialistic things, and seek out things that simplify our lives and free us to focus on manifesting our spiritual potential.

Another quality we can develop includes obedience. Unfortunately, obedience is seen as a sign of submissiveness and weakness by many people in today's society. The spiritual seeker believes that obedience, when exemplified in the spiritual context, means alignment and protection. It means we are aligning ourselves to receive divine blessings in our lives. And it means we are protecting ourselves from our lower nature while freeing our spirits to strive toward acquiring greater capacity.

Moderation means living simply by only consuming as much as we really need of the world's resources and of people's attention.

Moderation is about finding a balance in our lives where we live in peace with nature and our own spirits.

Selflessness means putting others first. If we put others first, then we are not dwelling on our own problems and tests. Selflessness helps us forget our trials and tribulations and live to help others become more fulfilled. The spiritual seeker believes that this is the key to a happy and contented life, and he works constantly to practice selflessness in his life.

Finally there is forgiveness. Forgiveness is about forgiving those who have hurt us without reservation. It means understanding that those who hurt people are often ignorant of the effects of their actions, and finding compassion in our hearts for them. We can realize through this process that we would not want to be in their shoes when they face the consequences of their actions, and we can even pray for God to be merciful to them, as we pray for God to be merciful to us.

The spiritual seeker can also use prayer to mitigate tests and difficulties in his life. He may pray to change the world to fit his desires. But he knows that the better prayer is the one that asks to change his desires to fit with the plan of God. Prayer is a powerful force for the spiritual seeker and it is something he is calling on constantly in everything he thinks, does, and wishes for in the world.

As the Bahá'í writings state, "Lord! Turn the distressing cares of Thy holy ones into ease, their hardship into comfort, their abasement into glory, their sorrow into blissful joy, O Thou that holdest in Thy grasp the reins of all mankind!" ('Abdu'l-Bahá, in *Bahá'í Prayers,* p. 23).

RECOGNIZING THE VALUE OF TESTS

Clearly, it is important to recognize the full value of tests and difficulties in our spiritual development. Tests and difficulties can help us make adjustments, adapt to change, remind us of what matters, and connect us to our fellowmen in deeper and more profound ways.

As the Bahá'í writings state, "To attain eternal happiness one must suffer. He who has reached the state of self-sacrifice has true joy. Temporal joy will vanish." ('Abdu'l-Bahá, *Paris Talks,* p. 179)

The fact is, tests and difficulties can help push us to make the adjustments that we may need to make in order to grow and develop properly. Sometimes a big test or challenge can wake us up from a rut. That is, there are times we get into routines in life with work, home, hobbies, and interests, and we forget the wider world and the needs of humanity. Facing a test or difficulty now and then helps change those routines, and wakes us up to the real world around us.

Tests can also force us to adapt. The reality is, life presents us with a series of challenges. Our role is to adapt to these challenges, learn from them, and find a way to prosper in the process. For example, many young people are going to have several careers in their lifetime. They may work at many different companies, in different skill areas, and even in different towns or countries throughout their lives. In order to succeed, they need to learn to constantly adapt to change, to develop new skills, to manifest new capacities, and to fit into new environments. Otherwise they will never be able to prosper in today's ever-changing economy. The same is true of spiritual matters. We have to learn to reinvent ourselves, our lives, and our world from time to time in order to succeed and prosper as spiritual beings.

Trials and tribulations of life can also remind us of what is important. For example, when we face health problems, it can remind us to appreciate good health. When we lose our jobs and come upon hard times economically it can help us appreciate having a job that pays the bills when we do find one. In spiritual terms, if we fall away for a time from the path toward awareness and peace, it can help us wake up and appreciate the value of the teachings that could have saved us from self-inflicted suffering.

Tests and difficulties can also help us connect to one another in deeper and more profound ways. When we struggle with our fellowmen and women in life we see them at their best and we see them at their worst. That is, at such times of great challenge we see the full spectrum of human capacity. Through these tests we may develop bonds with people that we cannot describe. By living and working alongside people who we care about, and helping them improve their situation in response to a crisis or difficulty in their lives, we truly get to know them. In turn, this helps us show compassion, understanding, and love to the people that we might otherwise not appreciate. Therefore, without the occasional test, we may never know how much we really can love and assist our fellowman.

Lastly, the spiritual seeker believes that growing spiritually in life does not mean you reduce the tests. Just because you live a virtuous life does not mean you will not have challenges to overcome in life. In fact, the spiritual seeker recognizes that sometimes the opposite is true. Sometimes the especially hard tests are reserved for the most virtuous of all. This is not because God is punishing virtue. Instead, it is because God wants to see the pure in spirit reach higher states of awareness in life. In this way, God helps those true spirits shine as bright as they possibly can by forcing them to manifest qualities such as patience, perseverance, and resignation in the world. In the end, such tests are a gift provided to the spiritual seeker to prove his faith, discover his capacity, and manifest his potential.

As the Bahá'í writings state, "O spiritual friends and loved ones of the All-Merciful! In every Age believers are many but the tested are few. Render ye praise unto God that ye are tested believers, that ye have been subjected to every kind of trial and ordeal in the path of the supreme Lord. In the fire of ordeals your faces have flushed aglow like unto pure gold, and amidst the flames of cruelty and oppression which the wicked had kindled, ye suffered yourselves to be consumed while remaining all the time patient. Thus ye have initiated every believer into the ways of steadfastness and fortitude. You showed them the meaning of forbearance, of constancy, and of sacrifice, and what leadeth to dismay and distress. This indeed is a token of the gracious providence of God and a sign of the infinite favours vouchsafed by the Abhá Beauty Who hath singled out the friends of that region to bear grievous sufferings in the path of His love. Outwardly they are fire, but inwardly light and an evidence of His glory." ('Abdu'l-Bahá in *Fire and Light,* p. 29).

THE UNLUCKY MAN LEARNS THE VALUE OF TESTS

There was once a very unlucky man. Since childhood he had endured many sicknesses and ailments. Because of all his health problems, the unlucky man struggled in school and had trouble keeping a job. His parents died when he was young and he had little support. For a long time he was bitter and resentful. But he was still a spiritual man. He believed in God and wanted to do the right thing with his life. Yet he could not understand why God had supposedly cursed him. He could not understand why he could never get a break in life, and why things never seemed to go his way.

One day, the man was in the hospital receiving care for one of his health issues. Next to him sat a young girl who had her own ailments. She was very sad. The unlucky man wanted to cheer her up. He began to talk with her and tell her some stories. He told her about all the ridiculous things that had happened to him over the years. Everything that could go wrong in his life seemed to go wrong. The sickly man and the little girl were laughing hysterically by the end of their time together. When it was time for the little girl to go in for her operation, she smiled and thanked the man for his time. Her eyes were glowing with warmth and confidence that whatever happened, she would be OK.

As the man sat there waiting for the little girl to come out of her operation, he realized that he had grown a lot from his problems in life. He recognized that if he had not had such a hard time in his life, he could never have connected with that little girl. He could never have made her laugh. He decided he was going to look for more ways to serve people in his life by sharing the experiences and insights he had gained.

The sickly man had spent many years investigating the Bahá'í Faith. Even though he did not understand everything about this faith, he decided to become a Bahá'í as a way to be of service to mankind. As he studied the Bahá'í Faith more, he started to read about the lives of some of the important figures such as Bahá'u'lláh. He realized that Bahá'u'lláh suffered imprisonment, banishment, and abuse for over forty years at the hands of religious and government authorities who were threatened by His Message of peace and fulfillment. The sickly man identified with the life of Bahá'u'lláh, and he felt a deeper connection to God in the process.

In the end the sickly man realized that tests and difficulties can offer a person perspective. They can teach people lessons about themselves and about the world. They can teach people about patience, resignation, and perseverance. They can help people connect to their Lord and identify with the lives of those who suffer for the cause of goodness. In this way, a life of trials and tribulations can lead to more spiritual awareness and divine inspiration in life.

ANALOGY OF THE GRASS AND THE TREE

One popular analogy from spiritual literature that helps people deal with tests and difficulties is the story of the grass and the tree in the windstorm. The tree is rigid, unbending, and unyielding to the wind. It stands its ground for as long as it can. The tree is proud and confident of its strength until the winds blow too hard and shatters it.

The grass, on the other hand, is not proud. The grass is humble. It bends with the wind. It yields under the pressure. It is not shattered by the tests of the windstorm. Instead, the grass lets the wind pass right through it and remains just as green and strong and beautiful as it ever was.

The spiritual seeker does not want to be full of pride. He does not want to try to resist the tests of life like the tree. He knows that this path only leads to destruction and suffering. When facing life's challenges and difficulties, the trick for the spiritual seeker is to live like that blade of grass. The blade of grass wants to grow tall and strong and beautiful. But it also wants to adapt. It wants to bend with the winds of the universe and survive the storms of life. Therefore it aligns itself with the forces of life in order to see a better day.

Finding humility to bend with the winds of life is essential to success in the spiritual path. As the Bahá'í writings state in a prayer, "If it be Thy pleasure, make me to grow as a tender herb in the meadows of Thy grace, that the gentle winds of Thy will may stir me up and bend me into conformity with Thy pleasure, in such wise that my movement and my stillness may be wholly directed by Thee." (Bahá'u'lláh, *Prayers and Meditations by Bahá'u'lláh*, p. 240)

CHAPTER 9:

LEARNING ABOUT LIFE THROUGH DEATH

"I came forth from God, and return unto Him, detached from all save Him, holding fast to His Name, the Merciful, the Compassionate."

—Bahá'u'lláh, *The Kitáb-i-Aqdas*, ¶129

FACING THE END

As mortal creatures in this material world, we all have to face death. Some of us try to prepare for it, but most of us try to not think about it. Death is something foreign to our modern world. Our lives today are about living. We focus on what we are, where we are, what we want, and when we want it. We leave death for another time. We may lose loved ones along the way including friends, family, children, and parents. For many of us, these losses are felt deeply and we are not always sure how to go on living with the loss. We miss these people with all our hearts and we are not always sure how to fill the void. We miss their presence, their voices, and their touch and we are not sure if it is OK to reach out to them once they are gone. We feel the loss of their immediate presence and we are not sure if we will ever be with them again. Yet, if we suffer, it is because that is where we focus: on what we cannot touch, cannot feel, or cannot hear anymore.

The fact is, death terrifies many of us. We fear the unknown. We fear the idea of nothingness and the darkness and emptiness that death appears to be. We fear being forgotten. We fear losing everything we are. We fear the loss of our experiences, our knowledge, our accomplishments, and our own sense of self that we've worked so hard to define in this world from the moment we first drew breath.

Most religious people do believe they are headed somewhere after death. They are comforted by promises of heaven and an afterlife. But many of them are not sure how that relates to the here and now. They are not sure how a promise in the future affects who they are, what they are doing, and how they are living in the present. They are not sure what it means for those who have passed on before them. Are they gone forever? Do they only exist in memories? They are not sure where they went, what they are doing, and how they relate to them.

Dealing with the end of life is difficult. Statistically, most of us will have to bury our parents. Many of us will lose friends and coworkers. Most likely, at least half of us who marry will lose our spouses. Some of us will even lose children. These losses are tragic, painful, and difficult to deal with. At a physical level we have to decide how to deal with their material legacy such as their properties, possessions, and their most precious belongings. At the interpersonal level, we have to learn how to live with the gaping hole that such losses leave in our lives. At the personal level, we have to decide how we are going to let this loss affect us and how we will continue to live our own lives. We have to deal with the fact that we too will die one day. We too will make that journey. We have to decide how we will face that door for ourselves. Will we face it with grace and dignity or will we face it with fear, dread, and anger? Will we live in a way that the end is perceived as a graduation from a life of service and love, or will we live in a way that we are dragged clawing and screaming from our material possessions and attachments?

The spiritual seeker does not see death as some great force of trauma and disruption in life. The spiritual seeker sees it as a natural phenomenon. He sees it as something that is normal and meaningful in our spiritual existence. Learning to deal with death in a positive, healthy, and balanced way helps the spiritual seeker. It helps him appreciate the time he does have, the memories he has acquired, and the friendships and relationships he has cultivated in his life. Death makes these elements of our lives precious, fleeting, and important. The spiritual seeker uses his meditation about death and the afterlife to help him make the most of his own life. It spurs him on to learn, overcome, and grow as a person in every aspect of his journey through this world.

WHAT IS DEATH?

The spiritual seeker senses that there is more to this world. He feels it in his soul. Many an artist, musician, writer, craftsman, naturalist has felt the evidence of something more in the perfection of their work, in the meditative trance they find through the excellence in their efforts, and in the poetic overtones that they find weaved throughout creation when their heart is attuned to a greater presence. It is an innate sense that there is something beyond this world, something underlying it, something driving it, and something reflected in it. It is a sense that crosses cultural and historical boundaries. The fact is, in most indigenous cultures throughout time, from the ancient tribes of Ireland, to the great civilizations of Egypt, to the modern followers of the world's great religions, people have felt the presence of another world acting on ours. Call it heaven, call it the spirit realm, or call it the endless worlds of God, the spiritual seeker believes this next world exists much in the way he knows truth exists.

In countless cultures and civilizations, death has been seen as the bridge between this material world in which we exist, and that other place where our spirits reside. Many spiritual seekers find the Bahá'í teachings on death to be comforting and meaningful. This is because Bahá'ís teach that death is an end and a beginning at the same time. That is, it is a moment of transition when our consciousness continues without a human body to restrain it. It represents a stage in our journey where we realize the impact of our lives in this world and then go on to the next realm of existence taking only the good we have developed along the way. Once we depart this mortal frame, we leave all our weakness, ignorance, and isolation behind, and we become light upon light.

The spiritual seeker sees the loss of loved ones as a temporary separation from those we care about. The Bahá'í Faith teaches that those who pass on before us are not gone, they are instead just one step ahead of us on the same path. Those who have lived lives of selflessness and spiritual awareness go on to develop a new kind of connection with us, a connection of the heart and soul. They still see us, but they see us as spiritual beings. They know us better than we know ourselves. They see our potential, our capacity, and our opportunity to better our lives and the world around us. They pray for us, guide us, and watch over us and long to see us succeed in service to humanity. Much like nurses in a newborn baby nursery, they care for us as the precious and wondrous bundles of light that we can potentially be. They are around us all the time, speaking to our hearts, guiding our minds, and inspiring our lives.

Bahá'ís are told that people who pass on who have not lived spiritually focused lives will find themselves impotent, small, and shrouded in the mists of attachments to the world they left behind. These souls are handicapped in the spiritual realms, aware of the suffering and pain they have brought themselves and those around them, and cognizant of the untapped potential and opportunity that they failed to realize during their time on earth. But again, this station is not the end of one's journey in the next world. These souls are not condemned to eternal damnation. Instead, they just have more to learn, more to atone for, and more to develop on their own personal journey toward God.

Hell, from this spiritual perspective, is found in ignorance of, and distance from, our Creator. In fact, in such a reality, hell can be found in this world as in the next. As the Bahá'í writings state, "The immortality of the spirit is mentioned in the Holy Books; it is the fundamental basis of the divine religions. Now punishments and rewards are said to be of two kinds: first, the rewards and punishments of this life; second, those of the other world. But the paradise and hell of existence are found in all the worlds of God, whether in this world or in the spiritual heavenly worlds." ('Abdu'l-Bahá, *Some Answered Questions,* p. 223).

The goal of the spiritual seeker is to live in a way that death is a beginning, not an end. The spiritual seeker wants his life to be one of meaning and purpose. He wants his legacy to be one of goodness in the world. He wants to take on a form of influence and love in the afterlife, and he lives a life in this world as if he is already in the next one. He believes that the spiritual capacity that people exert in the afterlife is a reflection of the spiritual power they can exert in this life. That is, human souls who achieve great things by helping, serving, and loving humanity to the fullest extent become inspirations to others. Through this process, they become sources of courage, empowerment, knowledge, wisdom, and constancy that others turn to for help in their paths. Their example lives on long after their presence in this plane of existence has expired. In this way we can affect others by living true to our values both in this world and in the afterlife.

WHAT WE KNOW OF THE AFTERLIFE

One question everyone wants to know is, what is the afterlife? Where do we go? The spiritual seeker can turn to an analogy from the Bahá'í writings for insight. Bahá'ís often use the analogy of a baby in the womb of its mother to describe the difference between this world and the next. As the Bahá'í writings state, "The world beyond is as different from this world as this world is different from that of the child while still in the womb of its mother." (Bahá'u'lláh, *Gleanings from the Writings of Bahá'u'lláh,* no. 81.1).

For example, a baby lives in the womb of its mother for about nine months, completely oblivious of the world outside. If one tried to explain what the outside world was like to the baby, that is, if one were to try to describe the sights and sounds of our world, the baby would not believe it. The fact is, all the baby knows is the womb world. The womb world seems pretty nice and cozy. Trying to explain a world beyond it to a baby inside the womb (if the baby could comprehend language and reasoning) would be like trying to explain sight to a blind man, or sound to a deaf man. Until they experience it, they will never fully understand it.

But there is a very important purpose for the womb world. Inside this perfectly warm and cozy bubble, the baby is growing arms, legs, eyes, ears, and organs for it to function properly when it is born. If the baby does not grow properly, if it does not develop completely, it is born into the world with a handicap.

The soul is in a similar state in this world. The soul exists in the womb-world of material existence. In this material world, the soul is surrounded by the spiritual realms, but it has no concept of those worlds. Even if someone came and told it how wondrous and peaceful those worlds were, the soul probably could not comprehend them. The spiritual realms represent totally different realities, just as the material world is totally different from the womb-world.

In addition, there is a very important purpose to life in the material world for all of us. That is, while the soul exists in the material world it is supposed to be acquiring spiritual qualities. These spiritual qualities include compassion, wisdom, love, empathy, and many more. These qualities will be of primary use in the afterlife, just like the limbs and organs developed by the baby in the womb are designed for this material world. If one does not develop these qualities, then, like a baby born without eyes or without hands, the soul will be handicapped in the next world.

In addition, the Bahá'í teachings explain that the human body is a temple for the soul. Therefore it is to be cared for and looked after and respected for the precious cargo that it carries. A soul is related to the human body like light is related to a mirror. The light is reflected in the mirror, but it is not in the mirror. The soul is reflected in our human temple, but it is not physically in the temple. They are together and apart at the same time.

The Bahá'í writings tell us that when the body ceases to function, the person dies, and the soul is released from this relationship. It is born into a new reality. Once the soul moves on to the next world, it leaves behind all sickness, pain, weakness, and suffering associated with the physical reality, and it takes on a new form. The reality of this new form is not limited by time and space. There are no physical limitations in the afterlife. In that place we see, hear, and think in spiritual terms with spiritual eyes, spiritual ears, and a spiritual perspective. We take nothing with us that is not used in that world.

In addition, Bahá'ís believe that at the time of death people face an ultimate accounting for their lives. In this process, they see every thought, act, and experience of life revealed back to them. At this moment people face judgment for who they are, how they lived their lives, who they helped, and who they hurt. Those souls who lived lives of virtue and service become luminous and influential in all the worlds of God. Those souls who did not develop as much are less luminous and less able to influence the worlds of God.

The Bahá'í writings explain that the world's of God are all around us, and that there are endless stages for development and growth toward God. The souls of the afterlife progress through these stages by the grace and mercy of God. As the Bahá'í writings, state, "The progress of man's spirit in the divine world, after the severance of its connection with the body of dust, is through the bounty and grace of the Lord alone, or through the intercession and the sincere prayers of other human souls, or through the charities and important good works which are performed in its name." ('Abdu'l-Bahá, *Some Answered Questions*, p. 240).

Bahá'ís believe that we are still connected to our loved ones throughout the spirit world. The bonds of love endure. Those who have passed before us look out for us, guide us, and pray for us from their reality. They see us from a spiritual perspective and exist in a state of utmost joy and radiance. We are told that the afterlife is beyond anything we can comprehend, but that for the humble and faithful souls it offers a wondrous and glorious reality. Souls in that reality can inspire us in this world like leaven inside of bread. As the Bahá'í writings state, "The nature of the soul after death can never be described, nor is it meet and permissible to reveal its whole character to the eyes of men. The Prophets and Messengers of God have been sent down for the sole purpose of guiding mankind to the straight Path of Truth. The purpose underlying Their revelation hath been to educate all men, that they may, at the hour of death, ascend, in the utmost purity and sanctity and with absolute detachment, to the throne of the Most High. The light which these souls radiate is responsible for the progress of the world and the advancement of its peoples. They are like unto leaven which leaveneth the world of being, and constitute the animating force through which the arts and wonders of the world are made manifest." (Bahá'u'lláh, *Gleanings from the Writings of Bahá'u'lláh,* no. 81.1).

DEALING WITH DEATH

The spiritual seeker sees his loved ones who have passed before him as colonists who have journeyed ahead to a new world to make a new life. While he misses them dearly, he also wishes them well in their new existence. He is happy for them because he believes they are now free of all cares, stresses, pain, and worry of the material world.

In dealing with the grief and suffering that comes from losing loved ones, the spiritual seeker learns to replace the pain of loss with the warm contentment that comes from gratitude. Instead of thinking about the time he does not have, he replaces it with memories of the time he did have. Instead of being resentful for what he has lost, he is thankful for what he gained from knowing these souls. He soon discovers that gratitude and grief cannot live in the same heart. Sometimes we know our loved ones for a lifetime, other times we only know them for a few years, or even a moment. But we can always find a way to be grateful for the good memories, the enduring lessons, and the wondrous presence that they will forever inhabit in our consciousness throughout all the worlds of God.

In some ways, the burial process of the Bahá'í Faith can help the spiritual seeker come to terms with the death of a loved one. For example, when a person dies in the Bahá'í community, the body is ceremonially washed, often with rose water. In addition, a special ring is placed on the finger of the dead that says, "I came forth from God, and return unto Him, detached from all save Him, holding fast to His Name, the Merciful, the Compassionate." Bahá'ís then wrap the body in silk or cotton and place it in the ground inside a coffin made of fine wood or crystal, along with more prayers. Burial is also required to take place within one hour's travel of the place of death. In addition, there is a special Bahá'í prayer, which we call *The Prayer for the Dead*, which is recited at the funeral ceremony. This is the only time in the Bahá'í Faith where congregational prayer (that is, where one person says a ritual prayer on behalf of others), is allowed.

Together these rituals provide Bahá'ís one last act of service to offer loved ones. We are also told to pray for the progress of their souls, as they are praying for us. We believe that our prayers will help them grow toward God in the spiritual realms. We can also render service or make contributions to good causes in their name. These are all things that will help their spiritual progress.

The spiritual seeker also uses the lessons of the burial process to face his own end. He knows that he too must die one day. He does not know when. In fact, his end could come in twenty years, or it could come in twenty minutes. Instead of putting off death until another day, the spiritual seeker learns to live every day as if it were his last. Instead of putting off service for another day, he struggles to live true to his beliefs, his ideals, and his dreams and aspirations in everything he does today.

In the end, the spiritual seeker uses death as a tool to be a better person. He finds ways to help those who are grieving the loss of loved ones. He tries to give meaning and comfort to those who remain behind. And when his time comes, he prays that he will have the grace, the dignity, and the courage to leave this world confident that he has given it his best. In fact, he might even learn to look forward to reunion with all of his loved ones who have passed on before him. In addition, he learns to live every day to the fullest. He smells every scent, appreciates every sound, and enjoys the company of every interesting and spiritually minded person that passes his way. Through this process, his life becomes a life of wonderment and joy. No matter what happens, he always has blessings to count, gratitude to express, and joy to manifest.

As the Bahá'í writings state, "Grant, O my Lord, that they who have ascended unto Thee may repair unto Him Who is the most exalted Companion, and abide beneath the shadow of the Tabernacle of Thy majesty and the Sanctuary of Thy glory. Sprinkle, O my Lord, upon them from the ocean of Thy forgiveness what will make them worthy to abide, so long as Thine own sovereignty endureth, within Thy most exalted kingdom and Thine all-highest dominion. Potent art Thou to do what pleaseth Thee." (Bahá'u'lláh, *Prayers and Meditations by Bahá'u'lláh*, p. 278).

THE MOTHER WHO LOST A DAUGHTER, THEN FOUND ANOTHER

There was a mother who lost one of her daughters to a long and terrible sickness. The year-long experience took everything out of the woman, so much that she barely had time to care for her younger daughter, the sister of the girl who had passed on. In truth, the mother was angry for what had happened. She could not understand why her little girl had to die. She was angry for the loss of all the experiences she was not going to have with her older daughter. She was resentful because she was never going to see her little girl grow up and make a life of her own.

One day, the mother was upstairs and she heard noises coming from the room of the daughter who had passed away. The mother had not set foot in that room since her daughter had died. At hearing the noises, she was very upset that someone was interfering with the room she wanted to leave as a shrine to her lost child. She marched right into the room to see who was disturbing her daughter's memory. But as soon as she went into the room she found her younger daughter playing in the corner with her big sister's dolls. The little girl was laughing and acting out some of the stories she had created with her sister.

Instead of saying anything, the mother just sat down on the bed and listened to her younger daughter play. Instead of getting upset, she began to smile through her tears. She too remembered the games and stories her older daughter constantly shared with both of them. Instead of feeling sad, she began to feel grateful. She was grateful for having the chance to know her older daughter during the time that she had been given with her.

At some point, the mother sat down and started playing alongside her younger daughter. In the end, she let the little girl move into her big sister's room and use all her big sister's toys and dolls as much as she wanted. Through this process, both mother and daughter found healing through remembering the good times, appreciating the memories, and thanking God for the time they did have with the daughter who had passed on. Together they prayed for the big sister every night, and called upon her spirit to cheer them up whenever they felt sad. They kept the girl's memory alive, helped heal one another, and grew together in the process.

ANALOGY OF THE BIRD IN THE CAGE

The analogy of the bird in the cage is one way to describe life and its relationship to death. That is, a bird outside a cage can potentially soar into the heavens and enjoy all the freedom and bounty of a wondrous world below them. But inside the cage all that potential is hidden. The bird in the cage does not know what life is like outside its walls. It does not need its wings. It does not know how to catch the wind and glide in the breeze. It is ignorant of the outside world.

Our souls in this world are like those birds. We are trapped in the human temple of our bodies. When the body dies, our souls are released to fly to our true spiritual homes. We discover all the capacities, powers, and influence we were meant to manifest in the world. Therefore, the spiritual seeker looks forward to his end as a bird looks forward to freedom from the cage. And when his loved ones pass on before him, he wishes them nothing but a speedy passage into eternity, as spiritual birds who fly home to heaven.

CHAPTER 10:

OFFERING A FULFILLING PATH TO EVERY SOUL

"Strive thou, that haply thou mayest achieve a deed the fragrance of which shall never fade from the earth."

—Bahá'u'lláh, *Epistle to the Son of the Wolf,* p. 115

WHAT FULFILLMENT IS AND WHAT IT IS NOT

Today's world offers few paths to true and lasting fulfillment. Many people wander through their lives never really feeling connected to their community, their world, or themselves. Some may find traces of something bigger than them in the world, but see it lost when the unifying spirit behind it moves on to the next fad, the next movement, or the next big cause everyone seems to care about. Some may struggle to find their place in society by fitting in or conforming to other peoples' standards. Others may strive to acquire riches and financial security only to find that money cannot buy the things that truly make life worth living. Some may turn to short-term pleasures or immediate gratification in ways that risk harming their most valued relationships. The fact is, there are countless distractions in life, especially in today's hyper-connected, hyperactive, and hyper-engaged culture. Sadly, none of these distractions leave us feeling truly fulfilled in our lives.

Finding spiritual fulfillment in life is about seeing past all the distractions of our world and focusing on answering the important questions in life. These questions include, "Why do we exist? What is our purpose? How can we add value in the world? What will be our contribution and our legacy? Who will I love and care for? And how can I become the person I was meant to be?" Spiritual fulfillment comes when we find deeply satisfying answers to these questions.

Spiritual fulfillment comes from a spiritually healthy and uplifting life. It is a result of living true to our values and our spirit. But true fulfillment is constantly under threat in today's world. It is being threatened by spiritual diseases. These diseases strike at the core of what it means to be a spiritual being. They often infect us when we least expect it. They often clothe themselves in virtue and seep into our lives with justifications and excuses that seem rational and logical at the time. Spiritual sicknesses include materialism, cynicism, self-absorption, apathy, licentiousness, fear, and closed-mindedness. Finding spiritual fulfillment, therefore, means we must heal these spiritual diseases that afflict us. Healing comes when we identify the symptoms, recognize the sickness, and take actions to bring us back into balance with our spirit.

Materialism is one of the greatest spiritual diseases of our age. It is constantly threatening to infect us with desires, wants, and cravings that can bring no lasting or enduring satisfaction. No one is safe from the ravages of this disease. It affects poor and rich alike. It can attack our hearts without warning and cause us to drift into an endless cycle of desire for things that do not endure. It drives people to buy clothes they may barely ever wear, electronics that they will hardly ever use, or homes with rooms they will never live in. It causes people to spend money they do not have, exhaust themselves shopping for things they may never utilize, and distract themselves with transient things that are gone in an instant. It is powered by a philosophy that tells us that we matter only as much as we consume things. It calls us to sacrifice friendships, family bonds, and relationships for the acquisition of material comforts that only serve to distract us from helping, serving, and caring for the ones we love.

Cynicism is another spiritual disease. Cynicism infects the hopeful and hardens their hearts. It creeps up on us when we surrender and when we stop believing it is possible to change our world for the better. It tells us that there are no answers, so we might as well not try. It shuts us down. It closes us off from the world. It is a protection mechanism that offers us safety from disappointment. It is seductive and easy but is it wrong. It leads us to accomplishing nothing. It makes no contribution. It adds no value. It leads us to resent those who try, to show disdain for those who struggle, and to belittle those who take risks. Cynicism darkens our spirit and leaves us hollow, empty, and alone.

Self-absorption is a spiritual disease that is disguised in false awareness. It is a sign of immaturity. Self-absorption puts our needs above those of others. It puts our own desires and wants at the center of our lives, and it leads us to make shortsighted decisions and pass up opportunities to grow, develop, and improve ourselves. It focuses our thoughts on whatever leads to instant gratification. Self-absorption leads us to a perpetual state of infantilism, where we think the world should satisfy our wants above the wants of all others. The selfish person never grows up. The selfish person never discovers the amazing bounties that come from a life lived in service and sacrifice for the greater good. And the selfish person never reaches his full potential.

Apathy is another spiritual disease where we leave the hard work to others. It is the easy path and the path of least resistance. It comes when we become comfortable in our lives. We see sacrifice as inconvenient. We see the needs of others as a nuisance. Apathetic people do not want to change. They would rather not deal with the pain and suffering of others. They often have a life filled with work, family, and friends that gives them a sense of stability and consistency that they do not want to interrupt. They are content to see the world around them suffer as long as they have their own needs met and their own desires satiated. Apathy leaves us cut off from the world. It makes us helpless to affect change. It means we never leave our nest and develop our full potential.

Licentiousness is a spiritual disease that leads us to debase ourselves by following our carnal desires. Licentiousness is when we disregard rules and standards that would ennoble and empower us. It is focused on satisfying our lower nature at any cost. Any rules that are inconvenient are set aside without worry about consequences or ramifications. We do what we want, and we disregard the cost. We turn to worshipping our animal natures. It means we never learn to restrain ourselves. We never learn to control ourselves. We find ourselves imprisoned by our bodies' physical desires. We turn to drugs, sex, gambling, consumerism, and unhealthy relationships that drag us deeper into emptiness and longing. The more we try to gratify the carnal desires, the stronger their hold becomes over our lives. They are like a rapacious parasite that attaches itself to our spirit, sapping our lives of the capacity to overcome our ego and reach our true potential. Licentiousness is an empty existence where we fill the void in our heart with frivolous distractions only to wake up the next day feeling empty and out of control in our lives. For the spiritual being, there is no worse fate than to be a prisoner of carnal desires, unable to break free and find true fulfillment in life.

Fear is a spiritual disease that takes many forms. While some fear may be a healthy thing that can keep us safe, too much fear can paralyze us. The fact is, if we let fear take hold of our hearts, we can end up fearing everything. We can come to fear change and we can come to fear the status quo. We can fear others and we can fear our own selves. We can fear commitment and we can fear uncertainty. The reality is that fear takes hold when we lose confidence in ourselves to deal with life. It comes when we see our own weakness, our own frailty, and our own ignorance as barriers between us and achieving success. Fear, in some forms, has the potential to make us weak and helpless.

Finally, closed-mindedness is a spiritual disease that limits us from appreciating the wonders and bounties of living a full and complete life. Closed-minded people are not willing to consider options, explore alternatives, test theories, or engage differences. Closed-minded people are content to hold onto their small and limited worldview. They believe that they know enough and therefore anything you offer is just a distraction and a waste of their time. Closed-minded people are never challenged, never pushed, and never awakened. They exist in their own little reality without growth and maturity. People who are closed-minded live as shadows of their full potential. They refuse to consider other paths, other philosophies, other cultures, or other ways of living. They shut themselves off from developing in the process. They become static and closed to the ever-changing world that offers the rest of mankind more meaning, purpose, and hope everyday.

So how does one deal with all the spiritual diseases? How does one overcome them, or better yet, become immune to them? The answer is the same as how we deal with physical diseases. With physical diseases, we have two ways to defend against them. First, we strive to stay healthy. And second, when we do become sick, we work to heal ourselves with medicine. The fact is, whenever our immune system is weak we become susceptible to disease. So the first thing to do in order to combat physical diseases is try to live a healthy lifestyle. This means eating right, exercising, and keeping a positive outlook in life. But even living well does not mean we will never become sick. We also need to deal properly with the sicknesses when we are afflicted. This means seeking medical advice, getting lots of rest, and taking our prescribed medicines (no matter how unpleasant the cure may be).

With spiritual diseases it is similar. We can build up immunity to them by living right. This means keeping our spiritual perspective clear, developing habits that lift us up, and holding ourselves to account each day. But even that may not be enough. Even the most spiritual person can slip into cynicism, materialism, fear, self-absorption, or the other diseases. When this happens the spiritual person needs to refocus on the spiritual reality, pray and meditate, and do the right thing, no matter how hard it may be.

QUESTIONS OF FULFILLMENT

Spiritual fulfillment comes from a sense of satisfaction within our soul. It cannot be bought or ordered. It cannot be won or taken. It cannot be found from just joining a group, a political party, a cause, or even a religion. Joining is not enough. We have to live it. This is because spiritual fulfillment is not a destination, it is a living condition. Spiritual fulfillment comes from living up to our values, from standing for something bigger than ourselves, and from sacrificing for a greater good. In order to find this deep and abiding fulfillment in our lives we need to answer some important questions about who we are, what we are doing, and how we are contributing to the world. If we never answer these questions, then we never have a basis for feeling fulfilled.

The first question to ask is about existence itself. Does it have a purpose? Does it have a meaning? Do we have a place in it? Where did existence come from?

Unfortunately, there is no label on the bottom of the universe that says, "Made in Heaven." Instead, the universe exists unto itself. It simply *is*. Many scientists speculate about when our physical universe of planets, stars, and galaxies was formed, how it was made, and why it is expanding. There are a multitude of theories regarding these questions; however, when discussing spiritual matters we are not dealing simply with a physical universe. The spiritual universe encompasses the physical one. It wraps it up with meaning and purpose. It provides it some context and grounding. But it is more. The universe, from the spiritual perspective, includes the physical and the spiritual realms. It goes on past this plane of existence into all the worlds of God. It is transcendent, unifying, and comprehensive. We can only know fulfillment when we know our place in this greater universe.

Of course, this is hard for us to understand. We live in material bodies. We see, hear, taste, touch, and smell this physical realm. And yet, we can transcend those senses. Look at the dream state. In the dream state we also hear, see, taste, touch, and smell, but we do not use our ears, eyes, mouth, fingers, or nose. It is entirely in the mind. In this way, we encompass another realm of consciousness. The spiritual world is like that. In that state we use our spiritual capacities to feel, intuit, analyze, and actualize things without the physical body.

Once we accept that there may be a wider universe, we want to find a purpose and meaning for it. The purpose that many spiritual seekers discover in the holy books of many faiths is of knowing our Creator. In all the world's great religions, the spiritual seeker discovers that God wants to be known. In order to be known, God brought the universe into being. Not just this planet, but all the worlds of God in this plane of existence and beyond it.

Once this purpose is realized, we need meaning for our lives in this world. We need to learn something from our existence in this realm. We need purpose to teach us lessons about right and wrong, good and evil, truth and error, and light and darkness. And we need the universe to guide us.

The spiritual seeker discovers that the universe will guide us with its rules and laws. When we live in alignment with the principles of the greater universe, we prosper in the spiritual reality. We learn its infinite lessons and we take those lessons with us through all the worlds of God. We appreciate its infinite variety, impossibly complex systems, and elegant simplicity all moving in orbit around the true purpose of all things, which is to know and love God.

Once we understand it, the next step is to harness it for good in our lives. Prospering in the spiritual reality means to live in that state of spiritual fulfillment. It means aligning oneself with all that is good, true, and right in the universe, and letting go of everything else. It means finding our place and making it our own by learning the lessons we were intended to learn, discovering the mysteries we were intended to discover, exploring the capacities we were intended to explore, and manifesting the potential we were meant to manifest.

UNDERSTANDING PRINCIPLES OF SPIRITUAL GROWTH

As we explore the path to fulfillment in our lives, it is important to understand the principles of that journey. If our purpose in the universe is to discover God, and our place in all things, then spiritual growth is the toolkit we use to navigate and tread this path. Spiritual growth is about acquiring the awareness, virtues, and capacity we need in order to function in the spiritual universe.

States of spiritual awareness include understanding the purpose and meaning behind the universe, appreciating the wonders and bounties of creation, and claiming our own place. Living with awareness means we live more purposefully. That is, we make better decisions that lead to healthier and more productive lives.

Another part of spiritual growth is learning to manifest virtues. Virtues in the path of spiritual growth include kindness, empathy, reverence, wisdom, mercy, openness, curiosity, restraint, humility, compassion, discipline, love, and countless others. Virtues are qualities that guide us to operate in the world. They are ways of modeling our behavior, standards for holding ourselves to account, and guides for making decisions on how we interact with others.

As we learn to manifest these virtues, we learn to ennoble ourselves. Ennobling ourselves is one of the most important tasks we have as spiritual beings. A truly noble person is someone we trust, someone we admire, and someone we look to for insight and wisdom. A noble person is someone we can rely on, ask for help, and count on to stand for principles even under the most difficult circumstances. Becoming such a noble person can take a lifetime. But there is no greater calling, no greater work, and no greater responsibility for the spiritual being than to set out on that journey toward a noble life.

Finally, developing spiritual capacities involves cultivating the capacity to serve others. This means we strive to become useful in the world. We manifest this capacity as we strive and struggle in the world to make a difference. Like an endless well of human potential, we must drop our bucket into its depths and pull up our share. That is, our capacity to add value in the world is manifested when we move, when we try, and when we act. Through this action, we are putting our own cup into the well and drawing up our own portion of the endless supply of capability stored up for mankind.

We call upon this capacity to add value in the world by setting goals, making a plan, and then implementing our vision in the world. We call upon it by crafting something unique or reflective of our innermost soul and offering it to the world. We call upon it by constructing something beautiful, practical, or useful that others can appreciate. We call upon it by designing something wondrous, elaborate, or amazingly simple that adds value to society. And we call upon it by serving others in a way that is selfless, humble, and honest. In these ways, we live to our fullest potential and we manifest the spiritual capacities pent up for us by the heavens above.

In the end, we find spiritual fulfillment when we truly contribute, grow, and love. Living a full life is about choosing to live for more than our own selves. It is about seeing bigger purposes in the things we do, deeper meanings in the things we discover, and wider implications for the actions we undertake.

In the end, living a full life is not about acquiring wealth for its own sake, rather we acquire wealth to serve, support, educate, and empower others. It is not about acquiring learning and degrees for egotistical reasons, but rather about making an ever more profound contribution to the human condition. It is not about enjoying momentary pleasures in selfish indulgences, but rather about creating important or precious moments that will deepen our bonds to others and our awareness for our place in the world. It is not about visiting places to check off a box on a list, but rather expanding our consciousnesses and worldviews by experiencing all that our world has to offer. It is not about creating and raising a family for our own emotional benefit, but rather about building a foundation for good that can contribute to the development of mankind. In all of these examples, it is a choice to see everything we do, everything we are, and everything we wish for in the world as part of building something better.

The fact is, just about anyone can live a full life by this standard. One does not need an elite education, an abundance of material goods, or access to special professional opportunities in order to live a full life. One only needs free will. One only needs a path to follow toward making some kind of contribution, manifesting virtues, and cultivating spiritual awareness in one's life through practical service to humanity.

FINDING FULFILLMENT IN THE BAHÁ'Í FAITH

In discovering paths to fulfillment, many spiritual seekers have discovered that the Bahá'í Faith provides the beliefs, the practices, and the vision that they need for manifesting spiritual fulfillment in their lives. Through these elements, the Bahá'í Faith offers the spiritual seeker a cause that inspires, teachings that guide, and understandings that give the proper sense of balance and awareness in life.

Indeed, Bahá'ís believe it is the duty of everyone to reach their potential and achieve this kind of fulfillment in life. As the Bahá'í writings state, "The whole duty of man in this Day is to attain that share of the flood of grace which God poureth forth for him." (Bahá'u'lláh, *Gleanings from the Writings of Bahá'u'lláh,* no. 5.4).

The beliefs of the Bahá'í Faith provide us with the understandings we need to find our way in this world. They protect us from fanaticism.

They help us bridge the gaps between the world's religions. They inspire us to change our lives, align our actions, and improve our characters. They teach us about God, religion, happiness, detachment, life, death, and dealing with tests and trials in life. With these understandings we lay the foundation for discovering a path that fulfills us in the ways that endure throughout all the worlds of God.

In addition to the beliefs, the Bahá'í Faith also offers practices to help us become better people. The spiritual seeker who investigates the Bahá'í Faith quickly discovers that the practices are both practical and profound. These practices offer a path to self-discovery, self-discipline, and self-awareness. They are specifically designed for our busy lives, our diverse communities, and our varied paths. The practices in the Bahá'í Faith include guidance for prayer, fasting, community life, worship, and work.

Finally, the spiritual seeker can also discover how the vision of Bahá'u'lláh offers a unifying element for Bahá'í life. This vision is the driving force behind the Bahá'í Faith. People may have differing understandings, insights, interpretations, and paths that they follow as individual Bahá'ís, but all can agree that realizing the vision of Bahá'u'lláh is the most important objective of all.

The vision of Bahá'u'lláh is for a world that is peaceful, educated, fair, self-disciplined, and full of equal opportunity for all men and women no matter where they live or what they look like. It is for a world where no child is unloved, where no life is disposable, where no capacity is untapped, and where no spirit is left empty and without a sense of hope and purpose. It is to create a world in which we could travel from one corner of the planet to the other and find every person we encounter full of kindness, courtesy, nobility, uprightness, and genuine brotherly love.

In the Bahá'í Faith, the role of each Bahá'í is to contribute something, however small, to make that vision a reality. Some may write books, others may speak out in the name of the cause. Some may train the children in moral virtues and spiritual awareness, others may build organizations that further the aims of the cause. Some may have people over to dinner to discuss spiritual matters and share the Bahá'í teachings, others may travel to faraway countries and live out their days pioneering for the Bahá'í Faith and serving some foreign community as spiritual brothers and sisters.

The point is, the Bahá'í cause is vast, but it is personal. It belongs to the Bahá'ís. It is a cause that inspires, channels energies, and drives its members forward toward creating a better life for all mankind. For Bahá'ís there is no more fulfilling path to tread than the path of service to this cause.

As the Bahá'í writings state, "Take heed lest anything deter thee from extolling the greatness of this Day—the Day whereon the Finger of majesty and power hath opened the seal of the Wine of Reunion, and called all who are in the heavens and all who are on the earth." (Bahá'u'lláh, *Gleanings from the Writings of Bahá'u'lláh,* no. 14.2).

THE WANDERING MAN'S PATH TO FULFILLMENT

There was a man who wandered through life, never staying in one place for very long. He was a restless soul. He became bored easily. He always wanted to be challenged and push himself. He always wanted to be learning new things, meeting new people, and mastering new skills. Every place, every person, and every job had something to teach him. He worked as a deck-hand on a boat, a guide in a nature preserve, a glass blower, a caretaker at an island hotel, a project manager on an oil rig, a teacher in an elementary school, even a businessman in an international trade company.

The man was also married and had several children. He loved them dearly. And through all this change and travel, the man struggled to keep his family together. His lifestyle was difficult for those who loved him. The man caused much suffering for his children and wife over the years through his choices. He tried to help them understand the value he placed on living a full life in which they could learn as much as possible about themselves and their world. It was difficult to keep things constant in such a lifestyle, however. He felt the need for some common values to guide him and his family, and inspire them as they journeyed through the world exploring different cultures and having different experiences.

The man carried his passion for discovery and exploration into his spiritual life as well. He investigated every faith he encountered. He read all the world's holy books and was open to spiritual truth from every tradition. After a long evaluation process, the man eventually decided to become a Bahá'í.

He chose the Bahá'í Faith because he agreed with the beliefs, practices, and vision of the faith. He also felt that the Bahá'í community provided consistency for him and his family throughout their journeys. Wherever they went, they could meet with the Bahá'ís and connect with a community of open-minded, spiritually awakened, tolerant, and loving servants of mankind. Of course, each community was full of people who were just as imperfect as they were, but the family always found things to learn and ways to grow in the process.

In the end, the Bahá'í ideals provided a guide for the man and his family to find fulfillment in their lives. The Bahá'í Faith helped the man on his quest of discovery. And at the same time it helped anchor his family to values that transcended every situation, every country, and every society that they found themselves in.

ANALOGY OF TRAINING TO BE A DOCTOR

Becoming a doctor takes a long time. One first learns about the basics such as anatomy, chemistry, and biology. When one has this foundation, one learns about the practice of medicine. One reads, studies, takes tests, works on non-human and non-living subjects, and writes papers. One may also do research and clinical analysis. All of this is done before one starts practicing on real people.

Up to this point, he or she is not yet a doctor—they are still a student. Once they have proven their capabilities in the classroom, they are tested in a controlled environment. They learn under the tutelage of more experienced doctors, and are guided, instructed, and supported by teachers along the way.

Only after years of this process is he or she finally ready to go out on their own and be a doctor. But even then, they are not finished. They are still constantly learning as science and techniques change, so does methodology. In the end, today's modern doctor often spends his entire lifetime learning, improving, discovering, and mastering his job.

Finding spiritual fulfillment is the same. Just knowing the basics about following a spiritual path is not enough. We must practice it. We must make it our own. We must strive to master it through service to our fellowman, and we must share it by helping others reach their potential in life. And we are never done. It is not a destination; it is a living reality. Like being a doctor, becoming spiritually fulfilled is not something we finish once we get a degree, it is something we practice over a lifetime.

PART II: PRACTICES

CHAPTER 11:

PRACTICING MODERATION IN ALL THINGS

"Whatsoever passeth beyond the limits of moderation will cease to exert a beneficial influence."

—Bahá'u'lláh, *Gleanings from the Writings of Bahá'u'lláh,* no. 110.1

SEEKING A BALANCE

We live in a world of continuous change and seemingly endless complexity. These changes affect how we live, how we interact with one another, and what we know about our universe and ourselves. Through all this change the spiritual seeker is looking for a way to find a balance. He is looking for a way to enjoy the benefits of an ever-evolving civilization without being overwhelmed by it. He knows the dangers of being consumed by technology, culture, and information. He knows that people can lose their sense of right and wrong, good and bad, healthy and unhealthy, when faced with so much visual, mental, and physical stimuli at once. He recognizes the dangers of being sucked into a world where there is no foundation to build our lives upon, no grounding to keep us steady, and no underlying vision to guide us.

It does not take much to recognize recent changes in the way we live in the world. In media and entertainment, we are faced with an infinite variety of choices to pass the time. This includes movies, music, art, literature, poetry, and dance. The spiritual seeker believes that all the changes within media and entertainment are not good or bad. For example, the arts can be used to expand, explore, or reflect the human experience. But the arts can also be prostituted. That is, the arts can become a tool used merely to shock, grab attention, and play off our basest desires in order to motivate people to purchase things. When the arts are used merely to make money, the result is that our stories are endlessly recycled, music is merely repackaged, and "new" content is merely a regurgitation of the old. In such a world, there is less true creativity in the arts. The result is that the arts are reduced to sensationalism, materialism, sensuality, and other pursuits of pleasure and empty entertainment that add nothing to the spiritual condition of mankind. Content like this too often leaves people feeling numb, abused, and gullible for enduring it. The spiritual seeker believes that consuming such mindlessly prostituted content only leaves a person less inspired, less capable, and less motivated to grow and develop as a spiritual being.

Technology, too, has affected every aspect of our daily lives. With more tools, more capabilities, more methods of communication and interaction being created every day, we live in near constant connection to one another. New methods of farming, logistics, and bioengineering have brought us food production on an unprecedented scale. Modern capabilities of travel and transport make movement between places faster and more convenient than ever before in history. And new forms of energy offer the capacity to power greater and more powerful tools then ever imagined.

These changes in technology bring many benefits to mankind, but they also bring risks. Mankind has to learn to use these powerful technologies wisely and responsibly. We need to protect ourselves from our own capacity to inflict harm on ourselves and our environment. Otherwise, such new methods of communication can be used to corrupt and destabilize. New methods of farming can be used to create unhealthy foods or even super germs. New methods of travel can bring plagues to the furthest corner of the globe. New methods of transport can provide channels for terrorists to strike and criminals to expand their field of influence. Finally, new forms of energy can be used to create weapons of unimaginable destructive power.

Along with changes in how we live our lives, there are many changes in the way we interact with one another. Relationships are changing because our families are more spread out and disconnected. We struggle to maintain a sense of community in our lives. Fewer and fewer people in the modern world know their neighbors. Suburban sprawl has spread people out to the point that they are not connected to anything. Some people join sports teams, clubs, or other community activities from time to time, but without much time or opportunity to develop deep bonds of support and affection between people these activities remain polite and distant.

Finally, there are constant changes in what we know about who we are and where we fit in the big scheme of things. Scientists, engineers, astronomers, philosophers, doctors, and others from around the world are constantly engaged in the act of discovery. They are constantly learning new lessons about how and why the world works. They are discovering new connections between people, society, and culture. They are helping to define our place in the wider scheme of things and realize how we affect the world (and how the world affects us).

All this knowledge and learning is important and scary at the same time. On the one hand it helps us grow collectively toward better understandings of our world and our place in it. On the other hand, the endless discovery causes us to question the underlying assumptions we have held, sometimes for thousands of years. These new questions sometimes challenge our beliefs. They can shake our concept of identity, threaten to divide us more than ever, and offer ever-wider variances for individual interpretations.

INTRODUCING MODERATION

To the spiritual seeker, our civilization is clearly out of balance. The goal of the spiritual seeker is therefore to find his sense of balance in this chaotic world. He needs to find a way to live in this world, but not be of this world. He seeks moral clarity that helps him break free of cycles of distraction and confusion. He wants a sense of right and wrong that transcends every message, every event, and every interaction he has in this world. He wants to better himself and to see his life as a path to spiritual awareness and perfection. He wants to keep his sense of perspective and not get lost in the materialism and self-absorption in this world.

The spiritual seeker appreciates that the Bahá'í Faith stresses the importance of moderation. Moderation sounds like a simple idea, but living it can have a most profound effect on our lives. Moderation means avoiding extremes. In spiritual terms, it means we do not become fanatical. In material terms, it means we are not gluttonous or greedy. In personal terms, it means we show self-restraint, self-control, and self-discipline. It is the act of keeping balance in our lives.

Moderation brings freedom. That is, it brings freedom from the unnecessary. When we live with moderation as our guide, we are cleansed from desires for things that we do not really need. We are instead focused on the things that are good for us at the times when they best fit. Moderation means we do not take too much, we do not use too much, and we do not desire too much. It means we appreciate the things that do matter, and we let go of the things that do not.

The fact is, living in a world of abundance has created new challenges for living a life with moderation. Moderation is likely a more tricky issue for those that enjoy economic privilege. Some people in more economically advanced regions of the world struggle with moderation. Many face the challenge of learning self-control and self-restraint in order to be healthy and balanced in life.

For example, in the United States, people throw away almost half of the food that is produced. They buy new clothing every season just to stay in style. They refurnish their homes just to entertain themselves, even when their old furniture was perfectly fine. They spend countless hours surfing the web, sending messages, and viewing content that leads to nothing, achieves nothing, and produces nothing. They are trapped in cycles of endless consumption without ever finding true satisfaction. They have at their disposal an endless array of choices in food, entertainment, and material possessions that add no value to society or to their own sense of fulfillment in life.

The spiritual seeker seeks a path to freedom from this cycle. The spiritual seeker seeks a tool that can help him find balance in all of this madness. He seeks a tool that he can use to measure how much he really needs and how much is actually good for him. Whatever does not fit within that measure he learns to let go of. He finds this balance through practicing moderation. Moderation teaches him to take only as much as he needs in order to reach his full spiritual potential.

IMPLICATIONS OF A LIFE LIVED IN MODERATION

In nature, everything exists in a state of moderation. Animals eat only as much as they need to survive, and then they stop. Trees take in only as much carbon and light and nutrients as they need to survive and grow, and then they stop. Water flows only until it is level with its source, and then it stops. Light fills up an area until it is in proportion to the source of light, and then it stops. The spiritual seeker is looking for this capacity in his own life. He is looking to take only as much as he needs to live, exist, and grow as a person. Anything more could make him sick, distracted, and not useful in the world. If he focuses too much on buying things, collecting things, and owning things then he has less time to focus on his spiritual life. If he focuses too much on eating and drinking then he becomes sick, immobile, and less able to be of service to others. If he spends too much time in fruitless pursuits of entertainment that does nothing to ennoble him, then he has less time to do things that inspire, challenge, and empower him to become a better person.

As the Bahá'í writings state, "For desire is a flame that has reduced to ashes uncounted lifetime harvests of the learned, a devouring fire that even the vast sea of their accumulated knowledge could never quench. How often has it happened that an individual who was graced with every attribute of humanity and wore the jewel of true understanding, nevertheless followed after his passions until his excellent qualities passed beyond moderation and he was forced into excess. His pure intentions changed to evil ones, his attributes were no longer put to uses worthy of them, and the power of his desires turned him aside from righteousness and its rewards into ways that were dangerous and dark. A good character is in the sight of God and His chosen ones and the possessors of insight, the most excellent and praiseworthy of all things, but always on condition that its center of emanation should be reason and knowledge and its base should be true moderation. Were the implications of this subject to be developed as they deserve the work would grow too long and our main theme would be lost to view." ('Abdu'l-Bahá, *The Secret of Divine Civilization,* p. 59).

Moderation is about learning to maintain that balance. It is about finding our own capacity to channel our energies into things that do improve us, and to show restraint when it comes to things that only distract us, or worse yet, that demean and degrade us as spiritual beings. Moderation means that we live in balance with what we have, what we want, and what we do.

Showing moderation in the things we have means that we learn to appreciate the things we start with. That is, we start our spiritual journey with capacities, possessions, and experiences. We have to learn to see them for what they are. Those things that help us, inspire us, and guide us to a better life, we learn to appreciate. We thank God for them. We cherish them. We take care of them. We look after them. We protect them.

But we can also learn to let go of those things that do not make us better people. We can learn to give our excess to others. That is, we can learn to see whatever we have that is above and beyond what we could ever use in a healthy way as things we should share with others. For example, if we have excess food, clothes, furnishings, and money, we can see it as an opportunity to be of service to our fellowman.

The fact is, showing moderation is about taking the right action. It is about what we create, build, and develop in the world. Living in moderation means we do things that matter. We work in professions that benefit mankind. We create art that uplifts, inspires, and ennobles people that experience our creations. We develop programs, institutions, and processes that provide the means by which the capacities of humanity can be harnessed in positive and meaningful endeavors.

LEARNING TO LIVE BETWEEN EXTREMES

Clearly, moderation affects all aspects of our lives. Learning to live a life of moderation can take a long time. It takes patience, perseverance, and resilience. By its very nature, we need to avoid being too extreme when we try to practice moderation. That's because moderation itself is about avoiding extremes. This means we have to avoid "shocking the system" and working to recognize those things that bring us out of balance in our lives over time. Anything that provokes extreme reactions in nature falls outside the bounds of moderation and may lead to trouble.

The challenge for everyone is to see the value of true spiritual wealth and to focus on that, instead of being focused on material things. True spiritual wealth is attainable by everyone. We do not need a fancy house or an elitist education to achieve spiritual wealth. We do not need to be poor and isolated either.

True spiritual wealth comes from developing spiritual qualities. No matter what situation we face in life, we are always capable of developing spiritual qualities. Spiritual qualities come from growing, learning, and experiencing life to the fullest. They come from interacting with people and living true to what is right and good in the world. They come from learning how to restrain our animal nature and overcome our ego. And they come from discovering the bounties of living a life of virtue and showering blessings upon everyone in our lives.

The fact is, to be spiritually wealthy is to be truly alive, to experience all the good and bad of life, and to do our best no matter what. True wealth is to discover our limits, to overcome our weaknesses, and to manifest our capacities that God has poured forth for each of us.

When we learn to live with moderation, we discover the beauty, peace, grace and balance that comes from simplicity. Simplicity is a state of mind. It is about noticing, appreciating, and choosing an elegant path in life. Elegance is about minimizing effort, maximizing value, and maintaining principles of grace. It is about working in our lives with the least resistance to the winds of change in the world. Through elegant living, we learn to adapt, to grow, and to transform our spirits into channels of spirituality in the world.

As the Bahá'í writings state, "Be not troubled in poverty nor confident in riches, for poverty is followed by riches, and riches are followed by poverty. Yet to be poor in all save God is a wondrous gift, belittle not the value thereof, for in the end it will make thee rich in God..." (Bahá'u'lláh, *The Hidden Words*, Persian, no. 51).

THE OBSESSIVE WOMAN WHO FOUND PEACE

There was an obsessive woman who would become very involved in whatever task she was doing. Whatever topic, subject, or goal she set for herself, she would give everything she had to mastering it. She felt that she had to be the best in everything she attempted. That meant that she had to be smarter, faster, and more accomplished at all times.

For example, when the woman studied music as a child, instead of settling for one instrument, she studied and mastered three. Later when she went to medical school, she took extra classes in order to finish early. When she became a doctor she tried to have all the answers for her patients. When she exercised, she would train hard so that she could run marathons and finish at the top. When she started her family, she put her children in extra classes and artistic and sporting activities. She pushed her kids to be the best.

Over the years, the woman achieved many goals, won awards, and brought home trophies. She was most often successful in whatever she strove to achieve. But as she aged, she also began to feel the stress of the lifestyle she had adopted. Her bones began to ache, her body started to break down, and her relationships began to suffer. Her husband grew distant. Her children resented her. Her coworkers felt stressed and overwhelmed by her expectations. Her life began to feel alien to her. She wasn't sure who she was most of the time.

One day, as she was preparing for a busy day of errands, work, exercise, family duties, and hobbies, the woman sat down and took a deep breath. Her husband came by and sat down next to her. She wondered to herself if she was pushing herself and her family too hard. She talked with her husband for a few minutes, and assured him she was OK. But something changed. Something switched in her. All this work wasn't making her happier. It wasn't making her more fulfilled. It wasn't giving her anything but more to worry about. And for the first time in her life, she realized it was not real to her. It was noise. What was real, she realized, was love. Not fake love, but real love. Love for her family, love for her friends, love for her patients, love for her coworkers, and love for humanity. She didn't need to be better than anyone. She needed to love them.

From that moment on, she relaxed. She realized that love did not require her to be the fastest, the smartest, or the most aggressive. Instead, love required her to be present. It required her to focus on the people around her, on their needs and their concerns. It required her to let go of her desires and focus on serving and caring for the people around her in a whole-hearted and open manner.

The woman began to look into a way to bring balance into her life. She searched the Internet for something that taught moderation and balance. She was open to anything. As she browsed different books, websites, and organizations, she came across the blog of a Bahá'í who had posted a note about the principle of moderation. It was a spiritual approach to balancing everything in life, and it was a teaching that resonated deeply with her.

The woman began to investigate the Bahá'í Faith and discovered several more key teachings that helped round out her understandings. For example, she realized that the purpose of life was not to achieve material trophies and goals. The purpose of life was not to be better than other people. Instead, the purpose was to acquire spiritual qualities and to become the best person she could. This meant that jumping through the hoops created by others (or herself) was not the objective in life. Instead, the objective was to map out what we she was inspired to do in service to mankind, and then go and achieve that.

With this new understanding balanced with the teachings of the Bahá'í Faith, the obsessive woman began to let go of the trivial goals she had become attached to. Instead, she adopted new and more spiritually healthy goals. She still realized the importance of achieving excellence in all things, but this did not mean she had to achieve excellence according to other peoples' standards. She only had to achieve excellence according to her own standards. She was only competing with herself. This took a lot of the pressure out of her life. She learned to let go of the stress and do the things that she enjoyed as she brought more happiness to those around her.

She then passed these understandings on to her children. She stopped pushing them to meet her standards, and started helping them set their own standards. She inspired them instead of nagging them. She encouraged them instead of dragging them. She empowered them instead of forcing them. In the end, both she and her children were happier and more successful because they did things they enjoyed.

At work, she learned to stop trying to be all things to her patients and coworkers, and instead she began to ask more questions and tried to help people to recognize issues for themselves. And she started exercising for the sheer enjoyment. She still ran in marathons, but it was because she loved the whole experience, not necessarily because she wanted to win.

In the end, the woman found more peace and balance in her life, and enjoyed her pursuits on a much deeper level.

ANALOGY OF EATING

If we look at the example of eating, we can see a clear and logical need for living with moderation. Those who do not slow down and think about what they are eating often end up eating too much. They eat out of instinct or habit. They may eat to satisfy emotional needs. They may eat until they are completely satiated and cannot stuff anything more into their mouths. When people do that, they quickly gain weight, become unhealthy, and develop diseases. They expend tremendous amounts of money and time in the pursuit of food and the gratification of their desires. Hunger comes to dominate their lives. It easily takes over their lives. They may find themselves powerless to stop it. The more they try to regain control by berating themselves, the worse they feel about who they are, and the more powerless they may feel to help themselves.

Those who learn to consume in moderation, however, find value in the experience of eating. They learn to appreciate every bite, to savor the flavors, to enjoy the company, to engage in conversation, and to explore the intricacies and differences of cultures. They learn self-control and to restrain themselves. They learn to eat before they are hungry and then stop before they are full. They look into the foods' nutritional content and learn to manage what they eat, when they eat, and how they eat so that they can remain healthy in all aspects of their physical lives. Truly, moderation in eating is a powerful tool for unlocking many hidden benefits of food. And when the principle of moderation is applied to other aspects of our lives, it can unlock the many hidden benefits of living a balanced, healthy life.

CHAPTER 12:

STRIVING TO FOLLOW THE BAHÁ'Í LAWS

"Think not that We have revealed unto you a mere code of laws. Nay, rather, We have unsealed the choice Wine with the fingers of might and power."

—Bahá'u'lláh, *The Kitáb-i-Aqdas*, ¶5

LEARNING THE VALUE OF STANDARDS

What is a law? Is it a standard? Is it a rule? Are all laws good? If not, then how do we know a good law from a bad one? Is it a tool of justice or a tool of oppression? Do laws guide and protect us, or do they restrict and restrain us? Does the importance of a law depend on who made it? Does it depend on whether it is enforced?

Philosophers have grappled with the wisdom and meaning of laws since time immemorial. They have debated the nature of laws, the types of laws, the sources of laws, the implications of laws, and the purpose of laws. They have identified and categorized laws as eternal vs. temporary, natural vs. scientific, manmade vs. universal, human vs. divine, and fair vs. unjust.

The fact is, everything in the universe has laws. In science and mathematics we know that every object has limitations, every movement has a trajectory, and every number has its quantity. In sociology and human behavior we see that every society has laws as well. That is, every community has standards and boundaries established in order to keep things ordered. Such boundaries set limits and restrictions for people. These limits and restrictions keep us civilized. Without them we would have chaos, anarchy, and destruction.

For example, without laws a game is not fun or productive. Without laws any game can result in a mob where the law of the jungle takes over and no one feels safe or fairly treated. The same is true in society. Society has to say what is right and wrong so that we can all achieve our potential. Therefore we need laws against murder, theft, and abuse. And we have to set the bar for how we interact with cultural and social norms. In civilized societies, we also strive to protect the rights of all people to live, think, say, and believe any way they want, as long as it does not infringe on the rights of others. In this way we can establish a baseline for what we value in society. Without such social standards we have nothing to strive for. Without clear boundaries we do not know what is right or wrong. And without rights we have no trust. Laws are an essential ingredient in creating a civilized society.

On the other hand, humanity is always testing its rules. We are always pushing up against boundaries. We are refining our existing laws, growing and developing new standards, and adapting old rules to the needs of a changing world.

Besides laws in the natural and social realms, the spiritual world also has laws and standards. Like nature and society, spirituality has principles upon which it operates. As spiritual beings, we develop when we live in alignment with those spiritual principles. As with driving a car, we have rules of the spiritual road that can guide us, keep us safe, and help us to become more productive. And as we live out our days, we grow and mature when we follow these spiritual principles. That is, when we restrain our animal nature and refine our spiritual capacity, we are ennobled and empowered. Throughout this process, we are constantly struggling to adapt and refine our character, and part of that process is coming to understand the spiritual laws of the universe. This is part of growth and maturity as a spiritual being, and we can learn to see it as one of our most important tasks in life.

The spiritual seeker looks at the laws of science for lessons about the spiritual laws of the universe. He studies the laws of physics such as those governing motion, force, gravity, energy, and mass. He studies the laws of electricity including those governing voltage, amperage, impedance, and wattage. He explores how humanity has discovered these laws over time, how we have learned to harness the powers of these laws to build great machines that can do incredibly complex calculations, to travel great distances, to instantly communicate anywhere in the world, even to journey into the stars. By discovering, studying, testing, and mastering these laws, humanity has become more capable, more aware, and more connected than ever before in our history.

But these scientific laws also have dark sides. If we do not respect them, if we do not keep our machines working within the limits of moderation, fairness, and balance, then we have problems. Sometimes if we break the scientific laws the machines will just break down and stop working. Other times they might explode or go off course and hurt people. The reality is, the same tools we use to progress can be used to oppress or destroy us. It is just a matter of approaching them with an ethical foundation.

In society, the spiritual seeker also finds spiritual truths. He studies how social norms can give us predictability, order, and balance in our communities. They offer guidance on the limits of civilized behavior. They aren't always easy to follow. They may require us to take the long road sometimes, and avoid the shortcuts to immediate gain. Social norms are not there for individual gain, they are there for social balance. This can be hard to appreciate sometimes. The fact is, social norms may mean we should not drive as fast as we want even if we will not get caught, we should not lie and cheat to get our way even if no one will get hurt, and we should not hurt and oppress anyone who might stand between us and our goals. Social norms may mean we have to pay our fair share of taxes and live up to our duties and responsibilities as citizens.

At a national and international level, when citizens live within societies governed by fairness and justice, our nations function better, our markets prosper, our homes are safe, and our lives are less fearful. When we do not follow laws, civilization breaks down, people lose trust, markets are corrupt, we do not feel safe in our own homes, and people are filled with fear. Sometimes this chaos gives rise to tyrants and oppressors who promise order but who end up bringing more suffering to the masses. Peace and security do not return until people take responsibility for their civic duties and show respect for law and order again.

The same is true of spiritual laws and admonitions. We need them to keep balance in our spiritual lives and to ensure everyone collectively can reach their full potential. Sometimes spiritual laws may mean we have to restrain our desires, but the spiritual seeker understands that this is for a greater good. To a person of faith, a spiritual law is a line in the sand. When we live within the bounds of our spiritual standards, we find ourselves empowered to do amazing things. We learn to recognize right and wrong, set limits on our own behavior, protect ourselves from our lower nature, channel our energies to positive outlets, and challenge ourselves to do great things.

As evidence for the power of spiritual laws to make our lives better, we can look back at all the world's great civilizations that have shaped history. The fact is, we can find religious faith at the core of all of them. Religion has undeniably been the guiding force for helping mankind channel the better natures of men to unite and bring prosperity, justice, and security to their citizens.

Of course, religions have also had negative effects in the world. Sometimes the power of religion to organize and motivate people is abused in order to further aims of domination, conflict, and destruction. Like the force of electricity, religion is a powerful energy employed by humans to achieve great things or dark things.

In order to resolve the disparity in religion, the spiritual seeker can learn to see a difference between religious laws and spiritual laws. He can turn to the Bahá'í teachings for insight into how these two might be different. Spiritual laws can be seen as eternal truths that encompass religious laws. Religious laws can be seen as fitting the needs and conditions of the age in which they appear. When we follow the religious laws of our time, we are fulfilling our spiritual obligations. We are living up to the standard for our age.

But when we follow spiritual laws, we are following eternal standards that transcend every religion. Spiritual laws are always relevant. They are the foundation upon which the world's faiths are built and sustained. An example of a spiritual law includes the commandments to be good people and true to our word. A religious law might be more specific such as following specific rules about marriage, prayer, fasting, and the like; whereas the spiritual laws underlying these religious laws are eternal and unchanging.

Religious laws change from age to age. Because of this, many laws of past religions may seem antiquated and outmoded in today's society. For example, in some ancient civilizations there were no prisons to isolate dangerous criminals from the rest of the people, and so they had to resort to the death penalty for many crimes. Later, people built facilities to isolate such people, and we created systems to try to rehabilitate people. So the death penalty today is seen as too harsh for most crimes. This is because we have become more civilized. Yet, in the future, the fact that our civilization locks people up for crimes that are often caused or accentuated by mental illness, lack of opportunity, and poor education, may be seen as barbaric. In the future we might be seen as an intolerant and ignorant society. When it comes to religious laws, sometimes humanity grows and develops and is ready for a new standard, and so God sends a fresh measure of guidance in the form of a new faith.

In another example, we can look at children and how their need for standards and guidance changes as they grow into adulthood. In the beginning of life, the smallest child is not allowed out of his mother's view. But as he grows, he can play by himself in his room. Soon he is ready to go to a friend's house to play. Later he can spend time with friends in another part of the city. In young adulthood he might even move out on his own to get an education or start a career. At each stage his parents (if they are living up to their responsibilities) are setting appropriate standards for his own good. They are giving him ever-greater spheres in which to grow and develop, but he is also kept within boundaries that will protect him.

The same is true with humanity. We are collectively growing and developing. We are learning and discovering new things about the world, about each other, and about ourselves. We have evolved from the tribe, to the city, to the nation, to the present day in which we are struggling to create a world community. We are entering an age of maturity for humanity. We have all the powers of an adult, but we have to learn to keep ourselves within the bounds of moderation, to restrain our lower nature, and to discover the value of virtue and civilized behavior if we are to reach our full potential.

Bahá'ís believe that today we are ready for a new standard—that the world is sick with materialism and selfishness, and that God has prescribed medicine for us. We cannot take medicine that was meant for different people living in a different time. It will not be effective, and it could even be dangerous. To Bahá'ís, today's ailments require a fresh measure of spiritual medicine that fits the problems of our age. Bahá'ís believe that the cure for mankind's ailments are found in the teachings, practices, and vision of the Bahá'í Faith. Together, these elements make up the religion of Bahá'u'lláh. Within the practices of this religion are included many laws and admonitions for how to live life individually and collectively in the current age.

HOW STANDARDS IMPROVE OUR LIVES

The spiritual seeker believes that spiritual laws protect us. They protect us from the actions of others. They protect us from the influence of others. And they protect us from our own lower natures. They guide us and help us mature as spiritual beings. They help us stay focused on positive aspects of life that can lift us up and empower us to do the right thing, even during the most challenging tests.

So how can spiritual laws protect us from our lower natures? First, we need to have trust. We need to trust that these laws are designed by an all-knowing Physician Who knows us better than we know ourselves. We may not understand every implication or reason for the laws' existence, but we can trust that God provides the tools that we need to grow. We can trust that by following them to the best of our abilities we can learn to appreciate them, understand them, and cherish them. Sometimes we do not recognize the value of something until we practice it.

The Bahá'í Faith teaches that humans have a dual nature. We have an animal nature that is instinctively small, selfish, and childish. It wants only to satisfy itself at any cost. But we also have a spiritual nature. This spiritual nature is all-encompassing, compassionate, and open. It wants us to live for the betterment of all creation, to sacrifice for our fellowman, and to rise to ever-higher heights of nobility and purpose. The Law of God provides the path that helps us overcome our lower natures and rise to our heavenly realities, thus becoming the best people we can be.

As the Bahá'í writings state, "They whom God hath endued with insight will readily recognize that the precepts laid down by God constitute the highest means for the maintenance of order in the world and the security of its peoples." (Bahá'u'lláh, *Gleanings from the Writings of Bahá'u'lláh,* no. 155.2).

Bahá'ís believe that the Law of God is above manmade laws. It cannot be half-heartedly applied. We can never escape from it. We will always be held accountable. But as we grow as spiritual beings we grow in our appreciation for the presence of God in all aspects of our lives. We recognize that we are never alone and never without judgment. Every action and every thought is being watched, recorded, and established as a testament to our faith. Bahá'ís believe that the all-knowing nature of God means that nothing we do is ever forgotten or missed. It means that everything we do has consequences in this life and/or in the next world. Understanding this helps motivate us to keep working at it, to keep striving, and to continuously pick ourselves up and try again.

Spiritual laws help us mature as spiritual beings by keeping us focused on the right things in life. They keep us from becoming distracted by the transitory things of life. The spiritual seeker believes that the laws of God are not intended to fill us with guilt and shame. Instead, they are meant to inspire us, to lift us up, and to ennoble us.

The Bahá'í Faith teaches that faith has two elements, belief and obedience. Both are critical elements. Belief gives us purpose, and obedience gives us a chance to achieve that purpose. Obedience is an important quality that the spiritual seeker believes he has to develop along with all the other qualities that give him a healthy and balanced spiritual life.

Another part of a healthy spiritual life is recognizing our weaknesses and humbling ourselves before God. Recognizing sin is an important element of that process. If we never sin, we could never appreciate God's forgiveness, mercy, and compassion. We could never learn humility and submissiveness. When we sin, it is most likely a sign that we have something to learn. Once we learn from our mistakes, we sin less. In this way, we overcome our faults, step-by-step, day-by-day, year-after-year.

When we learn to see the "big spiritual picture," we learn to turn away from bad influences. When we recognize the suffering we cause to ourselves and to our loved ones from our own bad choices, then we recognize the value of the laws of God. It is a natural and important part of growing as a spiritual being. The spiritual seeker believes that it is impossible to be perfect. Perfection is a quality of God alone. Instead, we were created to strive. We were created to struggle. We were created to appreciate all the qualities of God. Therefore, sinning is part of our natural development toward becoming more spiritual beings. To stop sinning, we have to overcome our lower nature. To overcome our lower nature is to grow into a better person. And to grow into a better person is to fulfill our potential as a spiritual being.

INTRODUCING THE BAHÁ'Í LAWS AND ADMONITIONS

Many spiritual seekers have willingly accepted the laws and admonitions of the Bahá'í Faith as standards that they aspire to live up to. These laws are not forced on us. They are seen as gifts that we can choose to strive to fulfill in our own lives. They include laws for prayer, meditation, and fasting. They relate to community life, marriage, and death. Bahá'ís believe that together they provide the means for a more complete, well-balanced, and ever-advancing spiritual life.

As the Bahá'í writings state, "The purpose of the one true God in manifesting Himself is to summon all mankind to truthfulness and sincerity, to piety and trustworthiness, to resignation and submissiveness to the Will of God, to forbearance and kindliness, to uprightness and wisdom. His object is to array every man with the mantle of a saintly character, and to adorn him with the ornament of holy and goodly deeds." (Bahá'u'lláh, *Gleanings from the Writings of Bahá'u'lláh,* no. 137.4).

Some of the Bahá'í laws include laws of prayer and meditation. Bahá'ís say an obligatory prayer everyday. They may choose from one of three prayers, but they must say one of them. These prayers help Bahá'ís reaffirm their belief and realign their spirits everyday. In addition, Bahá'ís should also meditate on the word of God every morning and evening. Meditation can take many forms, as long as it helps the individual reconnect to God. In turn, meditation helps focus on God's instructions for the creation of a better world.

Bahá'ís fast once a year for nineteen days. The nineteen-day fast involves abstinence from food and drink from sunup to sundown. Fasting is a time of spiritual renewal and alignment.

Bahá'ís are forbidden from backbiting. This law protects the community from negativity and unhealthy divisions.

Bahá'ís are forbidden from drinking alcohol or consuming mind-altering drugs. This law protects people from intoxicating substances that can cause poor judgment and the numbing of the senses. It also protects us from habit-forming and addictive drugs that can sap our capacity to grow as spiritual and productive beings.

In addition, Bahá'ís have laws for marriage that require the consent of all the living parents before a Bahá'í wedding can be performed. This law keeps families united and gives the entire community a vested interest in seeing the marriage succeed. Bahá'ís believe that strong families are the bedrock of civilization and that they must be supported, encouraged, and strengthened by the entire society.

Bahá'ís are called to a high standard of chaste thought and action, implying absolute chastity outside of marriage and complete faithfulness to one's partner within marriage. While many things contribute to a healthy marriage, this law assists in creating unity and trust between a couple. The sex instinct can form a strong and intimate bond between a husband and wife. Bahá'ís believe it should be preserved and respected in that capacity, and that if it is not kept sacred for marriage it loses part of its potency to keep a husband and wife intimately connected. Sexual relations outside of marriage, on the other hand, can also lead to the destruction of families, the spreading of disease, the birth of children out of wedlock, and an overemphasis of the sex instinct instead of focusing on the spiritual bonds between a man and a woman in marriage.

Bahá'ís believe that the soul is created and associated with the human body at the time of conception. Therefore, an embryo is considered to be a human life, but just in a different stage of its development. Abortion is therefore not seen as a legitimate form of birth control in the faith.

Like the followers of most of the world's religions, Bahá'ís are also forbidden from engaging in adultery, fornication, and homosexual acts. Of course, people are free to love, care for, and form deep and intimate bonds with people of all genders and backgrounds. Bahá'ís believe, however, that the sex act is to be used to bind a husband and wife together in the utmost intimacy, while they foster a more unified and balanced institution for raising children. Any sexual relationship outside of this condition, from a Bahá'í perspective, leads to our own suffering and often the suffering of the ones we love. If this law is something that troubles a person, Bahá'ís encourage deepening, prayer, meditation, and an open examination of the evidence around the issue.

Laws around sexuality can be particularly difficult to understand in a society that has overemphasized the sexual instinct and its role in living a full life. From a Bahá'í perspective, however, human beings are fundamentally spiritual beings living a physical existence. Therefore all of these laws are meant to help us rise to our spiritual potential.

Bahá'ís have burial laws including the law that bodies must be buried within one hour's journey of the place of death. In addition, bodies should be cleaned and prayed over with a special burial prayer before interment in the ground. These laws help us appreciate the mystical connection between the body and the soul, and to send the spirits of our loved ones off to the next world with respect and love.

Bahá'ís are forbidden to engage in actions that degrade the station of man including impure thoughts, slavery, begging, gambling, and showing cruelty to animals.

Bahá'ís are called to treat everyone equally. They should not be sexist, prejudiced, or judgmental toward anyone. They must treat people of all faiths as spiritual equals. They must work to show love and respect to all people regardless of race, gender, or ethnic background.

The Bahá'í Faith forbids the establishment of a clergy, the waging of holy war, the acts of asceticism and monasticism, engaging in fanaticism, confession of sins before others in an effort to seek absolution from anyone but God alone, proselytizing or forcing one's faith or belief on anyone else under any circumstances, and treating certain people (or things) as impure. These laws help bring people together as spiritual equals and aid Bahá'ís to avoid the temptations to divide the flock based on individual desires and understandings.

Bahá'ís are commanded to educate children in spiritual and material matters. Both aspects are critical to the proper growth and development of children, and it is incumbent on the parents (and the community) to ensure all children are educated properly.

Beyond contributing to the local, national, and international funds, there is the Bahá'í law of Huqúqu'lláh, which means the "Right of God." This law requires Bahá'ís to give 19% of their excess income and it is considered a great privilege to actively practice detachment and obedience, to cleanse ones' possessions and one's heart, and to contribute to the betterment of society knowing that these funds will be used by the administrative order to help improve the condition of humanity. Excess income is whatever is above and beyond what is needed for the basic necessities of life, after personal debts have been paid off. The calculation of this amount is confidential and completely left up to the individual. No one can solicit contributions from any individual in the community. It is completely voluntary and must be offered in a spirit of willing submission to God. If it is not offered willingly by the believer, Bahá'ís believe that the contribution is not acceptable to God.

Bahá'ís are called to go on pilgrimage at least once in their life if they are able to. This pilgrimage helps connect them with the global community and it helps them deepen their spirit of faith. The Bahá'í Pilgrimage is currently a nine day journey to the cities of Haifa and 'Akká, in Israel. It involves visiting the holy places of the Bahá'í Faith and offering prayers of visitation at the shrines of the central figures of the faith.

Bahá'ís cannot form different sects or divisions within the Bahá'í community. There is only one Bahá'í community. Bahá'ís believe that the authority of leadership was passed directly, through what is called the Covenant of Bahá'u'lláh, to the Universal House of Justice.

Together, these laws, and a few others, make up what it means to live the Bahá'í life. They are goals to aspire to. Of course, no Bahá'í lives up to all of these laws perfectly all the time. The point is not to be perfect. The point is to strive for perfection. Bahá'ís believe that until we align our lives with the law of God for this age, we cannot manifest our full potential.

Like many things in the Bahá'í faith, the consequences of not obeying the laws of our faith are nuanced. Generally speaking, if we fall short in living up to the standards of our Faith, we believe that we ourselves suffer, our loved ones can suffer, and the world around us suffers because we fail to manifest our full potential in the world. We each have something unique and important to offer the world of humanity, and when we fail to live up to our spiritual potential, we rob the universe of the special light that we alone were created to reflect.

On the other hand, we also understand that there are times when our institutions do need to get involved in order to protect society and the community from the actions of those who flagrantly disobey the laws and standards of our faith in a way that affects others directly. As the Universal House of Justice has clarified, "It would seem to be important to make clear to the friends that the 'laws' of the Faith must be regarded in various lights. There are laws, ordinances, exhortations and principles, all of which are sometimes loosely referred to as 'laws.' All are very important for the life of the community and the spiritual life of the individual, but they are applied differently. Some affect the society and the social relationships, and the Spiritual Assemblies are responsible for their enforcement. If a believer breaks such a law, he is subject to the imposition of sanctions. Others, although of very great importance, are not sanctionable, because their observance is a matter of conscience between the individual and God; among these fall the laws of prayer and fasting and the law of Huqúqu'lláh. Then there are those high ethical standards to which Bahá'u'lláh calls His followers, such as trustworthiness, abstention from backbiting, and so on; generally speaking, obedience to these is a matter for individual conscience, and the Assemblies should not pry into people's lives to see whether or not they are following them; nevertheless, if a believer's conduct falls so far below the standard set by Bahá'u'lláh that it becomes a flagrant disgrace and brings the name of the Faith into disrepute, the Assembly would have to intervene, to encourage the believer to correct his ways, to warn him of the consequences of continued misconduct, and possibly, if he does not respond, to deprive him of his administrative rights.

"In other words, the friends should realize the importance of following all the teachings and not assume that merely because an offense is not punishable it is therefore less grave. Assemblies, on the other hand, should distinguish clearly between those laws which it is their duty to enforce, those which should be left strictly to the conscience of the individual, and those in which it may have to intervene if the misbehavior is blatant and injurious to the good name of the Faith..." (*Messages from the Universal House of Justice, 1963–1986: The Third Epoch of the Formative Age, par. 405.2-405.3.*)

TIPS FOR FOLLOWING THE BAHÁ'Í LAWS

Following all the Bahá'í laws is challenging, even for the strongest Bahá'ís. There are a few tips and suggestions that can help on this journey. These tips include developing an understanding of the laws and standards and why they are important, cultivating an understanding of ourselves and our limitations and our potential, making a clear plan and following through, and learning to forgive ourselves while developing a healthy sense of humility in the process. It should be noted that following the Bahá'í laws, and the manner in which one does so, is a personal matter. The laws are clearly defined by Bahá'u'lláh in the *Kitáb-i-Aqdas*, and any tips offered here are merely suggestions based on the personal experience of the author.

We can study the laws and admonitions of the Bahá'í Faith to help us see the wisdom behind them. We can accomplish this by meditating on the holy writings. This meditation can also be reinforced by studying the effects of living without these laws in the world around us and recognizing the suffering, pain, confusion, and desperation of a world that lacks standards. In addition, we can learn through consultation with other spiritual seekers. We can ask questions, discuss experiences, share stories, and collectively explore the laws and admonitions of the Bahá'í Faith to help us crystallize our own understandings and to encourage others to live spiritually healthy lives as well.

Understanding the laws and admonitions is important, but we also need to understand our own selves. We need to recognize what laws and admonitions are hard for us to follow. That means we need to recognize what tempts us on our own paths. If we know our weaknesses, then we can learn to identify the triggers that lead us to break the laws of God. Triggers can take many forms. Perhaps we feel weak when we are around certain people, in certain situations, or experiencing certain feelings. When we recognize the triggers that can throw us off course, then we can learn to avoid them.

Once we understand the laws and why they are important, and after we have recognized our own weaknesses and the things that tempt us, it might help to make a personal plan. It can be helpful to set goals, objectives, and measurable standards to which we hold ourselves. We can work on replacing bad habits with good ones. We can change routines. We can build on our capacity one day at a time, and work constantly on overcoming our weaknesses. And we can take it at our own pace. If this means working on one law per month, then so be it. If it means we struggle with the same law over and over and never seem to overcome it, then we can focus on other things until we build up the strength to tackle the bigger tests.

Finally, our most important task in learning to follow the laws and admonitions of a high standard is to develop a healthy sense of humility. It helps to recognize that failure is part of the process, and that we can use mistakes to learn, grow, and develop. This helps us to learn how to show forgiveness and love to our own selves. We need to trust in God, ask for His help and His guiding hand at every step of the journey.

For the spiritual seeker, asking for help is not showing weakness. Instead, it is expressing our humility and desire to do better in our lives.

Once we have cultivated a healthy sense of humility then we can also turn to helping others in their spiritual paths. The humble spiritual seeker realizes that we are all in this together, and that spiritual success for one of us is a victory for all of us. Therefore we can learn to inspire, aid, and guide each other as we learn to navigate our own paths to spiritual development.

In the end, the most valuable source of inspiration for following the Bahá'í laws is to see the benefits of living with them first-hand. As the Bahá'í writings state, "Were any man to taste the sweetness of the words which the lips of the All-Merciful have willed to utter, he would, though the treasures of the earth be in his possession, renounce them one and all, that he might vindicate the truth of even one of His commandments, shining above the day spring of His bountiful care and loving-kindness." (Bahá'u'lláh, *Gleanings from the Writings of Bahá'u'lláh,* no. 155.3).

THE PARTY-GIRL WHO CHANGED HER LIFE

There was a girl who went off to college with some of her friends. Together they joined a sorority and took part in many of the wild things that happen on today's modern college campuses.

For her, college life was pretty crazy. It was the first big chance for her to live away from home and experience real freedom and responsibility. At first, the girl wanted to fit in with her friends more than anything. She took all the same classes that her friends took. She went to all the big parties and college activities. She experimented with alcohol and drugs a bit. She even met a young man who seemed to like her.

Overall everyone around her in college seemed to feel as though they were entitled to go crazy. They acted as if they had a right of passage to enjoy in the college experience in such a crazy way. But for the girl, all the parties, alcohol, and wildness of the time was not fulfilling. She wanted to change but she wasn't sure how. All her closest friends were caught up in the madness. She did not really know where to start.

At some point the girl decided to take a comparative religion class. This was not a class her friends approved of, but she did it anyway. She had always been interested in different religions. Her grandmother had been a very important influence on her when she was younger, and she had always engaged with her in the study of religion.

In the comparative religion class, the girl learned about all the world's faiths. She thought they were beautiful and wondrous expressions of the diversity of the human world. Eventually she learned about the Bahá'í Faith and she realized that this religion taught everything that she already believed. She wanted to learn more about this religion and perhaps join it.

The girl started attending campus Bahá'í club meetings and was befriended by the Bahá'í students at the university. It became very clear very fast that these students were not like the friends she had been spending her time with. She realized that if she wanted to be a Bahá'í that she was going to have to change her lifestyle. After some deep soul-searching, prayer, and meditation on the matter, she decided to become a Bahá'í.

Unsurprisingly, most of her friends could not understand her decision to become a Bahá'í. But she did not care. She decided to start trying to live the Bahá'í life in her own way, even if her friends could not comprehend why anyone would want to miss out on all the "fun" they were having. But for her, it was much more important to live a life she felt good about living than to engage in the mindless diversions of college life.

In trying to live up to the Bahá'í laws, her first step was to stop backbiting. This was a lot harder than she anticipated. She soon realized how much of the conversations in her sorority and among her friends were negative. In the process, she had to learn to spot backbiting when she saw it. She worked at this in many ways. Sometimes she would try hard to steer conversations in positive directions by saying positive things about other people. When she could not change the tone of a conversation, she would leave it and do something else. She also stopped drinking alcohol, which meant that she did not have a lot to do at the big parties that were going on.

She also told her boyfriend that she was now on a spiritual path and working to discover her spiritual qualities. This meant that she would no longer have a physical sexual relationship with him. She still wanted to spend time with him though. Unfortunately, her boyfriend did not understand her decision. They decided to end their relationship. This hurt her very much, but she realized it was probably for the best. If all he was interested in was a physical relationship, then he could find that with someone else. She wanted to find someone who was interested in learning about who she was as a human being instead.

As she disengaged from her old sorority life, the girl began to spend more time doing things that interested her. She took more classes that taught her about the world and its endless diversity. She studied philosophy, art, and international relations. She wasn't afraid to take hard classes anymore. She wanted to learn about new things, explore deeper meanings, and expand her perspective. In the process the girl began to make new friends. She went to poetry readings, art shows, special speaking engagements, and other events that the college had to offer that were actually things she could learn from. She started to spend time with people who had a lot of intellectual and spiritual things to discuss. These new friends wanted to talk about thought-provoking topics and have engaging debates. It was all very refreshing to her.

Of course, as she grew in her faith, the girl still struggled with many of the Bahá'í laws. In particular, she struggled most with the laws about chastity before marriage, avoiding backbiting, and not drinking alcohol. But she knew the Bahá'í laws were not there to make her feel guilty. Instead, they were there to give her a standard to strive for. She did her best with the laws on a daily basis. And in the end, she appreciated that the laws had given her a reason to change her life, to focus her spirit, to expand her mind, and to protect herself from her lower nature. She knew that these laws were there to make her a healthier and happier person, even if at certain moments it meant that she had to restrain herself from things she desired. She knew that God was always watching, and that there would be consequences for every one of her actions, either in this world or the next. This was not something she feared out of dread and guilt, but it was something that motivated her to live well, even when she didn't appreciate the wisdom at the time. She believed that because these were the instructions of the Manifestation of God for this Age, that she was living in alignment with His Will for her. And in that, she trusted that her life would be better because of it.

ANALOGY OF THE HORSE AND THE RIDER

Think of a horse and a rider. If the horse is not tamed and restrained, it is useless to the rider. The man cannot even climb on the back of the horse before he gets thrown off and trampled beneath its hooves. But if the horse is tamed, he becomes a noble and graceful creature. The tamed horse lets the man ride on his back. It helps the man travel, build, and develop the world around them. The two become helpmates for each other. The man provides consistency, guidance, and direction to the horse so that together they can do great things. Together, the tamed horse and his rider are light upon light and a bounty for all of creation.

The human spiritual condition is like a horse and a rider. The horse is the physical and animal nature of man. The rider is the spirit and soul of man. When the animal condition is tamed in us, it becomes a willing instrument of goodness in the world. Then the spirit of man has a tool to be of service to others.

In the end, the laws and admonitions of the Bahá'í Faith provide the spiritual seeker with the means to tame the animal nature of man. They help him learn right from wrong and to direct his energies toward things that will endure.

CHAPTER 13:

HARNESSING THE POWER OF PRAYER IN OUR LIVES

"Thou art, verily, the Almighty, the Most Powerful, Who art wont to answer the prayers of all men!"

—Bahá'u'lláh, *Prayers and Meditations by Bahá'u'lláh,* p. 247

WHAT IS PRAYER?

Almost every religious tradition has some concept of prayer. Like music, prayer is an international language that translates across culture and society. It can become a language of the heart, a song of the soul, and an intimate conversation with the infinite voice that is present in all things.

The spiritual seeker has a wide definition for prayer. For him, prayer is not just about words, but it is about feelings, insights, inspirations, and hope. Prayer is not just when he talks to God with words of respect, honor, and praise. Prayer is not just about asking for help, wisdom, or patience when he needs aid and assistance. Prayer is not only about asking God to change the world, ourselves, or our circumstances when things do not go our way. Prayer is something wider. It is something more encompassing. And it is something more engrained in the human experience.

For example, whenever the spiritual seeker feels awe standing on top of a mountaintop, or wonderment beholding the vastness of the ocean, or an open-hearted love for all mankind, this is prayer. Whenever he sees people caring for one another with unfailing love and pure-hearted charity, this is prayer to him. Whenever he aches for the suffering of the innocent or longs for the presence of a loved one that he deeply cares about or cries out in frustration at the inability of mankind to overcome its many problems, this is prayer to him. Whenever he achieves something good in his life not for reward or payment, but simply to add value in the universe, this is prayer. Whenever he sacrifices for others, whenever he offers his time or his money for causes or issues that he cares about, or whenever he provides something meaningful for a cause that is bigger than his own self, this is prayer to him.

Prayer, for the spiritual seeker, is about connection. It is about connection to God, the universe, and to his fellowman. It is a connection of the spirit that draws on spiritual forces that exist to help us, guide us, change us, unite us, and inspire us. Prayer is also about communication. We communicate through words of prayer. But we also communicate through our thoughts and actions in a spirit of prayerful engagement. That is, our thoughts can be mental prayers and our actions can be living prayers.

Prayer is directly related to meditation. If prayer is how we talk to God, then meditation can be thought of as how God talks to us. Prayer calls forth the divine forces in the universe. Meditation helps us direct those forces to the right places in our lives. Prayer asks for guidance; meditation implements that guidance. Both are important and inseparable.

For the spiritual seeker, prayer is not an act of the weak. Instead, prayer is an act of the spiritually empowered. Prayer for the spiritual seeker is something he uses to call down unseen powers that guide him in his daily life. It is a source of strength, wisdom, and energy. It helps him overcome himself, let go of his earthly desires, and focus on the things that really matter in life.

For the spiritual seeker, prayer is the ultimate act of personal responsibility. It is claiming his place as a spiritual being. And it is recognizing that he can be an active agent of change and goodness in the world. It is not about asking the universe to solve all his problems and bend to his desires. Instead, prayer is about asking for the power to face his problems with patience, confidence, and perseverance. Prayer is often about seeking assitance to align individual desries with the Will of God.

DISCOVERING THE POWER OF PRAYER

People can use prayer in almost any situation. What we pray for reveals what is in our heart. It defines who we are, what we want, what we care about, and what we are trying to accomplish in the world. We can pray for general things or specific things. We can pray for things we desire or for the things that God desires for us (they might not always be the same things). We can pray for health, healing, and wellness. We can also pray for detachment and contentment in life. We can pray for knowledge, understanding, or wisdom. We can pray for excellence, competence, and capacity. We can pray for forgiveness or mercy. We can offer prayers of gratitude, praise, thankfulness, awe, and wonder. We can pray for an end to suffering, whether that suffering is material or spiritual in nature, or whether it is our own suffering or the suffering of people we care about. We can pray to overcome tests and difficulties, trials and tribulations, and pain and loss. We can pray for those who have passed on, or for those not yet born. We can pray for our children, parents, siblings, friends, and coworkers. We can pray in any aspect of life where we need to focus our thoughts, clarify our desires, and realize our hopes.

In some ways, prayer is like the crying of a baby. When the baby cries, it receives milk, love, and attention. If it does not cry, the mother or father does not know that the baby is hungry or in need. The same is true in prayer. If we do not pray, then the universe does not know that we need assistance or attention. Prayer is that active force that draws forth the heavenly confirmations into our lives when we ask for them.

The spiritual seeker can turn to the explanations given in the Bahá'í Faith in order to understand what is happening when he prays. The Bahá'í Faith teaches that the purpose of sending Messengers of God into this world is to help people prepare themselves for the afterlife. To aid us in that process, we believe that wondrous divine forces are potentially available to us if we call on them through prayer. Like turning on a light in a room, when we pray we are flipping the switch and illuminating our world with light from divine power.

The divine forces can change the world around us. They can cause connections to manifest themselves. They can open doors to opportunities. They can influence people to make decisions that affect their lives. They can affect the natural world, causing elements to become excited and energized.

But more than changing the world outside us, these same forces can also affect our inner condition. They can change the way we see things. They can alter our perceptions. They can calm us and help us understand the bigger picture. Oftentimes the answer to our prayers is not in the form of changing the world around us. Instead, the answer to our prayers too often comes through the process of changing our own hearts. For example, we might pray for someone to get better from an illness. But if this person were to become better from this particular illness, he or she may go on to suffer even more from further complications. Therefore the prayer is not answered in the way we intend. The patient becomes sicker and may even die. This is not because God is not merciful. Instead, it might be that ending the suffering is truly merciful and beneficial. This is a reality we may not always be able to appreciate in this world, but it may be something we will understand when we pass on and join our loved ones on the other side.

Prayer can help us gain a new perspective. We might come to understand that this person will be at peace and be free from his or her situation. We can then find peace with the idea that our loved one will go on to an existence of unity with the divine and freedom from the cares and sufferings of this material life. In this case, the prayer helped us feel closure and peace in our own heart. "The prayers which were revealed to ask for healing apply both to physical and spiritual healing. Recite them, then, to heal both the soul and the body. If healing is right for the patient, it will certainly be granted; but for some ailing persons, healing would only be the cause of other ills, and therefore wisdom doth not permit an affirmative answer to the prayer." ('Abdu'l-Bahá, *Selections from the Writings of 'Abdu'l-Bahá*, p. 161).

True prayer helps align us with the spiritual worlds. It is an act that affects us on many levels. Not only does it unleash divine forces to work in our lives, but it also works to slow us down and causes us to reflect on what is important. It helps us take a moment out of our daily cares and concerns and turn to the infinite presence in our spirits. When we pray, we notice more. When in a state of prayer, we can take a deep breath and connect with the spiritual aspects of our lives. Prayer has the capacity to calm the mind, warm the heart, and inspire the spirit. In this respect, prayer serves us at both the material and spiritual levels.

THE FUNDAMENTALS OF PRAYER

The spiritual seeker can turn to the guidance offered by the Bahá'í Faith when it comes to understanding the dynamics of prayer. The Bahá'í Faith teaches that the content of the prayer matters, but that the content takes several forms. It is not just the words that matter. There is a complete language to prayer that we can learn to use in all aspects of life. It is a language of the spirit. Many people find that the power of prayer to transform us comes from more than the actual words, but also from the tone, the focus, and the underlying message inherent in the prayer.

The central figures of the Bahá'í Faith (Bahá'u'lláh, the Báb, and 'Abdu'l-Bahá) revealed countless prayers for a wide variety of occasions. These prayers are often written in a very formal tone. This is to help us raise our minds to a noble state. For someone who is new to these prayers, their language might seem a little strange at first. They are full of references to God and His endless qualities such as beneficence, mercy, love, wisdom, and power. In addition, Bahá'í prayers carry messages about who we are, why we exist, and what we are supposed to be doing with our lives. We are free to use our own words, of course, but for Bahá'ís the language of the prayers revealed by Bahá'u'lláh, the Báb, and 'Abdu'l-Bahá provide a guide to us. They teach us this language. They instruct us on what to pray for and how to address God in our prayers.

As the Bahá'í writings state, "I render Thee thanks, O Thou Who hast lighted Thy fire within my soul, and cast the beams of Thy light into my heart, that Thou hast taught Thy servants how to make mention of Thee, and revealed unto them the ways whereby they can supplicate Thee, through Thy most holy and exalted tongue, and Thy most august and precious speech. But for Thy leave, who is there that could venture to express Thy might and Thy grandeur; and were it not for Thine instruction, who is the man that could discover the ways of Thy pleasure in the kingdom of Thy creation?" (Bahá'u'lláh, *Prayers and Meditations by Bahá'u'lláh,* p. 282).

One important quality we learn from our moments of prayer is the quality of reverence. We show reverence when we quiet our minds and connect our hearts. Reverence in prayer means we show the deepest respect for the act of prayer, no matter if we recite it our self, or if someone else is saying it. We can show reverence no matter what language a prayer is being said in. Reverence means we listen to the tone, the spirit, and the words while we seek the deeper meanings in our spirits. We take these prayers into our hearts and let them work on us. Through this process, prayer changes and inspires us to a better life.

Of course, reverence takes many forms. In some cultures people show reverence by closing their eyes, crossing their arms, and sitting at attention. In other cultures, reverence can be shown with bright smiles and warm embraces for all people. In still other cultures, people show reverence by kneeling or bowing. Therefore, while the actual form of reverence may vary, the spirit behind it is what matters.

The point is, when we show reverence for the act of prayer we are opening our spiritual hands in order to catch the waters of divine bounties. We are showing that we are ready to receive the inspiration and channel the forces of the universe that are called upon through prayer. If we do not show reverence, we might be closing our spiritual hands and letting the water of divine blessings land on our fists of pride or ignorance. Thus if we are not reverent we risk missing an opportunity to drink deep of these spiritual fountains of light that are unleashed through the honest prayers of all mankind.

Prayer is also about cultivating a relationship with God. As we know, successful relationships require time, attention, and effort to grow. Therefore, we need to make the time to pray. We need to create those moments that can affect us. This may mean creating a space in our home that is free of distractions. It may mean praying at times such as late at night or early in the morning when we are removed from the cares and concerns of life. It may mean we go for walks to places in nature where we can be alone with God. It may also mean we go to temples or churches to worship God. The point is, we often need to step out of our routines in order to cleanse our minds from distractions that can take us off course. Once we do create these special moments, we find our bodies refreshed, our minds invigorated, our hearts opening up, and our spirits taking over.

Other questions often asked by people are: Who do we pray to? What do we think of in our mind when we say a prayer? What do we focus on?

The Bahá'í Faith teaches that the essence of God is unknowable and beyond our comprehension. This is because a creation can never truly know its Creator. If it ever did, the creation would be equal to its Creator. And in the case of God, there can be only One. Baha'is do not subscribe to an anthropomorphic image of God, and therefore sometimes turn their thoughts to the divine Manifestations of God including Bahá'u'lláh, the Báb, Jesus, Muhammad, the Buddha, and others, while praying.

The spiritual seeker recognizes that some people do not need to think of anything in particular in prayer. For the spiritual seeker, the act of prayer itself is the answer. The act of tuning our heart to the infinite, of opening our consciousness to something more, of putting the content of our spirit on display are what prayer is about. How God Himself responds to our prayer is not really the point.

In truth there are many ways to pray. Prayers can be recited, they can be thought, and they can be sung. Prayers can be said with others or in private. The important point to remember is that we show respect, honor, and reverence to the words in the prayer, and we open ourselves to the answers of our prayers in whatever form those answers may take.

In practically every situation we can turn to the Bahá'í prayers for perspective, assistance, and guidance. During times of trials and tribulations we can say prayers revealed to help us with tests and difficulties. In our family lives we can use prayers revealed specifically for families, spouses, and children. In dealing with material problems or questions, we can use prayers revealed to help us find detachment and offer thanks for all the blessings and bounties of life. We can use prayers that bring us closer to God by offering us spiritual growth and development in the process. We can use prayers intended to help us be of service to God in everything we do.

Lastly, some Bahá'ís often refer to a series of suggestions known as "of the Dynamics of Prayer." (*Principles of Bahá'í Administration,* p. 90). While no one is required to use them in prayer, they offer valuable guidance. These steps include:

1. First, pose the question and pray about it. Once the prayer is done, remain in silence and await inspiration.
2. The second step is to arrive at a decision or answer to the question or concern. Once the answer is known, the spiritual seeker needs to accept it—even if it appears impossible.
3. Third, harness personal determination to see the answer through to the end.
4. Fourth, trust that the right path will appear. Sometimes it will be the path we set ourselves out on. Other times we will learn that this wasn't the right path and we will take those lessons learned with us.
5. Fifth, act as though the prayer has already been answered. This means to act in the world as if the divine forces are with us under all circumstances.

These suggestions can help make the most of time spent in prayer. They provide a helpful method for putting our prayers into action and in making them tangible and useful in the world.

In reality, prayer is a tool for helping us in all aspects of life. As the Bahá'í writings state, "O thou who art turning thy face towards God! Close thine eyes to all things else, and open them to the realm of the All-Glorious. Ask whatsoever thou wishest of Him alone; seek whatsoever thou seekest from Him alone. With a look He granteth a hundred thousand hopes, with a glance He healeth a hundred thousand incurable ills, with a nod He layeth balm on every wound, with a glimpse He freeth the hearts from the shackles of grief. He doeth as He doeth, and what recourse have we? He carrieth out His Will, He ordaineth what He pleaseth. Then better for thee to bow down thy head in submission, and put thy trust in the All-Merciful Lord." ('Abdu'l-Bahá, *Selections from the Writings of 'Abdu'l-Bahá,* no. 22.1).

THE FORMER COMMUNIST WHO LEARNED HOW TO PRAY

There was a man who grew up in a communist country in Eastern Europe without any sense of religion, God, or spirituality in his life. He had never been to any religious events, but he considered himself a good person and he aspired to do the right thing.

Soon after the fall of the Iron Curtain in the early 1990s, the man encountered the Bahá'í Faith. The Bahá'ís brought teachings that seemed very good to him. They taught about the unity of mankind, the equality of all people, universal education, and world peace. He loved the vision of Bahá'u'lláh and all the social and cultural teachings that it brought. He appreciated the moral teachings about how to live a more noble life.

The man struggled to connect with the spiritual aspects of the Bahá'í Faith, however. Specifically, he did not know how to pray. Whenever he would spend time with the Bahá'ís and listen to them say their prayers, he did not feel anything. He did not know who they were talking to, what they were experiencing, or how anything was changing in the world from the prayers.

One day he asked one of the Bahá'ís about this. The Bahá'í appreciated the man's honesty and said that there was no shame in his question. The Bahá'í went on to explain that prayer was just a conversation of the heart. He asked the man about what he said in his own head when deciding whether or not to do something. The man answered that he would just think about it and do whatever was the best thing that came to him. The Bahá'í told him that these moments could be thought of as prayers, and that these prayers meant that the man already knew how to pray. These internal conversations where actually spiritual moments where he was communing with a higher level of consciousness.

The Bahá'í went on to explain that prayer was not just about sitting and reading eloquent words. We pray whenever we ask questions in our heart. We pray when we strive to be our best. We pray when we aspire to live a more noble and righteous life. And we pray whenever we try to reach our potential and to be better people.

The Bahá'í asked the man to take it one step at a time. He suggested that he say one prayer every day to start with. The Bahá'í explained that prayer was a language, and that it took time to learn and master that language—often an entire lifetime. He also explained that prayer changes and evolves as we grow and develop. As we discover more about who we are, why we exist, and what we are here to accomplish in this life, our prayers accompany us in this journey. They are a tool we use to guide us, inspire us, and protect us from ourselves. They set us right whenever we fall short or become distracted.

The man followed the Bahá'í's advice and began to practice prayer every day. His life did not change overnight. But over several years he did begin to speak the language of prayer better and better. In the end, the man learned to pray in his daily life, and in the process he added an invaluable new tool to help him overcome himself and harness the strength, confidence, and empowerment that comes from the power of prayer.

ANALOGY OF PRAYER AND MUSIC

Many songs have two main components: melodies and lyrics. Sometimes the melody and the lyrics of a song reinforce each other. In these situations, it is light upon light, and we are moved to ever-higher heights of enjoyment from the song. Other times we listen to a song and we only hear the melody because our mind is distracted. And still other times, we focus more on the words of the song because the melody has faded into the background for us.

The fact is, what we appreciate from a piece of music often depends on what we have going on both inside us and around us. People take in music, comprehend it, and let it affect them in different ways. Sometimes it depends on the way the music is presented and the atmosphere. Sometimes people listen to the notes, other times people just listen to specific instruments, still other times people listen for poetic sentiments expressed in the lyrics. Whatever we listen for when we hear music, we might not all have the same experience from the same music.

This is because we all bring our own personal experiences to compare, contrast, and augment the music with.

Prayer is the same. Prayer has a spiritual melody and it has inspired lyrics. The melody of the prayer is found in the tone of the language, the reverence in the voice of the speaker, and the general spirit that is conveyed during the act of praying. The lyrics of the prayer are the second component. These words can awaken, educate, empower, and change us in many ways. Together, the tone and content of our prayers can lift us up to ever-higher heights of nobility, awareness, and purpose in life if we learn to listen to them fully.

CHAPTER 14:

ALIGNING OUR LIVES WITH MEDITATION

"O people of Bahá! The source of crafts, sciences and arts is the power of reflection. Make ye every effort that out of this ideal mine there may gleam forth such pearls of wisdom and utterance as will promote the well-being and harmony of all the kindreds of the earth."

—Bahá'u'lláh, *Tablets of Bahá'u'lláh,* p. 72

EFFECTS OF MEDITATION

There are many forms of meditation in the world. While some religions, philosophies, and schools teach different methods and techniques for meditating, the purpose of all meditation is generally the same, and that is to find peace within ourselves and alignment with the world around us. To that end, when we meditate we are reflecting, we are contemplating, we are thinking, and we are feeling. Meditation can be seen as a natural complement to prayer, and a tool that enables us to discover meanings, purposes, and realities that help us live better lives.

For people of faith the world over, meditation offers tremendous benefits in all aspects of life. Meditation helps clarify what is important, realign thoughts and actions, strengthen connections, increase capacity, deepen understandings, recommit to our efforts, and find balance and peace in our hearts.

Meditation can help us clarify what is important by continuously forcing us to question all aspects of our lives. That is, whenever we feel stressed out by the cares or tests of life, we can meditate about them. Meditation can help us look at the sources of our cares and tests and ask, "Does this really matter in the big scheme of things?" It forces us to cleanse ourselves of the dross of the material world. It helps us identify and be grateful for the things that do matter. Through meditation we can focus on things that lead to more love, more unity, more strength, and more courage. In the process, we let go of the things that divide us, weaken us, and cheapen our existence. Once we clarify what matters in our lives we can turn to helping others do the same. Our path becomes one of service to others and the education of mankind. Through meditation we turn to helping people overcome the suffering that comes from attachment to the material world and enslavement to our lower natures.

Meditation helps us realign our thoughts and actions by calling ourselves to account each day. Once we start holding ourselves to a higher standard, we begin to follow a path toward bettering ourselves. We can ask what we have done during the day to be of service to others. We can ask what we can do tomorrow. And we can ask how we can change, what we can learn, and who we can help. These questions force us to align everything we do in life to the path of service to humanity. And when we fall short, when we fail, when we show weakness and frailty, meditation can help us make it right. Meditation and reflection can help us correct mistakes and overcome our frailty.

Meditation can also help us strengthen our connections to the spiritual realm. It helps us focus on our strengths and not be overwhelmed by our weaknesses. It helps us discover our capacity and harness our abilities. We can meditate on examples of others who have lived and served mankind in ways that we want to emulate. We can turn to people that we respect and admire and ask ourselves how we can be more like them. As we learn lessons from all those souls who have overcome hardship and become the true glory of mankind, we can find ways to inspire others in the same effort.

Meditation is also about learning. It is about deepening our understandings of who we are, why we exist, and what we are here to accomplish in this life. Meditation can help people in different ways to do this. For example, meditation can help us discover spiritual lessons in tests we may face. It can inspire us to seek meanings and purposes in creation. And it can help us find ways to channel the spiritual forces of our world and make it a better place through our efforts. Meditation can also help us quiet our souls and empty our minds of extraneous thoughts while focusing on spiritual things.

Meditation helps us recommit to higher goals. No matter how far off course we may find ourselves in life, no matter how distracted we may become by things, meditation can help bring us back on course. When we find ourselves becoming depressed, angry, or anxious about things, we can meditate on them to help us remember the spiritual purposes behind things. As we meditate on what our goals should be, we can let go of the goals that are not healthy for us. We free ourselves from lower aims, and discover the power and strength that comes from living for the greater good of the world.

Finally, meditation helps us find balance and peace in our lives. Balance comes when we put things in their proper perspective. It comes when we detach ourselves from material things and attach ourselves to spiritual things. We learn to love the right things, and not become caught up in love of self or in the desperate search for approval from others. Meditation gives us a place to step out of ourselves for a few moments and look at things objectively. We can look at our choices, the people we surround ourselves with, and the paths we are taking and make sure that we are doing the right things. Each of us has a unique path to tread in this world, and meditation helps us tread that path with peace and composure. When we live in balance with nature and the universe, then whatever happens in life cannot disturb our inner peace. No test can defeat us. No trial can overcome us. No abuse can weaken us. No weakness can sway us. Meditation helps us reach this state of absolute awareness of who we are and what we are here to accomplish in life.

HOW CAN BAHÁ'ÍS APPROACH MEDITATION?

There are no set rituals or techniques for meditation in the Bahá'í Faith. Bahá'ís are called to find whatever works for them as individuals. For Bahá'ís, the form is not as important as the objective, and that is to make meditation a constant companion in life. Meditation in the Bahá'í Faith is meant to be practical, useful, and rational and thus lead us to better our lives and our world at the same time.

The Bahá'í writings prescribe meditation on the word of God twice-daily—in the morning and evening. For many Bahá'ís, this time of reflection is focused on resolving problems, dealing with issues, and manifesting spiritual qualities. Some Bahá'ís meditate when they sit alone in a room, others while they take walks, and still others meditate when they engage in manual tasks such as cleaning, gardening, exercsing, or traveling. The fact is, whenever our minds find themselves liberated from the cares and concerns of the immediate they can become open to inspiration and renewal through meditation.

Meditation is useful for many Bahá'ís because it helps us become more aware of ourselves. That is, it is often focused on our own contribution to the betterment of the world. During the process of meditation we may work to cleanse our minds of thoughts and ideas that are not helpful, but the goal is not to empty our minds for the sake of being empty. That is, Bahá'ís strive to clear their minds in order to become hollow reeds through which the spiritual waters of divine inspiration can pass. As the Bahá'í writings state, "O SON OF SPIRIT! Noble have I created thee, yet thou hast abased thyself. Rise then unto that for which thou wast created." (Bahá'u'lláh, *The Hidden Words*, Arabic, no. 22.)

Meditation for Bahá'ís is also rational. It is not something where the mind checks out and is left behind by the heart. True meditation requires that both the mind and the heart be aligned in the same state of awareness. Meditation for Bahá'ís is a potentially logical practice because it can be used to investigate issues, reflect on evidence, and discover new solutions in a systematic way.

As the Bahá'í writings state, "O people of Bahá! The source of crafts, sciences and arts is the power of reflection. Make ye every effort that out of this ideal mine there may gleam forth such pearls of wisdom and utterance as will promote the well-being and harmony of all the kindreds of the earth." (Bahá'u'lláh, *Tablets of Bahá'u'lláh*, p. 72).

HOW WE MEDITATE

As stated, there is no formal "technique" prescribed for meditation in the Bahá'í writings. Some people may make a special effort to create peaceful and meditative atmospheres for their times of reflection. Sometimes they may use candles, incense, or soft lights. Many will take a few moments prior to beginning their meditation to take several deep breathes and prepare their bodies to be silent and relaxed. They may also concentrate their thoughts on a word, a phrase, or an image. Many Bahá'ís use the word Alláh-u-Abhá, which means "God is All Glorious" in Arabic, which is also prescribed by Bahá'u'lláh to be said ninety-five times a day, in order to bring oneself into alignment before meditation. But none of these items are required for meditation. Each individual is free to find their own way to meditate in the faith.

Bahá'ís meditate on the holy writings of the Bahá'í Faith as a starting point. Individuals use these words as a guide, a template, and a continuous source of inspiration in meditation. By meditating daily on the word of God, they often find goals to strive for, states of mind to achieve, realities to explore, and stories to connect with. They then take the wisdom gained from such meditative experiences and set goals for their own lives that align with God's plan in the world. The purpose in such meditations is to find the purposes and meanings hidden within the word of God.

As the Bahá'í writings state, "Meditate upon that which hath streamed forth from the heaven of the Will of thy Lord, He Who is the Source of all grace, that thou mayest grasp the intended meaning which is enshrined in the sacred depths of the Holy Writings." (Bahá'u'lláh, *Tablets of Bahá'u'lláh*, p. 143).

As the spiritual seeker learns to meditate throughout the course of his spiritual life, he learns to make it a constant companion in all of his endeavors. It becomes a habit. It becomes something he does every morning to set himself on a clear path for the day. It is also becomes something he does at the end of the day to call himself to account, to ask what he contributed during the day, to think about what he learned and discovered, and to plan for the next day's efforts.

In this process, the spiritual seeker finds an infinite number of topics and subjects to meditate on. He can meditate on his actions including what he did, what he said, what he contributed, and what he accomplished. He can ask what the results were of his actions. He can also meditate on his inactions, where he fell short, what he forgot, what he failed to accomplish, and how he can try harder tomorrow. He can mediate on his thoughts and on his hopes and aspirations in life. He can meditate on life and death, and let the reality of his own mortality guide and inspire him to make the most of the time he has on this earth. He can meditate on his work and profession and find ways to solve new problems and be of service to his workmates and his customers. He can meditate on his family and think about ways he can show them more love, appreciation, and support. He can meditate on his community and think of ways that he can be of service to his neighbors and countrymen. And he can meditate on his own self. He can make sure he is living a healthy and productive lifestyle. He can foster his own connection to God and strengthen his personal faith. And he can look deep into his soul to find ways to cleanse the mirror of his spirit so more of the light of God can reflect into the world of existence.

The spiritual seeker can also meditate on ways he can help the Bahá'í community grow and develop so that it can be a continuous source of peace, love, and justice in the world. He can meditate on ways to connect with the Central Figures of the Bahá'í Faith, to deepen his love for Bahá'u'lláh, and to increase his capacity to follow the example of 'Abdu'l-Bahá. He can meditate on the role of religion in the world and discover how he can help ensure that the Bahá'í Faith is a source of unity for mankind. He can meditate on the laws and standards of the Bahá'í Faith and find ways to bring himself more into alignment with them. He can meditate on the changes and chances of the world and recognize how they help him find the eternal truths of existence. The fact is, there is a lot of work to be done in the path of regenerating the spiritual foundation of all mankind, and meditation offers a critical tool for the spiritual seeker to make a lasting difference in the world.

As the Bahá'í writings state, "It is incumbent upon you to ponder in your hearts and meditate upon His words, and humbly to call upon Him, and to put away self in His heavenly Cause. These are the things that will make of you signs of guidance unto all mankind, and brilliant stars shining down from the all-highest horizon, and towering trees in the Abhá Paradise." ('Abdu'l-Bahá, *Selections from the Writings of 'Abdu'l-Bahá,* p. 240).

THE WOMAN WHO MEDITATED ABOUT HER PROBLEMS AND FOUND A SOLUTION

There was a woman who had many problems in her life. She struggled financially to pay her bills on time and to save for the future. But the woman was also on a lifelong spiritual search to answer some of her deepest questions about why religion existed and why she needed it in her life. She was an honest soul and she desperately wanted to overcome her problems.

One day, the woman met a Bahá'í and was very intrigued. She liked the teachings of the faith, and she thought its logical and practical approach were beneficial. She instantly felt in her heart that there was divine truth in this message, and that there had to be something there. But she was also distracted by all her problems in her life. She did not think she could accept a new religion as long as she could not get her financial situation in order. She felt that she was too imperfect and her life was too chaotic to incorporate a whole new faith into it.

Her Bahá'í friend suggested that the woman meditate on the Bahá'í writings and she gave her a copy of *The Hidden Words* of Bahá'u'lláh, which is a book of spiritual wisdom and guidance.

The woman began to read this book every morning and evening. The passages in this book covered all aspects of life. They helped her to rethink how she approached work, service, and sacrifice. They also helped her prioritize things and focus on her spiritual search as a path to resolve her material problems. That is, when she put her material problems into a spiritual perspective, she began to see things more clearly.

For example, *The Hidden Words* offered the woman insight into why she existed and what she was here to do. This helped her be more objective in evaluating her life. She realized she didn't need all the material things she thought she needed. The woman began to see that her spending habits were unbalanced and that she was often too impulsive and focused on instant gratification rather than on achieving spiritual connections and being of service to humanity.

But the change did not happen overnight. It took time. The woman meditated every day on these words. She would then think about them all day long. She would remember them when she faced difficulties or challenges. She would be reminded of them when she had to make decisions about what was important. And she was inspired by them when she felt unworthy or tired of trying.

Daily meditation on the word of God helped the woman over time to change the way she thought, acted, and lived in the world. Through this process, the woman realized that becoming a Bahá'í was not about incorporating another set of responsibilities into her life. Instead it was about realigning all her responsibilities around a new spiritual reality that unburdened her and helped her set the right priorities in all aspects of her life.

As *The Hidden Words* state, "O SON OF MAN! Be thou content with Me and seek no other helper. For none but Me can ever suffice thee." (Bahá'u'lláh, *The Hidden Words*, Arabic, no. 17).

ANALOGY OF THE SHIP

As individual spiritual beings, we all sail our own ships across the great ocean of life. Prayer can be seen as the sail, and meditation as the rudder. When we pray we are opening our sails and letting the divine winds carry us, move us, and inspire us in our lives. Prayer harnesses the wind that blows across the sky and meditation helps determine the direction we go upon the sea.

When we meditate, we are deciding how we are going to use our spiritual capacity in the world. We may pray for strength, and then meditate on how to use that strength. We may pray for wisdom, and then meditate on how to put that wisdom to work. We may pray for opportunity, and then meditate on how to take advantage of that opportunity.

If we never pray, then our meditations are not powered by this eternal and powerful force. And if we never meditate, then our prayers may not bring us to any productive destinations. Both are essential in the process for achieving balanced spiritual growth and development.

CHAPTER 15:

ENJOYING THE LASTING REWARDS OF FASTING

"There are various stages and stations for the Fast and innumerable effects and benefits are concealed therein. Well is it with those who have attained unto them."

—Bahá'u'lláh, in *The Importance of Obligatory Prayer and Fasting*

FASTING AND FAITH

Throughout human history, people have used fasting from food and drink for spiritual, political, and personal purposes. In religion, fasting is often used to help detach people from the material world, unite people together in a common cause, and make certain occasions and celebrations sacred and special. As a result, people of all faiths have found that fasting offers many bountiful effects including physical benefits, mental benefits, and spiritual benefits. Together, these benefits help make us more aware, more empowered, and more capable spiritual beings.

The stories of many faiths have examples of spiritual leaders and their followers using fasting on various occasions. For example, Moses fasted for forty days and forty nights before receiving His divine revelation. Paul fasted for three days after his conversion experience on the road to Damascus. Siddhartha Buddha fasted for a period before He achieved enlightenment. And in the Bahá'í Faith, Bahá'u'lláh would often take almost no food and water during times of intense spiritual revelation.

Fasting is also an element in many religious practices. Muslims fast for the Islamic calendar month of Ramadan as a sign of submission and to bring solidarity within the Islamic community. Hindus practice a variety of fasts for particular festivals. Some Jews fast for Yom Kippur as a sign of repentance. Some Christians fast during Lent. Some Buddhists fast once a week. And Bahá'ís fast for nineteen days, once a year.

As people fast, they discover that there are many physical benefits of fasting. During most periods of fasting people do not consume any food. In some faiths, such as Islam and the Bahá'í Faith, during the fasting period people refrain from both food and water between sunrise and sunset. While this can be very challenging, faithful followers soon discover that there are benefits for their bodies from such a fast. The fact is, when we stop taking in food and water, our bodies take the energy we would otherwise use to digest food and use it to repair organs and cells that need attention. Additionally, during a fast the body turns from consuming food to consuming its own stored up fat. In the process the body releases toxins stored in that fat. Many believe that fasting is one way to help detoxify the body. Even in nature we see that when an animal becomes injured or sick, that animal will often lose its appetite. This is because the animal needs to spend its energy fighting the sickness or repairing its injuries, not digesting food. A regular period of fasting once a year can be an important source of health and renewal for the body.

There are also many mental benefits from fasting. Fasting strengthens our will power. It reminds our physical body that the spiritual self is supreme. It teaches us how to resist physical urges and impulses. It flexes our muscles of restraint and obedience. Fasting has the potential to make us more disciplined, more controlled, and more aware of our bodies. As we develop such capacities some of us might find that we have stronger will power to do the right thing, achieve our goals, accomplish tasks, and live a healthier life.

In addition to the physical and mental benefits, the spiritual seeker realizes that there are many spiritual benefits to fasting. Usually during a period of fasting people take time to say more prayers, read more of their holy writings, and generally reflect on life. This can be a useful time to realign our lives and refocus our spirits. It can help us gain clarity in what is important and work to improve ourselves in the path of spiritual development. In addition, many people of faith believe that fasting unleashes unseen spiritual forces in our lives that serve to inspire us, create deeper spiritual connections between us, open doors in our lives, and provide the means to make a greater contribution to the world.

Lastly, fasting together with others in a community can help unite us with our fellow believers. This is because when we sacrifice together we find a greater sense of camaraderie and cohesion.

THE BAHÁ'Í FAST

The Bahá'í month of fasting takes place during the Bahá'í calendar month of 'Alá, which is between March 2 and March 20. During these nineteen days, Bahá'ís refrain from consuming food and drink from sunrise until sunset. Every Bahá'í who is fifteen or older, and under the age of seventy, is required to fast. There are a few exemptions for people who are sick, women who are pregnant or nursing, those who are traveling, and those who have physically demanding jobs.

As with many aspects of Bahá'í life, the individual's decision to fast is a sacred and personal obligation. It is a matter that is ultimately between oneself and God. While community members can encourage and inspire each other to enjoy the benefits of fasting, generally speaking no one should check to make sure others are fasting, and no one should make another feel guilty if they are not fasting.

The Bahá'í Fast is described as a very important law of the faith, together with that of the obligatory prayer. In fact, in the *Kitáb-i-Íqán*, Bahá'u'lláh calls fasting the sun of religion, and obligatory prayer the moon. Fasting is also one of the most physically challenging obligations that Bahá'ís perform all year. It is an act of faith. It is a time for reflection, prayer, and meditation. It is an opportunity to align one's life and recommit oneself to the vision of Bahá'u'lláh in the world. And it is a reminder and a testament to God that one believes in His cause for this age.

For many Bahá'ís, the arrival of the Bahá'í Fast is like the visit of an old friend who comes back each year. Sometimes we prepare for our friend's visit. We get the guest room ready, we clean the sheets, prepare the bathroom, and buy food and supplies that we will need to entertain and provide for the guest. When we are ready for the guest then we can enjoy the visit more, appreciate the time, and get the most benefit from the experience.

Other times we are not ready and the guest arrives and throws our whole life out of balance. At these times it becomes harder to find perspective and make the most from the visit. We cannot put off our fulfillment of this sacred obligation until we feel ready. The Bahá'í Fast can only be fulfilled during the Bahá'í month of 'Alá. Bahá'ís are free to fast for their own personal efforts anytime during the year, but those days do not count toward fulfilling the sacred obligation to fast during the full nineteen days of the Bahá'í Fast. The friend is visiting, whether we like it or not.

Therefore, many Bahá'ís work to prepare themselves for the Bahá'í Fast before it begins. They make the effort to have the right attitude, adjust their routines, and prepare their bodies physically so that when the fast does arrive it is less of a shock.

In order to get the most from the period of fasting, Bahá'ís often find that the attitude they manifest during it is critical. As the Bahá'í writings state, "Even though outwardly the Fast is difficult and toilsome, yet inwardly it is bounty and tranquility. Purification and training are conditioned and dependent only on such rigorous exercises as are in accord with the Book of God and sanctioned by Divine law, not those which the deluded have inflicted upon the people. Whatsoever God hath revealed is beloved of the soul. We beseech Him that He may graciously assist us to do that which is pleasing and acceptable unto Him." (Bahá'u'lláh, in *The Importance of Obligatory Prayer and Fasting*).

To that end, many Bahá'ís learn to look forward to the Fast, to focus on its benefits and positive aspects, and to let themselves become excited about an opportunity to prove their faith to their Lord in such a tangible way. For example, if we remember that the Fast exists to help us grow and develop as spiritual beings, it helps us have the right perspective. Of course, we need to be balanced when we look to discover any gains from fasting. We need to make sure we set the right expectations for ourselves so we are less likely to be disappointed when we realize how hard fasting can be. Everyone's experience with fasting seems to differ depending on many factors. Sometimes it can even differ from year to year in our own lives depending on the stage of life we are in.

Along with having the right attitude comes cultivating the right habits. Many of us become set in our ways. We wake up and follow the same routines every day. Fasting often upsets these routines. It might mean we wake up earlier, eat later, and change our daily activities. It might mean we have to break our established schedule and move things around. But most of all it forces us to step out of our daily routines and question how we live. Breaking routines is often a refreshing and energizing aspect of the Fast for many Bahá'ís. It can help us appreciate moments, think about where we are at from a different perspective, and reevaluate the habits that we fall into oftentimes without even thinking about it.

Finally, many of us might want to make sure that we cleanse our bodies before the Fast. Modern life does not always encourage the healthiest lifestyle. Sometimes it is just easier to eat the unhealthy snacks to fill us up when we are hungry. In addition, many of us rely on caffeinated drinks or sodas to wake us up, and find that our bodies become addicted to the caffeine or sugar in ways that give us unpleasant withdrawal symptoms if we suddenly stop consuming them. Therefore, many Bahá'ís will try to wean themselves off of caffeine before the Fast instead of enduring terrible headaches that can come from withdrawal. Sometimes people will make sure they have healthy and filling food for breakfasts so that they do not find themselves hungry and tired throughout the day. The fact is, preparation is important in helping our bodies and spirits deal with the changes of the Fast.

BENEFITTING MORE FROM THE FAST

Fasting is a source of great bounties in our lives. As the Bahá'í writings state, "Verily, I say, fasting is the supreme remedy and the most great healing for the disease of self and passion." (Bahá'u'lláh, in *The Importance of Obligatory Prayer and Fasting*).

For many Bahá'ís, their relationship with fasting changes as they grow and develop in their lives. For example, fasting can be challenging for youth. It can be difficult to fast and feel different from friends and classmates. But it can also be challenging later in life when we work and only have a limited time to eat in the mornings or evenings. It can also be a struggle when we have children who are not fasting and we have to provide them food throughout the day, even while we ourselves are trying to avoid thinking about our hunger or thirst. In addition, it can be more challenging for some physically as they age and lose their stamina. The law of fasting is binding on all Bahá'ís from the ages of fifteen to seventy. Individuals must find their own way to make it work, to struggle through it if they find it difficult, and to do their very best to realize the most from every minute of fasting, no matter where they are in the various stages of life.

Some of the most beautiful and inspiring prayers and meditations in all of Bahá'í literature were written specifically for use during the Fast. These prayers can be very long, very moving, and very transformative if we take the time to say them and let the words and spirit seep into our hearts. For the spiritual seeker, prayer and meditation during the Fast can become spiritual sustenance. That is, they can become the spiritual food and water that we need to help us throughout the hardest times of the Fast.

Many Bahá'ís also enjoy the opportunity to use lunch breaks to go to a quiet place and say prayers. Lunch breaks during the Fast can be something unique, empowering, and refreshing. Many also enjoy starting their day with the fasting prayers to be a wonderful way to set the right tone for the rest of the day. And when sunset comes, many Bahá'ís say a prayer before eating as an opportunity to reflect on the day, thank God for the bounty of fasting, and appreciate the whole experience more completely.

Another important benefit of the Fast is the capacity it has to bond individuals with their fellow believers. Collective struggle can bring communities together. For many, the opportunity to break bread together during the Fast in the morning or in the evening provides a unique bonding experience with others in the community.

The Bahá'í Fast also provides people with an opportunity to reflect. It helps us reclaim our spiritual nature. It helps us take stock of who we are, what we are, and where we are going. We can use the annual nature of the Fast to think about the previous year and analyze what we have accomplished and what we have left undone. We can also take the time to set new goals, renew commitments, and reconnect with our spirit. Together these benefits can make the fasting period one of the most important annual events in our spiritual lives.

In the end, the Fast is a spiritual experience and a testament to one's belief. As the Bahá'í writings state, "We have fasted this day, O my Lord, by Thy command and Thy bidding in accordance with what Thou hast revealed in Thy perspicuous Book. We have withheld our souls from passion and from whatsoever Thou abhorest until the day drew to an end and the time arrived to break the Fast. Wherefore, I implore Thee, O Desire of the hearts of ardent lovers and Beloved of the souls of them who are endued with understanding, O Rapture of the breasts of them that yearn after Thee and Object of the desire of them that seek Thee, to cause us to soar in the atmosphere of Thy nearness and the heaven of Thy presence, and to accept from us what we have performed in the pathway of Thy love and good-pleasure. Write down our names, then, among those who have acknowledged Thy oneness and confessed to Thy singleness and who have humbled themselves before the evidences of Thy majesty and the tokens of Thy grandeur, those who have taken refuge in Thy nearness and sought shelter in Thee, who have expended their lives in their eagerness to meet Thee and attain the court of Thy presence, and who have cast the world behind their backs for love of Thee and severed every tie with aught save Thee in their eagerness to draw nigh unto Thee. These are servants whose hearts melt in ardent desire for Thy beauty at the mention of Thy Name, and whose eyes overflow with tears in their longing to find Thee and enter the precincts of Thy court." (Bahá'u'lláh, in *The Importance of Obligatory Prayer and Fasting*).

THE YOUNG MAN WHO LEARNED TO FAST IN STAGES

There was an eager young man who became a Bahá'í in a small remote town. He wanted to receive the most from all the teachings and practices provided by the Bahá'í Faith. For example, he had learned about the tremendous spiritual, mental, and physical benefits of fasting, and he wanted to see what it could do for him.

When the time of fasting finally arrived, the man was eager to begin. The first day of the Fast the man woke up early, ate a big breakfast, drank lots of water, and said prayers. He then went about his day as he normally did. For most of the first day he did not think about eating or drinking very much. He did feel a bit of indigestion from his big meal, but he got over it. He was tired and a little weak when sunset came, but he was thankful for the opportunity to prove his faith to God, and to himself.

The second day was a little harder. He felt himself becoming hungrier than the first day, but he made it through that day unscathed.

The third day was much harder. By this time his body was not happy with the situation. He started to really feel weak and tired, and by the end of the day he was having pretty intense mood-swings. He did not realize that not eating could affect him so much. By the end of the third day he was not sure he was going to make it.

The fourth day he nearly broke down and drank some water to make it through the afternoon of work. He could barely think. At the end of the day he was pretty disappointed in himself. That night he called one of his Bahá'í friends for advice.

His Bahá'í friend told him that it was the spirit that counted during the Fast, and that fasting was an acquired skill. It was not something most people were accustomed to. The Bahá'í told the man to use his own judgment on how he should proceed, but suggested that things would become easier once his body learned to adjust to this new reality.

The Bahá'í friend promised the man that if he stuck with it, that eventually the new routine would set in and fasting would be less of a burden. He also told the young man that this was what being a Bahá'í was all about. We often start off life as a Bahá'í very excited to practice all the teachings and to benefit most from the new life. But soon we realize that it is a lot harder than it looks. We find the laws are sometimes challenging to follow and the standards can be difficult to live up to. But if we stick with it, if we persevere, if we show patience with ourselves, if we are resilient when we fall, then Bahá'í life becomes part of us. It not only becomes habit, it becomes an aspect of life that makes us stronger, healthier, and happier. It just takes time.

The man learned to have patience with himself, and work on it. For the next few days he was not always able to fast completely, but he did not let it dim his enthusiasm. He still said the fasting prayers in the morning and in the evening. He still thought about the Fast all day long. And he still tried his best not to eat or drink. To his relief, it did become easier. By the last few days of the Fast, the man found his body had adjusted to the new reality and he was able to fast for the full day.

By the end of his first Bahá'í Fast the man was very excited about his accomplishment. It was one of the hardest things he had ever physically done for his faith, and it meant something to him. It meant that the Bahá'í Faith was materially real to him. It set the tone for the rest of his year. It helped him adjust and conform to the teachings and standards of his new faith. Additionally, the Bahá'í Fast taught the man to be patient with himself and to not let his own weaknesses and frailties hold him back from striving to be a better person.

The next year when the Fast arrived the man was a lot more prepared. He did better the second year, and improved in every fast after that.

ANALOGY OF PLANTING SEASONS

The period of fasting each year is like preparing a spiritual garden. In a garden we must first do the hard physical labor of tilling the soil and preparing the ground. Then we need to plant the seeds carefully in the soil. Finally we need to provide plenty of water and sunlight to see the plants grow and develop for a harvest.

The Fast is like this planting season. The hard physical labor is the abstaining from food and drink. This can be a struggle for many people, but it is necessary to prepare the ground for the seeds. The seeds of the spiritual fast are found in moments of meditation during the Fast. These come from the thoughts, ideas, plans, goals, and aspirations that we set for ourselves. And finally, the water and sunlight we need for our spiritual gardens come from unleashing the divine forces through prayer. Prayers call forth all kinds of energy in our lives, and they are an essential element of planting a fruitful garden for our spirits.

Over the course of the next year we will then harvest this garden. We will find the fruits we planted to be sweet, meaningful, and refreshing. And when the year is over, we will go through the process all over again as one of the most wondrous elements of Bahá'í life.

CHAPTER 16:

CHERISHING THE DAILY BENEFITS OF OBLIGATORY PRAYER

"As for obligatory prayer, it hath been sent down by the Pen of the Most High in such wise that it setteth ablaze the hearts and captivateth the souls and minds of men."

—Bahá'u'lláh, *The Importance of Obligatory Prayer and Fasting*

LEARNING TO FOSTER THE RIGHT ATTITUDE WITH OBLIGATORY PRAYER

Our attitudes determine the degree of bounty we allow into our lives from spiritual efforts. If we are bitter, resentful, spiteful, and suspicious then love cannot reach us, the Holy Spirit will not fill our hearts, and our souls will be isolated from the spiritual bounties of the world. On the other hand, if we are grateful, open, joyous, and full of spiritual curiosity then the spirit will gush out from our beings and fill the world with a light that only we can reflect.

If we see daily prayer as a chore or a mere duty, then we might see it as an unpleasant burden in our lives. But if we can teach ourselves to see it as a bounty, a gift, a wondrous reminder, and a daily chance to reconnect to our source, then we can learn to look forward to it with the right attitude.

Bahá'ís spend a lifetime developing a deep and abiding relationship with daily prayers. Apart from being enjoined to pray and meditate every morning and evening, Bahá'ís have a responsibility to say a daily obligatory prayer. The Bahá'í obligatory prayers are a continuing source of love, connection, and contentment for countless believers worldwide.

As with all personal teachings in the Bahá'í Faith, no Bahá'ís should ever compel others to say the obligatory prayers. The obligatory prayers offer the individual a daily opportunity to align his or her inner self with the Creator.

WHAT ARE OBLIGATORY PRAYERS?

Obligatory prayers are special prayers that followers of a certain faith are obliged to say. The prayers may have special requirements when we recite them. Only two faiths have obligatory prayers that were revealed by their Founders: Islam and the Bahá'í Faith. In Islam, daily prayer is considered one of the five pillars of the religion. It was mandated by Muhammad Himself, and Muslims are required to pray five times a day.

Each time they do so they turn to face Mecca, perform ablutions (washing their hands and face), and say their prayer accompanied by a series of motions including standing, kneeling, and sitting. For Muslims, daily prayer is a key element in the process of confirming a believer.

As stated above, the Bahá'í Faith also has the institution of obligatory prayers revealed by its Founder, Bahá'u'lláh. As a bounty to His followers, Bahá'u'lláh revealed three different obligatory prayers: a short one, a medium one, and a long one. Bahá'ís can say any one of these three as long as they follow the instructions for the one they choose.

For all the Bahá'í obligatory prayers, believers must perform ablutions (washing their hands and face). These ablutions are a symbol of clearing the mind and freeing oneself from the cares and worries of the day. When saying the prayer, Bahá'ís turn to face the direction of the resting place of Bahá'u'lláh, which is located just outside the city of 'Akká, in Israel. This is a symbol of their faith and a reminder of their commitment to its Founder, Bahá'u'lláh.

For each of the three prayers, there are specific requirements for how they are to be said. The short obligatory prayer, which is only a few sentences, must be said between noon and sunset. The medium prayer is only a few pages long and is to be said three times a day. It includes movements such as standing, kneeling, and bowing. The long obligatory prayer is to be said once in twenty-four hours, and it is almost five pages long (depending on the prayer book it is in). Many Bahá'ís have memorized this prayer and prefer to say it because of its beauty and expansiveness. It also has movements such as raising your arms, kneeling, and bowing down before God.

The Bahá'í obligatory prayers are binding on every Bahá'í from the age of fifteen. The three prayers range in content. The short prayer talks about why we exist, why God created us, and what our relationship is to Him. The longer prayers include more detail about how God relates to us and how we relate to Him. They also explore how we can detach ourselves from this world, cleanse our spirits of our sins and transgressions, recommit ourselves to trying to be good people, and remind ourselves to continuously appreciate the bounties that God provides.

All three prayers are daily statements of praise and gratitude that in turn honor our Creator and affirm belief in His faith. Saying the obligatory prayers can be seen as an act of spiritual fulfillment and one of the most important acts of belief that a Bahá'í can offer in his personal journey toward his Creator.

BENEFITING THE MOST FROM OBLIGATORY PRAYERS

As with all aspects of spiritual alignment, reciting obligatory prayers takes practice. As the Bahá'í writings state, "O My brother! How great, how very great, can the law of obligatory prayer be, when, through His mercy and loving kindness, one is enabled to observe it. When a man commenceth the recitation of the Obligatory Prayer, he should see himself severed from all created things and regard himself as utter nothingness before the will and purpose of God, in such wise that he seeth naught but Him in the world of being. This is the station of God's well-favored ones and those who are wholly devoted to Him. Should one perform the Obligatory Prayer in this manner, he will be accounted by God and the Concourse on high among those who have truly offered the prayer." (Bahá'u'lláh, in *The Importance of Obligatory Prayer and Fasting*).

Just as with exercise, prayer is something that needs to be done consistently for it to have an effect upon us. The moment we stop saying our daily prayers is the moment we cut ourselves off from their benefit. It is similar to daily exercise. If we keep it up, then we remain fit and healthy. But if we stop exercising we quickly become weak, tired, and we do not feel as good. The same is true if we stop saying our daily prayers. We quickly get spiritually weak. We start to slow down in our spiritual development. And we do not feel as good about who we are, what we are doing, and where we are going in life. The obligatory prayer is a helpful companion in all aspects of life, but only if we work at it. As with exercise, we have to put in the time to enjoy its benefits.

Many Bahá'ís designate a special place in their homes where they say their obligatory prayers. Some will try to set aside a regular time each day for their daily prayers and meditation in the morning or in the evening. As is the case with meditation, there is no one way to say the obligatory prayer. It is left up to the believer to decide when, where, and how they say the prayers as long as they follow the guidance for each.

As stated before, consistency is key to success with the obligatory prayer. The reality is that some days we will feel these prayers bringing light and inspiration to our lives as the words and the spirit overwhelm our beings and illuminate our souls. Other times they might not have such a dramatic and tangible effect upon us. Like a song with both a melody and inspiring lyrics, some days the melody may inspire us, other days the words will capture our attention, and still other times we may not get much out of the song at all. The benefits that can be experienced from the act of saying the obligatory prayer are many, as it provides a daily opportunity for obedience, submission, and an affirmation of belief.

In the end, the spiritual seeker learns that these daily prayers are not there to make us feel guilty and bad about ourselves. Instead, as with all Bahá'í prayers, they are full of promises of forgiveness, mercy, and love from our Creator. They are filled with words of encouragement and inspiration for us. They are a guide to us whether we are strong that day or not. The spiritual seeker learns to hold on to the obligatory prayer even during the worst tests of his spiritual life because it helps him find his way.

The obligatory prayer can be seen as a gift. It is a tool we can use to help improve our lives and develop our spiritual capacity. As the Bahá'í writings state, "Concerning obligatory prayer, it hath been revealed in such wise that whosoever reciteth it, even one time, with a detached heart, will find himself wholly severed from the world." (Bahá'u'lláh, in *The Importance of Obligatory Prayer and Fasting*).

THE WOMAN WHO LEARNED TO MAKE AN EFFORT FOR HER FAITH WITH THE OBLIGATORY PRAYER

There was a woman who had recently become a Bahá'í but did not feel as though it had changed much about her life. She had studied the Bahá'í Faith for many months leading up to her decision to join it. She had weighed many of its beliefs and teachings in her heart, and she had decided that this was a cause that she wanted to be a part of.

But to her surprise, right after she joined the Bahá'í Faith, she did not feel very different. She did not have any new visions or epiphanies that solved her problems or made her a better person. She was still the same person. The reality was, she just had a new membership card and attended a few new events during the week.

One night she met up with one of the more experienced Bahá'ís who had taught her about the faith. She explained her situation and her disappointment with how things were turning out. She talked about how she had expected the Bahá'í Faith to change her and to make her life better.

The more experienced Bahá'í asked the woman what she had been doing since becoming a Bahá'í. She asked the woman if she was saying her daily prayers, practicing meditation, and working on developing spiritual qualities in her life. The woman said she had tried a few of those things, but that she just did not feel inspired by them. She did not feel as though those things were very easy to do.

The more experienced Bahá'í then asked if the woman saw a connection? The woman was confused. Should not being a Bahá'í itself make her want to do those things? The more experienced Bahá'í responded that belief was only part of the equation, and that to truly receive the benefits in our spiritual lives from the Bahá'í Faith, effort was required. Belief was often the easy part. The hard part was actually doing the work.

The more experienced Bahá'í suggested that the woman start with saying her obligatory prayer every day, no matter how tired she was, and no matter how unspiritual she felt. She said that this practice had helped her learn the qualities of self-discipline, obedience, and trust in God. These qualities formed the bedrock for her faith, and without them, it was very hard to grow spiritually.

The woman took the more experienced Bahá'í's advice and started trying to say her obligatory prayer every day. After several months she found that this daily prayer helped her stay on course. It helped change how she thought and adjust how she felt. No matter what mood she started in, once she had said the prayer she felt a bit more refreshed and realigned. Soon she was inspired to start meditating in the morning and evening too. And after that she started to really think about her spiritual life and how she was living up to the Bahá'í standards.

The woman discovered that by taking that first step of saying the obligatory prayer every day she opened the door to the power of the Holy Spirit to inspire her in her spiritual journey. She realized that the daily prayer helped reconnect her to what was important in life and remind her of why she became a Bahá'í in the first place. Over time she came to love saying the obligatory prayer, and saw it as one of the most important moments of her day.

ANALOGY OF THE TRAINING ROD ON A PLANT

Sometimes a gardener will place a rod next to a sapling and tie the sapling to the rod. As that sapling grows and matures into a full plant, that training rod is there to guide it upward. Obligatory prayer serves the same purpose in our lives. We tether ourselves to the rod of daily prayer, and in return that training rod keeps us focused on growing upwards. It keeps us moving forward toward spiritual awareness and development. It is our guide and companion as we grow and mature as spiritual beings.

CHAPTER 17:

EXPERIENCING PILGRIMAGE AND DIVINE CONNECTIONS

"The purpose of God in creating man hath been, and will ever be, to enable him to know his Creator and to attain His Presence."

—Bahá'u'lláh, *Gleanings from the Writings of Bahá'u'lláh,* no. 29.1

MAKING A JOURNEY SACRED

A religious pilgrimage can be a journey we undertake to connect with our faith. It can be a spiritual journey of body, mind, and spirit. It can be a chance to learn about our faith and grow as a person. It can be an opportunity to bond with our fellow believers and connect with our spiritual heritage. It can be a personal quest for answers, redemption, and fulfillment.

All of the world's religions include some concept of pilgrimage. Many Christians make pilgrimages to sites related to Jesus' life, crucifixion, and resurrection in Israel. Many Christians journey to the Church of the Holy Sepulcher, which is believed by some to be the site of the burial and resurrection of Jesus Christ. Some others might go to Bethlehem where Jesus was born or to the Sea of Galilee where Jesus preached. During medieval times many Christians made pilgrimages to various churches and monasteries that claimed to have relics from the life of Jesus. These journeys can be tremendously meaningful for Christians who want to see and touch the same ground that their beloved Jesus Christ walked.

Many Jews make a pilgrimage to Jerusalem to see the sites related to their faith's history. They often visit the Western Wall, which is all that remains of their most sacred temple that was destroyed many years ago. This is the most sacred place for Jews, and it is a place where they bring their deepest hopes, prayers, and aspirations as offerings to their Lord.

Muslims also make a pilgrimage, which is in fact an obligatory element of their faith. All those who are physically able to go are told to make what is called "the Háj." It is a sacred duty that takes place during one month of the Islamic calendar. At that time, millions of Muslims come from all over the world go to the twin cities of Mecca and Medina. There they visit the sacred places of Islam associated with the life of Muhammad and the ancient prophets. In addition, Muslims can make pilgrimages to other sacred spots. Many Shiite Muslims journey to Iraq to the shrine of the Imám Ali. Others journey to Jerusalem to visit the Dome of the Rock, which is where Muhammad took His Night Journey into heaven with the angel Gabriel. These pilgrimages offer Muslims opportunities to come together as equals in peace, brotherhood, and true spiritual unity. They are an important right of passage for the people of Islam and they make up a critical pillar of belief in their faith.

Buddhists also make pilgrimages for their faith. Many travel to Lumbini, the birthplace of the Buddha. Many also journey to other important sites associated with His life, including the place where He achieved enlightenment, the place where He first preached His message, and the place where He died.

Hindus have numerous places of pilgrimage all across India. Generally, most Hindus place particular importance on the making of a pilgrimage to the four sites of the Chardham. But there are other sites associated with certain festivals, other sites established to commemorate certain times of the year, and still others associated with particular rites of passage for individuals.

In reality, pilgrimages have been around a long time in all the world's religions. Even in ancient times people would journey to oracles, temples, monuments, or other special places in nature where they made sacrifices, posed questions, and looked for answers in their lives. Whether it is visiting the Delphi in Greece, the Karnak in Egypt, the volcanoes in the islands of Hawaii, the mountaintops or mystic waterfalls in the Americas, or to countless other sacred places where humanity has found special meaning, making a quest for deeper knowledge and wisdom is a continuing part of our collective spiritual existence.

Pilgrimages do not even need to be mass movements of people to singular places of worship. They can be personal journeys we make for personal reasons. People can make a pilgrimage to the land of their ancestors to discover their roots and honor the sacrifices of those who came before. People can make pilgrimages into nature seeking peace and solitude where they can seek answers to life's biggest questions. And people can make pilgrimages back to places of their past where they might try to make peace with who they were, what happened to them, and how they remember it. Whatever the reason, people make journeys of the spirit all the time, and it is an important part of spiritual development.

WHAT IS THE BAHÁ'Í PILGRIMAGE?

The Bahá'í Pilgrimage is something that Bahá'u'lláh Himself instructed all of His followers to undertake at least once in their lifetime. As the Bahá'í writings state, "The Lord hath ordained that those of you who are able shall make pilgrimage to the sacred House, and from this He hath exempted women as a mercy on His part. He, of a truth, is the All-Bountiful, the Most Generous." (Bahá'u'lláh, *The Kitáb-i-Aqdas*, ¶32). While only men are obligated to perform this right, today both Bahá'í men and Bahá'í women are encouraged to make the pilgrimage at least once in their lives, if they can afford it.

For many, the Bahá'í Pilgrimage is an act of faith and an important part of living a full and balanced Bahá'í life. It is a physical and a spiritual act that breaks the routine of daily life. It offers a deeply personal experience that connects Bahá'ís to their spiritual heritage and unites them with the entire worldwide Bahá'í community.

Today the Bahá'í Pilgrimage takes Bahá'ís to several locations in Israel including sites in the cities of Haifa and 'Akká. These cities contain many important buildings, shrines, and gardens associated with Bahá'í history. In the future, the Bahá'í pilgrimage may take believers to sites in modern-day Iraq and Iran, but for now the pilgrimage to Haifa and 'Akká are enough to satisfy the requirement for Bahá'ís.

The Bahá'í Pilgrimage offers believers a chance to have a personal experience with the faith's history. Bahá'ís do not believe that visiting all the places of significance for all of the world's religions is necessary in this day and age. This would not be a practical or productive requirement of mankind. Instead, today Bahá'u'lláh has washed away ancient traditions and brought humanity a new common homeland for all. The spiritual seeker believes that the true value from pilgrimage is not found in visiting a physical location. Instead, the true value comes from the meaning, understanding, and purpose that we find when we align our lives with the spiritual forces of our time. These forces come into the world with the latest Manifestation of God for the age and are realized by the community of believers that rise up to make a new world civilization around His Message.

To that end, the Bahá'í Pilgrimage is the same for all Bahá'ís. It offers a clear and compelling opportunity to see places that have been touched by the Holy Spirit in this day and age. Because Bahá'ís believe that the same God sent all the Messengers and Manifestations of God for all religions, to visit the places of Bahá'í Pilgrimage is really the same as visiting the places of pilgrimage for all faiths. The Bahá'í Faith brings them all together in one. No matter what country, race, religion, or class a person comes from, when they make the Bahá'í Pilgrimage they are making it as a citizen of the world, as a believer in all the world's faiths, and as a sign of their commitment to realizing the vision of Bahá'u'lláh for a better world.

THE SITES OF BAHÁ'Í PILGRIMAGE

Bahá'ís have three types of places that are visited during the Bahá'í Pilgrimage. The first are the sacred shrines of the central figures of the faith. The second are the historical buildings associated with the lives of the central figures. And the third are the institutional buildings that house the administrative bodies of the Bahá'í World Center.

There are three central figures of the Bahá'í Faith. The most important is Bahá'u'lláh, the Prophet and Founder. His name means, "The Glory of God." The second is the forerunner of Bahá'u'lláh, the Báb (which means "the Gate"), Who is considered to be a Prophet in His own right. The third central figure is the son of Bahá'u'lláh, known as 'Abdu'l-Bahá, meaning "Servant of the Glory." All three central figures are buried in Israel. Currently, the remains of 'Abdu'l-Bahá are interred in the Shrine of the Báb, which is on Mount Carmel in Haifa, Israel. In the future 'Abdu'l-Bahá's remains will be moved to a separate shrine. The remains of Bahá'u'lláh are located in Bahji, which is just outside the city of 'Akká. There is no more sacred place in the world to Bahá'ís than the Shrine of Bahá'u'lláh.

Like the Founders of all the world's religions, Bahá'u'lláh was seen by the leaders of His time as a threat to their authority because He brought a new world religion, a new message of peace and tolerance, and a new cause for the unity of mankind. Bahá'u'lláh and His family were persecuted, banished, and imprisoned throughout the Middle East. They were eventually banished to the city of 'Akká, which, at the time, was a penal colony of the Ottoman Empire. The historical sites of the Bahá'í pilgrimage include the prison cell in 'Akká where Bahá'u'lláh and the holy family were locked for several years, and the homes where they were imprisoned for decades once they were allowed to leave the prison cell.

Bahá'ís on pilgrimage also visit sites associated with the life of 'Abdu'l-Bahá and His grandson, Shoghi Effendi. 'Abdu'l-Bahá worked to guide, develop, and protect the Bahá'í world community for decades after the passing of Bahá'u'lláh. Shoghi Effendi was appointed to be the Guardian of the Bahá'í Faith after the passing of 'Abdu'l-Bahá, and he worked for several decades to translate the word of God and guide the worldwide community until the Bahá'í world was ready to elect its supreme governing council, the Universal House of Justice.

Bahá'ís visit sites associated with these blessed souls' lives during their pilgrimage in order to connect with the sacrifices made for the cause. They hear the stories, see the relics, and connect with the spaces in which the history of the faith played out. For many Bahá'ís it can be a very moving and confirming experience.

Finally, Bahá'ís visit their institutions during pilgrimage. Bahá'í pilgrims have an audience with their international institutions. Most important of all is in the Seat of the Universal House of Justice, where the governing council of the Bahá'ís of the world meets with the pilgrims and welcomes them to the Holy Land.

THE ISOLATED BAHÁ'Í AND HIS FIRST PILGRIMAGE

There was a man who became a Bahá'í in an area where there were no other Bahá'ís around him. He had learned about it on the Internet and realized that this was the religion for him. He read books, studied the teachings, and worked hard to refine his character to live up to the Bahá'í standard, all without ever meeting another Bahá'í. It was a lonely struggle for the man. He wanted to share the excitement and energy he felt. But no one in his small town seemed interested. Instead, many of them were suspicious and some were even hostile to him and his new religion. His new belief began to make him feel very alone.

At one point the man decided that he wanted to make the Bahá'í pilgrimage. He saved his money for many years and waited with great anticipation. When the time finally came for him to go, he was both excited and nervous. Not only was he excited to fulfill this sacred obligation and connect with the deep and rich heritage that the pilgrimage offers, he was also excited to at last meet other Bahá'ís and find out what the Bahá'í community was really like. On the other hand, the man was nervous because he was afraid that the Bahá'ís would not accept him and would see him as not worthy. He had very high expectations about what being a Bahá'í meant, and he was afraid that he could never live up to those standards.

When he finally arrived in Haifa and met the other Bahá'ís for the first time, he was profoundly impacted by the deep spiritual experiences he had visiting the sacred sites of pilgrimage. In addition, the man was overwhelmed by the warmth and unity he experienced. Having lived in a small town his whole life, he had never met such a diverse group of people. There were believers from every corner of the globe joining him in this deeply personal and spiritual experience. As he visited all the holy places, he connected with the lives and experiences of the central figures of the Bahá'í Faith and deepened his understandings of the sacrifices made for this cause. He also opened his heart in prayer and meditation and recommitted himself to service to humanity. In addition, the man renewed his strength and certitude so that he could go back to his small town and live more confidently as a Bahá'í.

The man also learned about the Bahá'í world community and experienced the love and encouragement of the Bahá'í institutions. He truly realized that the Bahá'í Faith was much more than just his "own" little experience in his small town. It was a thriving, growing, and developing worldwide community of people transforming the world from the ground up. Like him, these people were not perfect by any stretch of the imagination. They all had their faults and weaknesses. But they were all united in the work of revitalizing the spiritual reality of mankind. And they were all just as excited as he was by the vision of Bahá'u'lláh for a better world.

The man returned to his small town with a whole new understanding of his faith. He knew more than ever that he was a part of something much bigger in the world, and this inspired him when he felt lonely. The fact was, he was not alone anymore. He knew of people just like him all over the world who were engaged in the same efforts to build a better world. His pilgrimage gave him a lifeline in his spiritual journey that ended up sustaining him for the rest of his life as a Bahá'í.

ANALOGY OF APPRECIATING THE TREE

If the Bahá'ís of the world today are the fruit of the Bahá'í Revelation, then the pilgrimage helps us appreciate the roots of this tree. The roots of the tree of the Bahá'í Faith are deep and strong. They dig deep into the ground of significance and meaning. These roots are the sacrifices made, the pain endured, the banishments inflicted, and the torment endured by those early Bahá'ís who laid the foundation of the cause. These roots offer an example of sacrifice and devotion that will inspire generations to come.

CHAPTER 18:

CULTIVATING A NEW MODEL FOR MARRIAGE AND FAMILY LIFE

"Enter into wedlock, O people, that ye may bring forth one who will make mention of Me amid My servants. This is My bidding unto you; hold fast to it as an assistance to yourselves."

—Bahá'u'lláh, *The Kitáb-i-Aqdas*, no. 63

THE FAMILY AS THE FOUNDATION OF CIVILIZATION

At the bedrock of society lies the family. Everything in society depends on its health, dynamism, and resiliency. It is the beginning of everything. It is the beginning of life. It is where we learn our first lessons about who we are, why we exist, and what we are here on earth to do. Studies have shown that healthy personal development is dependent upon children receiving the proper love, attention, discipline, guidance, and care from the earliest stages of life. In a perfect world, every child would have loving parents and a supportive community to help them reach their fullest potential.

Unfortunately, we do not live in a perfect world. Many families today have been ravaged by a world out of control. In some countries, more children have been born out of wedlock than within it. And many studies show that children in such households have a harder time. This evidence shows that children from single-parent households struggle more in school, relationships, and life. And once the family unit has broken down, it becomes even more likely that the trend will continue.

The spiritual seeker has seen the deficiencies of the modern world's concept of family. He's seen what materialism, self-absorption, anger, lust, and stress can do to people and how it can ravage family life. When it comes to starting and cultivating his own family, the spiritual seeker is looking for a new model. He recognizes that forces of modernity are changing everything. He sees how education is empowering men and women like never before with knowledge and capacity. But education and training often means that both husbands and wives need to learn how to treat each other as equals, to set aside their egos, and to sacrifice for each others' growth and development.

The spiritual seeker sees change in society and culture requiring a new approach to marriage and family life. The old models where men were the sole breadwinners and could find jobs that sustained a family are not viable. Today it often takes two parents to work, compromise, and support each other in order to sustain a family. Today people move away from family and support systems for their work and studies. Their communities are more divided and disconnected and this makes raising a family more challenging. Increasingly diverse communities no longer have common values that all can relate to. A world that is converging in every way, presents incredible challenges. People do not know how to overcome their cultural, religious, racial, social, and community differences and support and care for each other.

The spiritual seeker believes that the whole system is broken, and not just in a material way. It is not a problem that a new technology or a new government program can fix. The situation cannot be solved by reading one book or by taking one class. It is a systemic breakdown that fails society on every level including materially, mentally, and spiritually.

Today's marriages require a sense of equality and balance in order to deal with all this change. It requires sacrifice, compromise, and healthy communication. It means we have to be open and supportive. It means we have to give up some of our ego. It means we have to take responsibility for our own happiness and not expect someone else to make us whole. This equality is hard to create in our marriages. People often need a higher standard to live up to in order to accomplish it.

The spiritual seeker recognizes this. He realizes that we need a new approach to marriage and family life that is adaptive and resilient and that can help us thrive and grow as spiritual beings in our modern and ever-changing world. The spiritual seeker looks for new values to live by, new teachings to guide him, new standards to live up to, new tools to help him, and a new vision to work for.

The spiritual seeker is ready to build a new model for our marriages and family life that is founded on spiritual principles. That means seeing every person as a spiritual being above all else. It means seeing marriage itself as a union of two souls and helpmates, not as some superficial exercise in romantic fulfillment. It sees the work of raising children as the most sacred spiritual responsibility any of us could ever undertake. The spiritual seeker wants to help children grow so that they can reflect their own light in their own way. He wants to see them manifest their fullest potential in life, and this means building a family that is healthy and balanced from the very beginning.

BUILDING SUCCESSFUL MARRIAGES IN THE BAHÁ'Í FAITH

Many spiritual seekers find the model provided by the Bahá'í Faith for marriage helps them thrive in our modern world. The Bahá'í concept of marriage involves two equal helpmates working to raise a spiritually healthy family. Marriage is described in the Bahá'í writings as a "fortress for well-being." It calls for simplicity, balance, and moderation in our relationships from the very beginning.

As the Bahá'í writings state, "Bahá'í marriage is the commitment of the two parties one to the other, and their mutual attachment of mind and heart. Each must, however, exercise the utmost care to become thoroughly acquainted with the character of the other, that the binding covenant between them may be a tie that will endure forever. Their purpose must be this: to become loving companions and comrades and at one with each other for time and eternity." ('Abdu'l-Bahá, *Selections from the Writings of 'Abdu'l-Bahá,* no. 86.1).

For example. when Bahá'ís get married, besides fulfilling the laws of the country in which they live, the only Bahá'í requirement is that the bride and groom stand before one another (and two witnesses approved by the Local Spiritual Assembly of the area) and they say one phrase. Oftentimes, Local Spiritual Assemblies will also offer to provide information, consultation, and guidance to couples as they prepare for their married life together. Once they have done this, by Bahá'í Law, they are married. That phrase is "We will all, verily, abide by the Will of God."

This is a simple statement, but it has an incredibly potent message behind it. For when we look at what the will of God calls us to do, it can be very daunting. The will of God is that we forgive others. It is that we never give up. It is that we live to serve each other, and all of mankind. The will of God for us is that we become better every day, that we work at perfecting our own selves, and that we strive constantly to acquire the spiritual qualities we need to manifest more of the light of God in the world.

Additionally, there is one requirement that a couple must fulfill before they can get married in a Bahá'í ceremony, and that is to obtain the consent of all the living parents of the bride and groom. This places a huge responsibility in the hands of the parents. Many Bahá'ís see two main lessons for the law of consent. A first lesson is that it can help provide a safety valve for two young people who may not have thought through the consequences of their actions. Parents can help ensure that the couple understands the scope of the choice they are about to make, and make sure that they have the maturity and capacity to make it work.

A second possible outcome of the law of consent is that it binds the parents to the couple. The parents are taking a measure of responsibility to help support, encourage, and aid the couple to stay married throughout all the ups and downs in marriage. This is because successful families understand the importance of community. They understand that a strong marriage is a pillar of the community, and that together strong marriages hold up an entire society. In an ideal world, this law of consent is a sign of commitment of not just the couple to see it through, but of two families coming together in a common bond.

In the Bahá'í community, every marriage should be seen as a precious asset for society. Bahá'ís are encouraged to use the writings of the faith as a foundation in their relationships. These writing can be a guide in the way we treat each other, and a tool for perfecting our unions with others. Bahá'ís believe that true marriages last throughout all the worlds of God. Therefore, seeing marriages survive, thrive, and become healthy and magnetic forces of good should be the responsibility of everyone in the community. Bahá'ís have many resources they can turn to, including the Local Spiritual Assemblies—the annually elected councils that oversee the affairs of the local communities. Many couples have turned to the Assemblies to consult about their family's issues. The Assemblies' role is often to provide a measured voice of reason.

The spiritual seeker believes that one of the keys to success in the spiritual journey is learning to sacrifice oneself to something bigger. The same is true to building a successful marriage. In a Bahá'í marriage, both members must learn to sacrifice themselves for the sake of the marriage.

In fact, Bahá'ís believe that the marriage itself is a new entity that should be cared for. Like a newborn baby, a marriage must be nurtured, listened to, and shown infinite patience. Just as with a baby we must understand that couples will make mistakes and that they will learn, grow, and develop throughout the life of the marriage. And just as a child grows into adolescence and adulthood, marriage changes over time. It goes through stages. There are good years and there are challenging years. But just like a parent would never give up on a child whom they truly love, a couple should be just as committed to seeing their union succeed throughout all the trials and tribulations of life.

One of the most important things in marriage is to learn to overlook the faults of our spouses, to forgive our partners, and to avoid setting unrealistic expectations. The fact is, we cannot expect our partner to fulfill us or to make us happy or whole. That is our own responsibility. We must complete ourselves so that we bring a healthy, strong, and wise person to this union who is an asset, not a burden on our spouse. If we are unhappy, we have to look within ourselves to find the source of that unhappiness. If we are unsatisfied, we have to look to our own lives to find what makes us feel fulfilled. If we are incomplete, we have to discover what will complete us on our own terms, and not wait for our spouse to solve our problems for us. Each of us is responsible for our own spiritual well-being, whether we are married or not.

On the other hand, if both parties in a marriage sacrifice for the sake of the marriage, and strive to create a union in which trust, support, and encouragement are fostered, then the marriage can truly become a vehicle for growth.

RAISING SPIRITUAL CHILDREN

In today's society, many people focus on giving their children a material education. They want to see their children go to the best schools and find the best jobs. Many parents spend a great deal of money to see that their children are provided the tutoring, education, and guidance that they think they need to succeed materially in the world.

A material education is not enough, however. Unfortunately, too many of these parents live to see all this time and money spent on the material aspects of their children's education to have been spent in vain. Often those who only receive a material education find themselves perpetually unfulfilled, unhappy, and disconnected from anything meaningful in this world. As the Bahá'í writings state, "Thou didst write as to the children: from the very beginning, the children must receive divine education and must continually be reminded to remember their God. Let the love of God pervade their inmost being, commingled with their mother's milk." ('Abdu'l-Bahá, *Selections from the Writings of 'Abdu'l-Bahá,* no. 99.1).

The spiritual seeker believes that it is essential for children to have a spiritual element to their education. It is a spiritual or moral education that teaches the child right and wrong. It teaches the child discipline, patience, self-restraint, and wisdom. It teaches the child to be resilient in the face of spiritual challenges and difficulties in life. And it teaches the child to value detachment, balance, and moderation in all things.

In the Bahá'í Faith, a great deal of attention is paid to the issue of raising spiritual children. Bahá'ís throughout the world are engaged in classes catering to the needs of the young in their communities. The classes place focus on the need to assist children in manifesting the qualities and virtues of God. Such qualities include patience, trust, discipline, righteousness, spiritual awareness, closeness to nature, self-respect, resilience, adaptation, detachment, faithfulness, and forgiveness.

The spiritual seeker sees teaching spiritual qualities to our children as the way to motivate, train, and develop them to be true citizens of the world. Through this effort, he finds the Bahá'í Faith provides an endless source of encouragement, inspiration, challenge, and a path to service that he and his family can undertake together. In the end, his family builds on its physical bonds of flesh and blood with spiritual bonds of hope and purpose. The spiritual seeker then helps create a service-oriented family where the work of building a new world civilization is the work of all the members of the family. Such a family then becomes the bedrock of a better world.

As the Bahá'í writings state, "In this glorious Cause the life of a married couple should resemble the life of the angels in heaven—a life full of joy and spiritual delight, a life of unity and concord, a friendship both mental and physical. The home should be orderly and well- organized. Their ideas and thoughts should be like the rays of the sun of truth and the radiance of the brilliant stars in the heavens. Even as two birds they should warble melodies upon the branches of the tree of fellowship and harmony. They should always be elated with joy and gladness and be a source of happiness to the hearts of others. They should set an example to their fellow-men, manifest true and sincere love towards each other and educate their children in such a manner as to blazon the fame and glory of their family." ('Abdu'l-Bahá, in *Family Life, a compilation of the Universal House of Justice*).

THE FAMILY ADJUSTS TO BAHÁ'Í LIFE

There was a husband and wife who became Bahá'ís when their children were young. The children did not quite understand their parent's decision, but they definitely experienced the effects in their family life.

The first big change for the children came when the family started attending Bahá'í events. They went to the Nineteen-Day Feast together. The Feasts were unlike religious events they had attended in the past. There was no preaching by ministers or clergy. There were no separate programs that isolated the children from the rest of the community. Instead it was a completely communal event. There were prayers, songs, and readings shared by many different Bahá'ís, even the children. There was a consultative portion where the entire community discussed freely all the activities of the community in an open and consultative process. Finally there was a social portion with refreshments and fun. Everyone was invited to participate throughout the whole event.

This experience with the Nineteen-Day Feast carried through to all aspects of the family's new Bahá'í life. They began to attend devotional gatherings and study classes together. They worked together as a family to serve the community by hosting their own events in their home. They strived together to learn how to consult as a family to resolve difficulties and to work together as a united group. They learned that with consultation, everything was transparent and open in the family as it was in the community. When there was a question about life, laws, or standards in how we treat each other, the entire family would turn to the Bahá'í writings as a guide. The parents still had roles to fill as parents, and they had veto authority of many elements of life, but they tried to give the children an ever-growing sphere of influence in family decisions. Sometimes even if the parents knew the answer to a question, instead of telling their children what to do they would take that opportunity to turn to the writings for clarification and inspiration. When the children had issues with their parents, they too could turn to the writings as a guide. This made everyone feel involved in the new religion and it helped all the members of the family gain a sense of ownership over their newfound faith.

The model of family consultation also helped when the family had to deal with challenges. For example, when the father lost his job, the entire family came together to consult on ways to save money and make ends meet. When their grandmother passed away the entire family came together to share their grief, understand death, and to grow closer from this experience as a family. When the kids grew older and faced challenges in friendships, school, or life in general the entire family would come together to consult and help one another

As the children grew up they began to make their own way in life and define their own relationship with the Bahá'í Faith. The parents encouraged their children to travel, explore the world, offer service, and own their own spiritual development. To that end, the parents supported their kids financially to provide service, travel teach, and study overseas when they could afford it. If they could not financially support it, they would help their children find work and support them and encourage them to save their own money for their own service projects.

As the family went through different stages of growth and development, they strove to keep unity and peace among themselves as much as possible. Life was still messy. There were still problems, challenges, setbacks, and tests. But the family learned to deal with their problems together. And as the children grew up and started families of their own, it just meant that the collective responsibility to serve, consult, inspire and encourage each other in spiritual development expanded. Of course, none of this was impossible without the Bahá'í Faith, however, the faith served as an empowering model for the family, and they found that its principles aided them greatly in all aspects of their lives.

ANALOGY OF EXERCISE AND FAMILY UNITY

Unity is not an endpoint; to strive for it is an active state. That means that we do not discover unity, we create it, maintain it, and work at it. Just like a body must exercise its muscles constantly to stay fit, so a family must exercise its commitment to unity in order to stay united.

When we exercise our muscles it means we put them under strain, we push them, challenge them, work them, and energize them. The same is true if we want to practice family unity. In a family, we need to challenge ourselves to serve humanity together. We need to create situations that test us, push us, and make us uncomfortable. We need to step out of our comfort zones and together find the strength and capacity to unify. Therefore, if we do not challenge our families from time to time, then just like a muscle that never gets any exercise, our families will become weak and flaccid.

A spiritual family needs to find ways to exercise its commitment to unity through all the stages of life. This means going out into the world and serving humanity together. It means bringing people into our home and serving them, caring for them, and offering them love and encouragement as a cohesive unit. It means that everyone has a responsibility to serve our guests, welcome strangers, and love mankind in whatever way we can. Throughout this process our families become strong, healthy, and resilient pillars of goodness in our communities.

CHAPTER 19:

MASTERING A SPIRITUAL PERSPECTIVE IN WORK AND CAREERS

"O people of Bahá! It is incumbent upon each one of you to engage in some occupation—such as a craft, a trade or the like. We have exalted your engagement in such work to the rank of worship of the one true God."

—Bahá'u'lláh, *The Kitáb-i-Aqdas*, no.33

WHY WE WORK

In today's world, most people spend a large portion of their waking lives engaged in some kind of work. The spiritual seeker understands the value of work. He does not want to be a burden on anyone. On the contrary, he wants to be a contributor. He wants to add value to society through his profession. He understands the fundamental need society has for everyone to take personal responsibility for their own material well-being. Another responsibility is to care for our families. After we have accomplished that we can turn to care for our communities, and then care for the world. If everyone feels an obligation to add value in this way, it becomes light upon light upon light. People start to take care of themselves and of each other, and the world becomes a better place for everyone.

In many ways, peoples' professions define them. Our work often dictates who we spend time with, the social circles we join, and the way we see the world. Each of the countless professions available to us offers us a path, a way of life, and a culture unto itself that defines an aspect of who we are and how we contribute.

But the working world is also fluid, adaptive, and sometimes disruptive. Sometimes people switch careers and professions. Some work in more than one job at the same time. As the world becomes more technologically complex, interconnected, and educated, it requires an increasingly diverse and adaptive workforce to sustain it.

Work is also often a primary source of challenges and difficulties in our lives. Much stress in life comes from our bosses, coworkers, or changes in the economic landscape that add uncertainty and disruptions to our daily lives, our families, and our communities.

The spiritual seeker recognizes the challenges and opportunities of working in such a changing world. The fact is, most of humanity struggles just to survive and to put food on the table and provide for their families. Some people find themselves in jobs because of family traditions, social pressures, or just a lack of opportunity. Other people pick professions because they want to live a certain material lifestyle.

Still others choose a path that they think will lead to fame, power, or prestige. And some others find the profession that is the best match to their skills, capabilities, and interests.

A SPIRITUAL APPROACH TO WORK

The spiritual seeker strives to be detached and adaptive when he chooses a path for work. Of course, he is aware that while not all people have many choices in terms of what career options they have available, we all have a choice in how we approach our work. And so, as with all aspects of his life, he is constantly striving to learn new things, develop new skills, and look for new opportunities to grow and develop in his professional life. As a spiritual being, he values a sense of spiritual fulfillment over the accumulation of wealth and riches for purely materialistic motives. And if great material wealth is acquired through his work he is inspired to use such bounty to serve humanity and discover new ways to alleviate the suffering of others. Instead of approaching his work as a burden, he looks for opportunities to serve others in whatever he does. He desires a path that manifests his full potential in whichever direction life leads him. He constantly looks for ways to care for, love, and inspire others in his work. He finds ways to make even the simplest of jobs inspiring and challenging, always looking for new ways to benefit humanity, to reach new heights of excellence, and to develop his capacities in a spirit of service. The point is, the spiritual seeker takes the initiative to explore his full potential and contribute his full measure of capacity to the world no matter what his circumstances.

When it comes to considering a spiritual perspective on his work, the spiritual seeker can turn to the Bahá'í Faith for guidance. From a Bahá'í perspective, work performed in a spirit of service is the same as worship of God. This means that the countless hours we spend in the factory, on the road, in the office, meeting with clients, designing and creating products, and building things of value is equal to spending that time praising, thanking, and otherwise worshiping our Lord, provided it is performed in a spirit of service. This is because Bahá'ís believe we are created to manifest God's qualities. When we work in the world to the best of our abilities, we are doing just that. We are manifesting perfections of the spirit such as a sense of duty, attentiveness to detail, responsibility to our fellowman, accountability to our community, integrity in our dealings, wisdom in our decision-making, and more.

As the Bahá'í writings state, "Let your acts be a guide unto all mankind, for the professions of most men, be they high or low, differ from their conduct. It is through your deeds that ye can distinguish yourselves from others. Through them the brightness of your light can be shed upon the whole earth. Happy is the man that heedeth My counsel, and keepeth the precepts prescribed by Him Who is the All-Knowing, the All-Wise." (Bahá'u'lláh, *Gleanings from the Writings of Bahá'u'lláh,* no. 139.8).

To this end, it does not matter what our jobs are if we are there to manifest spiritual qualities. Most jobs do add some kind of value to the world. If our goal is to work for the benefit of mankind in everything we do, this helps us achieve a stage of maturity and empowerment that elevates and ennobles us as spiritual beings.

In some jobs this connection may be easier to draw than others. For example, in some professions such as teaching, nursing, or social work the connection between service to mankind and daily work is obvious. People engaged in this type of work are continuously presented with opportunities to inspire, love, and care for people in their lives in a very direct way.

But in other jobs the connection needs to be more actively cultivated in our hearts and minds. That is, sometimes our role is to support others, and it can be hard to realize how important our efforts are in the big scheme of things. For example, those who build products but who never see the impact of those products in customers' lives, those who clean buildings at night but never see who works in them in the day, those who wash laundry but never see people wearing the clean clothes, those who write books but who never meet their readers, those who calculate numbers but who never see the material change of their analyses, and those who gather resources but who never see those resources used, may not get to see the direct effects of their efforts in bettering others' lives. These people need to remind themselves of the bigger picture from time to time. They work to benefit themselves and their families, and they strive to do this work in a spirit of service to God.

In any case, in almost every job or profession, it can be easy to find ourselves caught up in the day-to-day affairs of the workplace. Wherever there are people trying to work together, there can be office politics and drama that can make it challenging to perform work in that true spirit of service. That is, it can be tempting to let ourselves be absorbed in the politics and maneuvering that goes on in work environments, and forget the service we are rendering to humanity. The spiritual seeker appreciates the Bahá'í Faith's writings that call us to pray, meditate, and connect with the divine forces in the world on a daily basis as critical elements of maintaining a spiritual perspective.

In all aspects of our lives, it is important to remember where we came from and where we are going as spiritual beings. As the Bahá'í writings state, "True reliance is for the servant to pursue his profession and calling in this world, to hold fast unto the Lord, to seek naught but His grace, inasmuch as in His Hands is the destiny of all His servants." (Bahá'u'lláh, *Tablets of Bahá'u'lláh,* p. 155).

TOWARD MORE SPIRITUAL WORK

Depending on the opportunities available to us, our options may be limited or they may be expansive. Opportunities are partly provided based on a combination of chance and choice. We have some opportunities based on where we live, who our parents are, what kind of education we have access to, and what the economic conditions of our community are like. But we also have opportunities that we can create or manifest. We can create opportunities by taking calculated risks, opening doors, and developing the skills we need to succeed in our chosen paths. In this way we can better ourselves everyday, and constantly seek new ways to get ahead in our path to add value in the world.

When it comes to capacity, we are all born with a unique combination of strengths, abilities, and talents. Each of us has a mixture of God's spiritual capacities that is distinct. Some of us are born with more capacity; others are born with less. Some of us are more artistic while others are more logical. Some of us are outgoing while others are more cautious. But all of that capacity is latent within us. It must be discovered, harnessed, and perfected through our efforts. The degree to which we develop our own capacity is up to us. It is up to our choices. If we practice, learn, and develop our own capacities in the arts, sciences, and crafts of the world then we can strive to manifest a fuller measure of our inborn capacity.

In addition, we receive certain values from our parents, our communities, and our society that drive us in our careers and professions. These values can include an appreciation for hard work, perseverance in the face of tests and difficulties, honesty and integrity in all transactions, adaptation to a changing world, and the desire to grow and learn throughout our entire lives. Our parents can work to instill these values in us from an early age. Our communities can offer us examples to follow. And our society can create opportunities for people who live up to these values to succeed. But we also choose our values. We decide what is important to us in our lives. We look at the opportunities we have and choose how important material success is in comparison to direct service or artistic expression. Each of us has to decide how much of our values we will sacrifice or manifest in our professional careers.

There are various principles of the Bahá'í Faith that help set a standard for Bahá'ís in the workplace as well as in all other aspect of life. Bahá'ís are called to show excellence in all things, and are forbidden from backbiting. Striving daily to uphold these standards offers an opportunity to grow spiritually while advancing in our careers. It also offers us an opportunity to change the work environment into a far more positive and noble place for everyone.

In addition, we can work to serve our coworkers as true spiritual friends. As we do this, we contribute not only to the success of our efforts, but to the betterment of the world. This is the highest aspiration for any truly ennobled being in the workplace—to want to be more than just another coworker; to be a spiritual friend; to help our coworkers grow and develop as spiritual beings, to overcome hardships, to find inner peace, and to be the best people they can be.

Together, when we work in a spirit of service, we become active agents of change in every endeavor. As the Bahá'í writings state, "Make ye a mighty effort till you yourselves betoken this advancement and all these confirmations, and become focal centres of God's blessings, daysprings of the light of His unity, promoters of the gifts and graces of civilized life. Be ye in that land vanguards of the perfections of humankind; carry forward the various branches of knowledge, be active and progressive in the field of inventions and the arts. Endeavour to rectify the conduct of men, and seek to excel the whole world in moral character." ('Abdu'l-Bahá, *Selections from the Writings of 'Abdu'l-Bahá,* no. 102.3).

THE UNHAPPY WORKER LEARNS TO SEE HIS JOB IN A NEW LIGHT

There was a man who hated his job on an assembly line. He found it mundane and boring. He felt as though he added no value in his job. He just showed up every day, put in his time, accomplished his assigned tasks, and went home.

But the man was looking for more out of life. He wanted to feel fulfilled. He thought a job where he served people directly would do that for him. He looked into doing international service, but he felt he was too old. He looked into teaching children, but he could not afford to go back to school. He looked into the medical profession, but he did not have the stomach for it let alone the finances. In the end, he decided to keep his day job and volunteer in the local schools as a weekend tutor. This volunteer work still left him feeling unfulfilled when going to his assembly-line job every day. He wanted to do more with himself.

Then one day he was talking with the mother of one of the children that he tutored and learned that she was a Bahá'í. He learned about all the activities that the Bahá'ís do to serve mankind, starting with improving their own selves. He liked that the solution started with changing one's inner condition first and foremost. That really attracted him because he felt too many people wanted to fix everyone else, but never really took the time to fix their own inner realities. He felt that if people would first stop to look at who they were, what they were about, and how they could come to peace in their own lives, that we would be halfway to a better world. Such an accomplishment could then radiate out to the rest of mankind as those people helped other people do the same thing.

The man joined the Bahá'í Faith and looked to be inspired to a life of service in the world. He prayed and meditated on how he could make his contribution. He was ready for inspiration to strike for him to resolve his inner spiritual problems. He expected that he might be compelled to free himself from the troubles of the world and leave his mundane work.

But his spiritual growth did not lead him to that choice. What he realized instead was that people do not resolve their inner spiritual issues with magical pixie dust. Prayer and meditation are nice, but without action we do not change anything. Instead, he learned to adjust priorities, realign values, and effect change the hard way. He learned that it takes a long and difficult struggle against our own selves in order to become the spiritual beings we want to be.

As he started to work at fixing his existing situation, the man realized that he had to try to fix his day job and try to make it a spiritual endeavor. He realized that he could not run from it. He realized that every job was going to have tests, so he might as well figure out how to make this one work. He believed that turning his mundane and boring job into a spiritual experience was actually a personal challenge that he wanted to take on.

Therefore, the man started to spiritualize his job by helping the people he worked with. He began to try to get to know his coworkers. He learned their names and the names of their family members. He asked about their lives outside of work and what challenges and struggles they faced. He started up daily conversations and showed sincere interest in people. And he worked extra hard to stop backbiting about the boss and other coworkers.

The results of his efforts began to pay off rather quickly. As he showed care for his coworkers he began to feel a deeper connection with them. As he stopped backbiting he found that people trusted him more and that they opened up more. He started to develop deeper friendships in the process. As he strove to become a better coworker, he was expressing spiritual qualities in the process, and fulfilling his spiritual potential at the same time.

Once the relationships began to change, the man started to turn to the work itself. He read a passage in the Bahá'í writings that called him to strive for excellence in all things. To him, this meant that he would have to work harder at excelling in his job. He started paying more attention to details and focusing on producing a better product. Nobody really seemed to notice his higher productivity at first, but that did not matter to him. He was doing a good job for God, not for his manager or the company per se. As time went on, the man did gain a reputation for dependability and reliability. People liked having him on their team. His managers appreciated his responsiveness.

But there were still hard days for the man. He struggled to make it interesting for himself some days. He would invent games to play in his mind (as long as they did not endanger anyone). For example, the man would invent stories in his imagination about how the products he was assembling would get used and cared for by people. This helped him stay engaged and intrinsically motivated to do a good job. Eventually his high performance got him recognized and promoted by the company, but that was not why the man did it. He did good work because he wanted to fulfill his potential and because it made him feel good about who he was and what he was offering to the world.

ANALOGY OF POTTERY AND SPIRITUAL DEVELOPMENT

In some ways, the spiritual condition of a man who makes a clay pot is revealed by the pot he creates. The person who creates a pot for simple economic gain does not put his heart into it. He makes something he can sell, nothing more. His pots might be simple, plain, and often not of the best quality. His days are boring, mundane, and trivial. He often dreads going into his workshop in the morning, and he cannot wait to get out at the end of the day. His work is unhappy and unfulfilling.

But the person who puts his heart into his craft, creates something more. His pot is handcrafted with care and precision. He is not just creating something he can sell, he is creating something he is proud of, something he can put his name on, and something he can hold up to his Creator as an offering of worship. The person who creates the piece of art for the sake of beauty and perfection is tapping into forces of inspiration and spirituality. His work is an act of faith. He has faith in himself, in his work, and in his fellowman. He believes he is contributing to the betterment of all men by doing the best work he can. He loves waking up in the morning and going to his workshop, which is his place of worship and creative expression. His life and work is happy and fulfilling. The choice is all his: Will he work to live, or will he live to serve?

CHAPTER 20:

EMBARKING ON A LIFETIME OF STUDY

"Immerse yourselves in the ocean of My words, that ye may unravel its secrets, and discover all the pearls of wisdom that lie hid in its depths."

—Bahá'u'lláh, *Gleanings from the Writings of Bahá'u'lláh,* no. 120.2

APPROACHING THE STUDY OF FAITH

For much of humanity's history, most people received their religious instruction through priests, ministers, imams, monks, gurus, and the village shaman. In fact, organized religion is one of the prime reasons learning, science, and philosophy ever developed over the millennia. The first universities and centers of learning were often founded on religious grounds. The first questions they were trying to answer were often religious questions such as "where did we come from," "why are we here," and "why are things the way they are?"

The spiritual seeker appreciates the benefits of scholarly research by religious leaders, but he also understands the risks. When he studies a religious question or a problem in light of his understandings of faith and spirit, he is willing to consider the ideas, interpretations, and concepts offered by religious leaders (both modern and ancient). He is always curious to hear, read, and share ideas from those people of faith who have dedicated their time to reading, understanding, and interpreting the religious truths of the world's faiths. He appreciates the challenges they offer him in his own interpretations, the inspiration they provide him in his own studies, and the encouragement they give him based on the fundamental truths of all faiths.

But the spiritual seeker also understands the risks of scholarship by religious leaders, especially when it comes to the study of spiritual matters. First and foremost is the fact that even the most devout scholar is a human being. This means he is fallible and not all-knowing. Second, human beings in positions of religious leadership are products of their own experiences and knowledge. This means their interpretations may be colored by cultural perceptions, historical understandings, and subconscious prejudices. Additionally, human beings in positions of religious leadership are susceptible to the same temptations that we all are. They can become attached to their positions of power and influence in a community. This attachment can hinder them from being truly open to spiritual truth, especially truth that might challenge their own prestige and/or livelihood.

In fact, because of all the reasons listed above, religious leaders do not have a very good track record when it comes to recognizing the spiritual Messengers of their age. Moses was persecuted by the Egyptian religious leaders. Jesus was persecuted by the Jewish and pagan leaders. Muhammad was persecuted by the Christian and Jewish leaders. And most recently, Bahá'u'lláh and the Báb were ruthlessly persecuted by the Islamic leaders of Their time.

The spiritual seeker knows that he must take personal responsibility for his faith. He reads and studies things for himself. He is open to all sources of spiritual wisdom. He is not prejudiced against one faith or tradition. He takes time to think, meditate, and pray about questions. He is also open to discussion and consultation about spiritual questions with people of all faiths. He loves sharing his understandings, being challenged in his interpretations, and being surprised by the wisdom and knowledge of people he meets in his daily life. But in the end, the spiritual seeker believes that he must make up his own mind about spiritual questions. He cannot rely on his parents, friends, or community to tell him what is true. He alone is responsible for how he lives his life, what he believes, and what he works for in the world. And he takes this responsibility very seriously when it comes to questions of faith.

A ROLE FOR THE INDEPENDENT INVESTIGATION OF TRUTH

For many seekers, one of the most attractive teachings of the Bahá'í Faith is the concept of the independent investigation of truth. For Bahá'ís this means that every person, no matter what their background, is solely responsible for answering life's big questions. To the spiritual seeker, this means that no one can tell him what to believe, why he exists, and what his purpose in life is.

As the Bahá'í writings state, "Arise in the name of Him Who is the Object of all knowledge, and, with absolute detachment from the learning of men, lift up your voices and proclaim His Cause. I swear by the Daystar of Divine Revelation! The very moment ye arise, ye will witness how a flood of Divine knowledge will gush out of your hearts, and will behold the wonders of His heavenly wisdom manifested in all their glory before you. Were ye to taste of the sweetness of the sayings of the All-Merciful, ye would unhesitatingly forsake your selves, and would lay down your lives for the Well-Beloved." (Bahá'u'lláh, *Gleanings from the Writings of Bahá'u'lláh,* no. 35.5).

For many millennia the only way people could receive spiritual wisdom and education was through the guidance and instruction of someone who had access to the word of God for the age. Today it is different. Today people can read. They can print or buy books and distribute them in digital form. Disparate ideas, ancient concepts, diverse philosophies, spiritual teachings, and divine realities that were once isolated by language and distance are now at humanity's fingertips. Therefore, with all this information available to each of us, the Bahá'í principle of the independent investigation of truth appears to fit the needs of the age on a universal level.

The spiritual seeker appreciates that in the Bahá'í Faith there is no clergy. This means that no one else is responsible for *our* spiritual development. There are no gurus or saints who tell us how to live, what to think, and what to believe. There are, of course, some Bahá'ís who are deepened in the spiritual and social teachings of the Faith. Individuals can turn to these people for insights, inspiration, and interpretation. In fact, Bahá'ís hold the wise and learned people of the community in very high regard. But as wise and experienced as these people might be, they cannot tell anyone else what to believe or how to live their lives. No one should blindly follow their advice or instructions. They should not be placed on pedestals, and no one should expect unrealistic virtue and spiritual insight from them. From a Bahá'í perspective, we are all equal in the eyes of God.

Bahá'ís approach learning not as a burden, but as a gift. We could spend a lifetime studying religious writings, meditating on their infinite meanings, and applying them to our lives and in the world around us, and have never exhausted their potential. The reality is, we are never done studying. If we strive to develop a taste for the holy writings that becomes insatiable and embedded in our lives, study of them can become ingrained in our spiritual realities and a key element to developing, cultivating, and mastering our spiritual capacities.

Spiritual education, however, is not just about mystical things and abstract questions. In fact, Bahá'ís believe that the study of spiritual things must be practical, meaningful, and purposeful.

WHERE TO START, WHAT TO STUDY

The spiritual seeker is open to truth wherever it comes from, no matter what names it carries, no matter what language it was originally revealed in, and no matter what religion it was part of. While the world's great faiths and spiritual traditions may differ in customs, laws, languages, calendars, rituals, and practices, they all share core truths that transcend every faith. The spiritual seeker, therefore, is a lifelong student of this truth revealed in many forms, and he actively seeks to find spiritual wisdom at the core of all the world's religions as a way to grow, develop, and extend his spiritual understanding of life.

The writings of the Bahá'í Faith offer the spiritual seeker a vast array of literature to explore, immerse himself in, and work to inculcate into his life. Bahá'ís believe that God has never left humanity without divine inspiration, no matter where we live, when we live, or how we live. Bahá'ís therefore believe that the writings of their faith not only uphold many of the same spiritual truths at the core of all the world's religions, but that the same spirit that animated the religions of the past has been renewed through the revelation of Bahá'u'lláh.

As previously stated, Bahá'u'lláh was the Founder of the Bahá'í Faith and He revealed the equivalent of over one hundred volumes of works including books, tablets, letters, and prayers. His works are the most important and foundational works in the Bahá'í Faith. They are both directly accessible and infinitely meaningful. Bahá'ís believe that the revelation of Bahá'u'lláh is the message of God for this age, and that reading His works is to read the divine wisdom for this day and age.

Therefore, Bahá'ís treat the writings of Bahá'u'lláh as a most sacred trust. These writings lay the foundation for the entire Bahá'í Faith by spelling out its fundamental teachings, core theology, basic laws, and basic organizational structure. While some of Bahá'u'lláh's works have yet to be translated, many of His writings are widely available in wide range of languages. They include His book of theology, also known as the *Kitáb-i-Íqán* (or *The Book of Certitude*), a book of mystical wisdom called *The Seven Valleys*, a book of laws called the *Kitáb-i-Aqdas* (*The Most Holy Book*), and a book of teachings and meditations known as *The Hidden Words*. Many of His most important tablets and letters are also collected in books such as *Tablets of Bahá'u'lláh* and *The Summons of the Lord of Hosts*.

The importance of the word of God as a source of inspiration and guidance in our lives cannot be overstated. It is our job to open our hearts and our minds to its influence. As the Bahá'í writings state, "Immerse yourselves in the ocean of My words, that ye may unravel its secrets, and discover all the pearls of wisdom that lie hid in its depths. Take heed that ye do not vacillate in your determination to embrace the truth of this Cause—a Cause through which the potentialities of the might of God have been revealed, and His sovereignty established. With faces beaming with joy, hasten ye unto Him. This is the changeless Faith of God, eternal in the past, eternal in the future. Let him that seeketh, attain it; and as to him that hath refused to seek it—verily, God is Self-Sufficient, above any need of His creatures." (Bahá'u'lláh, *Gleanings from the Writings of Bahá'u'lláh,* no. 120.2).

Secondary to the writings of Bahá'u'lláh are the writings of 'Abdu'l-Bahá. 'Abdu'l-Bahá was the son and appointed successor of Bahá'u'lláh. He is known as the perfect exemplar of the teachings of Bahá'u'lláh. He penned a high volume of writings and traveled widely giving talks and explanations of the foundational truths of the Bahá'í Faith. Some of his writings are compiled in a book called *Selections from the Writings of 'Abdu'l-Bahá*. In addition, he wrote the *Tablets of the Divine Plan* and *The Secret of Divine Civilization*. Lastly, many of his talks were compiled in several books including *Some Answered Questions*, *The Promulgation of*

Universal Peace, *Paris Talks*, and *'Abdu'l-Bahá in London*. Many Bahá'ís find the writings and talks of 'Abdu'l-Bahá to be more accessible and often easier to readily understand than the writings of Bahá'u'lláh.

After the passing of 'Abdu'l-Bahá, the leadership of the Bahá'í Faith fell to his grandson Shoghi Effendi who was appointed as the Guardian of the Bahá'í Faith. The Guardian was a special position in the history of the Bahá'í community. As the Guardian, Shoghi Effendi acted as the authorized interpreter of Bahá'u'lláh's revelation. Through this he gave the Bahá'ís of the world the context they needed to see their religion with the right perspective. He compiled and translated many of the most important works of Bahá'u'lláh and offered insightful interpretations. He also wrote some very important book-length letters offering instructions, guidance, and context for serving the Bahá'í Faith and building its institutions including *the Advent of Divine Justice*. His letters are also collected in some compilations including the *World Order of Bahá'u'lláh*. Lastly, Shoghi Effendi also helped put Bahá'u'lláh's revelation into historical context with books such as *The Promised Day is Come,* and his masterpiece of history entitled *God Passes By*. Through his correspondence with the Bahá'ís of the world, as well as the books he wrote, Shoghi Effendi provided an invaluable understanding of the faith's history as well as providing a framework for action through which the revelation of Bahá'u'lláh could essentially be put to use in the world.

In addition, the Bahá'ís turn to the writings and letters of the Universal House of Justice—the current head of the faith—to understand the goals, objectives, and plans currently in action around the world. As well as providing constant guidance to the Bahá'í world community, the Universal House of Justice has also written some important letters to the world at large such as "The Promise of World Peace" and "Message to the World's Religious Leaders," and has commissioned works including *One Common Faith*.

Together these works make up a large library for any believer. Later in this book there will be suggestions for a starting place for reading about the Bahá'í Faith. This list will include a few books that can be read, studied, and meditated on for an entire lifetime.

HOW TO STUDY THE BAHÁ'Í WRITINGS

The spiritual seeker approaches the study of spiritual matters with a mixture of process and intuition. He creates a plan, but he lets himself deviate from that plan as his heart calls. This is because spiritual study is not like studying engineering or mathematics. You do not learn something once and then move on. Spiritual study is cyclical. It builds on itself. It involves constant changes. This constant change means that our understandings of the same passage can evolve as we learn and grow as spiritual beings.

The point is, while there are many classes, courses, and institutes offered for people interested in learning about the principles of religions such as the Bahá'í Faith, there is no degree that you earn at the end of it that says you have become a "spiritual person." That is, there is no completion to our spiritual education. Spiritual education is a lifelong process. It becomes part of who we are. It becomes an inseparable part of our daily routine. It is a habit of living. And we have to remember that any habit requires practice, discipline, and some level of satisfaction or enjoyment for it to be maintained.

Therefore, Bahá'ís work at cultivating a healthy habit of spiritual study in their lives. They understand that we will not acquire all the spiritual knowledge we will ever need from one study class or from reading one book. Spiritual study, or what Bahá'ís call the process of "deepening," requires constant renewal. Deepening also requires self-discipline. This means pushing through "roadblocks," getting over the times when we feel tired or unconnected, and never letting lethargy or cynicism take hold in our hearts.

In addition, true deepening also requires enjoyment. Many Bahá'ís find great satisfaction from spiritual study. We see deepening as good for us. We see it as something uplifting, inspiring, and never-ending. Deepening offers us endless opportunities to creatively help recognize and realize the full potential of the Bahá'í Faith in the world.

Sometimes people new to the holy writings can find the language hard to penetrate. The sentences can be long, the words can be new, the tone can be unfamiliar, the structure can be complex, and the language can seem old-fashioned. Many new Bahá'ís have found that if they push through some initial awkwardness, however, that a new appreciation grows in them. As with the study of a foreign language, however, after a while the language of the holy writings stops sounding foreign and it becomes familiar. It becomes natural. It even becomes poetic. For many Bahá'ís, in fact, reading the writings of their faith is an experience that is majestic, powerful, and endlessly enriching.

The reward, once they learn this language is the ability to converse with God on a whole new level. Personal prayers begin to take a more exalted tone. Inspiration flows into their hearts, and over time the language of the writings become the language of their inner spirit.

As has been described, some Bahá'ís take a more systematic approach to deepening their understanding of the holy writings. Some might even write quotes on flash cards and work to memorize them. They may make lists of books and tablets to read and outline. They may gather quotes and concepts and make their own compilations and study guides. They might even learn a little Persian and Arabic so that the terms, names, and locations used in the Bahá'í writings sound a little less foreign. For many, even learning to count to ten in Arabic or to say a few phrases in Persian can offer a connection to the languages in which the writings were originally revealed, which in turn can enrich their study on some level.

In addition, Bahá'ís are always looking for ways to cross-reference their knowledge. Many of them love to explore the references made, metaphors used, analogies offered, stories told, and contexts set in the Bahá'í writings. They can also study the writings alongside the world's other holy books, cross-referencing ideas and concepts to give them a more complete picture of humanity's spiritual story. Throughout this process, they combine ideas, challenge traditional interpretations, and open up whole new arenas of understanding.

Bahá'ís also seek to take the wisdom they acquire from spiritual books, and apply them to the material world. They work to apply these principles in work, in family life, and in their approach to relationships. They are always looking for ways to add value to the world based on the spiritual principles they live by. In this way, their studies become more real, more relevant, and more empowering.

Finally, Bahá'ís are encouraged to study the holy writings in groups. Group study often presents a great chance to engage people of other faiths in open discussions of spiritual principles and religious themes. Many Bahá'ís will start their own book deepening groups. Other Bahá'ís will host a weekend retreat to study a tablet or theme. Many times Bahá'ís will try to come away with action plans on how to put what they learn into practice.

Bahá'ís also have what are termed "study circles." Today, Bahá'í communities are using study circles as not only a way to learn about the Bahá'í Faith, but as a foundational element of community-building. That is, people from all walks of life are encouraged to come together, pray, meditate, and discuss the writings and teachings of the faith in an open and loving environment. These study circles provide engines for the organic consolidation of communities as they grow and develop around the world.

From a Bahá'í perspective, spiritual truth is accessible to all people. There is no monopoly on spiritual wisdom in the Bahá'í Faith. Every person is responsible for discovering the meaning of their life and the purpose of their existence for themselves. This is a lifelong process that Bahá'ís consider one of our most sacred duties as spiritual beings.

What is important is that we let the word of God affect us, change us, inspire us, and guide us in our lives. We can do this, in part, through a lifetime of study, reflection, and meditation on the guidance provided by Bahá'u'lláh. As Bahá'u'lláh states, "The Word of God hath set the heart of the world afire; how regrettable if ye fail to be enkindled with its flame." (Bahá'u'lláh, *Gleanings from the Writings of Bahá'u'lláh,* no. 147.2).

THE STUDENT WHO LEARNED ABOUT SPIRITUAL WISDOM

There was a young woman who was investigating the Bahá'í Faith for a long time. She loved the teachings, she liked the practices, and she wanted to realize the vision of Bahá'u'lláh. But she still wasn't sure about it.

The woman was a life-long student. She approached every aspect of her life with a zest to know and understand. Whenever she chose to explore a new interest, master a new skill, or adopt a new hobby, she would read every book she could on that subject.

And so the woman investigated the Bahá'í Faith with the same systematic approach to all of her other endeavors. She felt as though she needed to know exactly what she was getting herself into before she could accept the new faith. She wanted to read everything written about it before she could be ready to join.

She set about reading every book written by Bahá'u'lláh that has been translated and published in English. She then read every book she could find by 'Abdu'l-Bahá. And she read all the published works of Shoghi Effendi. Lastly she read several history books about the lives of the central figures of the Bahá'í Faith. Her first pass through all of the Bahá'í writings gave the young woman a good sense for the scope and depth of the Bahá'í revelation. She understood the teachings, the history, and the vision of the Bahá'í Faith a lot more.

However, she did not really feel any different as a result of reading all that content. She did not feel any new spiritual powers developing within herself. Knowledge was good, but it was not wisdom. She realized that just reading the content was not enough; she needed to put the teachings into action for them to become real. Knowing about the Bahá'í Faith was one thing, but she had to see how being a Bahá'í affected her life in order to really appreciate it. The only way to really do that was to try to live up to the standards, practices, and expectations of this religion.

Therefore, she began to focus more on changing her life than on reading. She found that once she actually started changing the way she lived, once she started meditating and praying every day, once she started finding ways to spiritualize her work and career, and once she started applying the teachings in her family life and other relationships, she really started to appreciate the transforming power of the Bahá'í Faith. At that point she realized that words on a page were good, but they were not enough. They had to be combined with action. She realized that knowledge was not the end of things. Instead, it was the beginning.

ANALOGY OF SWIMMING AND STUDYING THE HOLY WRITINGS

One analogy often used in relation to the deepening and study of the Bahá'í writings is that of swimming. For example, if all we do is skim the surface when we swim, we will get tossed around by the rain, wind, and waves, and all the elements that affect the water.

But as we grow in our understandings, we begin to swim deeper into the ocean. And as we go deeper, the waves, rains, and winds of life have less of an impact on our spirit. We then find ourselves carried forward by the currents of the vast ocean. Here we find ourselves pulled into new places in the form of deeper understandings. The daily cares, tests, and difficulties of life are the storms of material existence. In the depths of spiritual awareness, such storms will fail to sway us from our spiritual path. In those deep places we remain calm in the storm and ever patient and resigned to the currents of the Universe. Our only objective in those peaceful depths is to swim ever deeper and keep ourselves on track by living a spiritual life.

But the depths of the ocean are not without tests. One thing to remember is that the pressure at the depths of the ocean is greater. For example, when we swim in a pool, if we swim to the bottom our ears and eyes begin to feel the pressure and weight of the water above. This pressure, in the analogy of deepening the spiritual depths of awareness, comes from our ego. That is, as we acquire knowledge and understanding, the pressure to think that we are more important becomes greater.

The spiritual seeker recognizes the danger of the ego when it comes to spiritual scholarship. He is aware of the temptations that come when people become attached to their positions of influence and power gained through knowledge. The fact is, many great men have fallen throughout the ages due to the temptations of the ego. Therefore, the spiritual seeker is always wary of this. He resists the temptation to think of himself as important. He continuously reminds himself that everything good is from God, and it all returns to Him. He is only acquiring this knowledge in order to do something good with it in his own lifetime. He is only a vessel carrying God's wisdom from heart to heart. What people may admire in the spiritual seeker is only what God allows him to attain. All praise, glory, thanks, and appreciation the spiritual seeker receives, he immediately reflects back up to his Lord, Who entrusted him with it.

CHAPTER 21:

GROWING FROM TEACHING THE BAHÁ'Í FAITH

"Guidance hath ever been given by words, and now it is given by deeds."

—Bahá'u'lláh, *The Hidden Words*, Persian, no. 76

OPENING A SPIRITUAL DIALOG WITH THE WORLD AROUND US

As the spiritual seeker grows in his own personal development, he looks for a way to translate that growth into an outward expression of faith. This is because how we express our faith to the world around us, to our families, with our friends, at work, and in our communities is at least as important as how we express our faith in private moments of prayer and meditation. In reality, for the spiritual seeker, there is no difference. The question for him is not whether he is going to share his inner spiritual condition with the world, but rather how he will do that. How will he engage with people in a way that informs, inspires, and encourages people to reach their potential in all aspects of their life? How can he engage with people in a spiritual dialog?

A spiritual dialog is a conversation of the heart. It is a discussion about life, spirit, and purpose. It is full of questions that have always been part of the human experience. It asks why we are here as human beings, what we are made up of as spiritual creatures, and where we are going as people who are constantly growing and developing. It ponders the purpose of existence. It wonders at the majesty of creation and the transcendence of love. It encompasses all aspects of life, from birth to death, from childhood to parenthood, from apprentice to master, from student to teacher. It is an ever-present dialog that continuously challenges us, inspires us, and remakes us as we learn and grow in our own spiritual development. It is a dialog that starts in the family, flows into our friendships, informs our workplaces, and unifies our communities.

For the spiritual seeker, the ideal place to start a spiritual dialog is in the family. Such a dialog can start from the earliest stages of life when children are just awaking to the world around them. As children discover the way the world works, parents can guide that discovery from a spiritual perspective. This means helping the children to see the world as a place of wonder, morality, and empowerment in the search for truth. A spiritual dialog can help educate children to see the world as a place to learn spiritual lessons, overcome hardships, and to work to cultivate a connection to God throughout every stage of life. In addition, spiritual dialogs can occur with other family members including parents, siblings, cousins, and grandparents in order to help people to deal with hardships in life, discover detachment from material things, and to see purposes behind all aspects of reality.

The spiritual seeker also has many friends to engage with in spiritual dialogs. As he moves from stage to stage in life, from school to work to community life, there are many opportunities to engage with friends on a variety of levels. Perhaps many of his friends have known about his spiritual path and spent time sharing insights with him into the deeper questions of life. Spiritual dialogs with friends can take many forms. Sometimes our relationships are deep and meaningful. We can ask honest questions of the spirit, and hope our friends will join us in a free, open, and nonjudgmental discussion.

Sometimes our relationships are not ready for such conversations, however. Sometimes our relationships remain superficial. Other times they need time to grow roots of trust before people will open up to enjoy the fruits of spiritual dialog with us. The spiritual seeker never rushes it. He shows his willingness to engage, he shares his openness to discuss spiritual matters, and he invites people to explore the deeper questions of life with him at their own pace. He holds himself to a high standard in his behavior, in his language, and in his beliefs, but he does not push that standard on anyone else.

In his work, the spiritual seeker also finds ways to engage in spiritual dialog when it is appropriate. Of course, sometimes his work requires focus and concentration, and there is not adequate time to veer off into conversations of the spirit. So he looks to create opportunities to earn the trust of his workmates. As he does this, he finds that the spiritual dialog begins to turn those coworkers from acquaintances into friends, and from strangers into the closest companions.

This is the power of the spiritual dialog. It brings people together around the most common and core elements of our existence, which is our spiritual path. It removes fear, suspicion, and distrust from our relations and replaces these feelings with openness, trust, and genuine love for people. The spiritual dialog deepens our relationships and enriches our lives, and so the spiritual seeker is constantly looking for ways to create the proper environment for this dialog with the people he meets throughout his life.

Lastly, even in his community the spiritual seeker longs to reach out to the people around him and engage in this dialog in a wider context. He recognizes that too many modern communities today are divided physically, socially, and economically. He believes that too many people keep to their own little groups, stay inside their homes when they are not at work, and avoid anything that might challenge their worldview. He sees people isolating themselves from one another and becoming distant and disconnected. Sadly, sharing faith and spiritual belief is often felt as threatening to people in today's society. This is because too many people have tried to convert us with aggressive means over the years. Too many people have been harassed by folks knocking on our doors, calling us in our homes, sending us unsolicited mail, or otherwise pushing their messages and worldviews on us in intrusive ways. As a result, the very act of trying to engage in meaningful spiritual dialog can then be seen as distasteful by some, because they think it might be some kind of trick to convert people to a different religious belief. It takes time to build up trust between people because of this in order to engage people in healthy, productive, and rewarding spiritual dialog where there is genuine love and respect between the participants.

The spiritual seeker wants to have a spiritual dialog within his family, friendships, work environment, and community that uplifts people. While there are many people he encounters across all age groups and demographics who are open to spiritual discussions, he also has to be mindful of sometimes having to do a little groundwork first in order to overcome cultural barriers and negative connotations. To that end, he is constantly looking for a way to engage people in meaningful conversations about questions that can truly help people help themselves, inspire them to follow their own spiritual paths, offer love and respect, and build trusting relationships over time.

WHAT IS TEACHING THE BAHÁ'Í FAITH?

One thing the spiritual seeker discovers about the Bahá'í Faith is the concept of "teaching," and its importance to a proper spiritual life for all Bahá'ís. In reality, teaching is one of the most critical duties prescribed to Bahá'ís. The spiritual seeker believes that teaching the Bahá'í Faith is not about going around trying to convert people to the faith, but instead, it is about engaging people in these spiritual dialogues and offering perspective.

As the Bahá'í writings state, "Consort with all men, O people of Bahá, in a spirit of friendliness and fellowship. If ye be aware of a certain truth, if ye possess a jewel, of which others are deprived, share it with them in a language of utmost kindliness and good-will. If it be accepted, if it fulfill its purpose, your object is attained. If any one should refuse it, leave him unto himself, and beseech God to guide him. Beware lest ye deal unkindly with him. A kindly tongue is the lodestone of the hearts of men. It is the bread of the spirit, it clotheth the words with meaning, it is the fountain of the light of wisdom and understanding ..." (Bahá'u'lláh, *Gleanings from the Writings of Bahá'u'lláh,* no. 132.5).

Bahá'ís teach the Bahá'ís Faith in two ways. First, they teach through words. Second, they teach through action. Both are absolutely essential for achieving success. For example, if Bahá'ís only told people about the faith but did not try to live it, they would fail to prove their belief could make a difference in the world. That is, if Bahá'ís do not strive to uphold the Bahá'í standards, work to transform their lives, and struggle to manifest their full spiritual potential, then they are not practicing what they call others to believe in.

Before we get into what teaching the Bahá'í Faith is, it is important to cover what teaching should not be from a Bahá'í perspective:

- Teaching is not preaching. It is not telling people what to believe or how to practice their belief.
- Teaching is not lecturing. It is not a one-way conversation where a Bahá'í unloads everything that he or she knows onto another person.

- Teaching is not arguing. It is not about convincing someone that his or her beliefs are wrong, and that the Bahá'í beliefs are right.
- Teaching is not selling. It does not involve watering down the core tenants of the Bahá'í Faith just to make it attractive to others. In addition, Bahá'ís can neither ask for, nor accept, financial donations from non-Bahá'ís. Teaching is never, ever, about asking for donations.
- And teaching is not converting. It is not the Bahá'ís responsibility to change hearts and minds, but rather to engage in a spiritual dialog and share valuable insights, guidance, and wisdom offered by the faith.

Teaching could be considered, on the other hand, many things, including the following:

- Teaching is questioning. It is asking the questions that matter to us as spiritual beings regardless of our religious or cultural background.
- Teaching is discovering. It is finding new realities, new answers, and new questions to explore with other souls.
- Teaching is confirming. It is about finding the things we have in common, realizing the connections we all share with one another, and recognizing the truths at the core of all the world's faiths.
- Teaching is humbling. It is about setting aside our own egos, our own understandings, and our own shortcomings and accepting that spiritual awareness comes from a higher source outside of our own realities.
- Teaching is healing. It is about finding the elements of life that make us whole, that complete us, and that give us a reason to awaken and draw breath in the morning.
- Teaching is loving. It is about opening our hearts to others and sharing the most personal of all connections with our source alongside another human being.
- Teaching is inspiring. It is about offering a clear, compelling,

and unifying path to a better world for every human being.

- Teaching is living. Without it, all of our spiritual growth, personal development, and spiritual understanding stays trapped inside us and unable to manifest itself in the world.

PREPARING OURSELVES TO TEACH

The fact is, any Bahá'í can teach the Bahá'í Faith. The most effective Bahá'í teachers are not always the people with the most book-knowledge, the most teaching experience, or the most personal connections. The most effective Bahá'í teachers are the ones who open themselves to the opportunity to truly engage another human soul in a spiritual dialog. They are the ones who can connect with people on a truly deep and profound level and offer them something healing and wondrous in the process.

Teaching the Bahá'í Faith is not about converting people to join a new religious club. It is not about gaining more followers just to have more followers. It is bigger than that. Teaching is about spreading ideas, inspiring action, and sharing the spirit of the Bahá'í Faith and the vision of Bahá'u'lláh. The aim of teaching is to make the world a better place, one heart at a time. A Bahá'í does not ask everyone they teach to become a Bahá'í. They ask them only to consider the Bahá'í Faith, its practices, beliefs, and vision as a legitimate path toward spiritual awareness. If the listeners agree, then the teacher might invite them to more activities. There must be no pressure, no compulsion, and no outside incentives in teaching. All are welcome to become Bahá'ís, become friends of the faith, or remain on their own path. Only the heart of the seeker knows what is right for him or her. As the Bahá'í writings state, influencing the hearts is truly up to God above all else: "Should such a man ever succeed in influencing any one, this success should be attributed not to him, but rather to the influence of the words of God, as decreed by Him Who is the Almighty, the All-Wise." (Bahá'u'lláh, *Gleanings from the Writings of Bahá'u'lláh,* no. 128.7).

HARNESSING THE BENEFITS OF TEACHING THE BAHÁ'Í FAITH

The benefits of teaching the Bahá'í Faith become real to the spiritual seeker the moment he engages in it. That is, the moment he opens his mouth to share the message of Bahá'u'lláh with someone, he finds himself discovering true and abiding friendships, living with a new openness to all things, and becoming a channel of divine love in the world. Throughout the experience of teaching he finds a new purpose for living that redefines what he thinks he is here to do in the world. That is, when he teaches, the spiritual seeker becomes an instrument building a new world community focused on healing the ailments of all mankind. He becomes empowered to change the world in a way that will last far longer than he can possibly imagine.

The spiritual seeker finds that teaching the Bahá'í Faith offers a new path to deeper friendships with everyone he comes across in life. The spiritual seeker creates relationships that are deep and more meaningful, and in the process he enriches his life in lasting ways.

The reality is, there is no one way to teach the Bahá'í Faith. Every path is different. Every conversation is wondrous and full of possibility. As the spiritual seeker shares this process with countless souls he encounters over his lifetime, he finds that every soul's journey is distinct and important. He opens himself up to each path as another source of inspiration and empowerment that he could never find if he were to remain isolated in his own journey to God. He finds that teaching is about renewing his own personal faith in new ways, expanding his own understandings, and experiencing the journeys of other seekers.

Lastly, through teaching the Bahá'í Faith, the spiritual seeker discovers the bounty that comes from being an instrument of a higher power. That is, as he teaches he finds doors opening that he could never have imagined. He finds that every relationship has the potential for a deeper purpose. As he teaches he purposefully puts himself in new situations that challenge him in new ways.

To become a teacher of this faith is to become an active instrument of its spirit for the age. As the Bahá'í writings state, "O Friends! You must all be so ablaze in this day with the fire of the love of God that the heat thereof may be manifest in all your veins, your limbs and members of your body, and the peoples of the world may be ignited by this heat and turn to the horizon of the Beloved." (Bahá'u'lláh, in *The Individual and Teaching: Raising the Divine Call*)

THE WOMAN WHO NEEDED TO TEACH OTHERS TO FIND TRUTH FOR HERSELF

There was a young woman who had attended many firesides about the Bahá'í Faith. She had several Bahá'í friends and considered herself a friend of the Bahá'ís. She appreciated the faith's teachings, beliefs, and vision for the world. But in her own spiritual path, she never felt the need to join the Bahá'í Faith. She had her own religious background that was part of her, and it never really occurred to her that she needed to change anything. No one ever told her she should become a Bahá'í, and so she never really thought she needed to.

One night at a fireside discussion there was an open discussion between the visitors and the Bahá'ís. At some point in the conversation, one of the visitors turned to her and assumed that the young woman was a Bahá'í. The visitor started asking her questions about the Bahá'í Faith.

The young woman had learned a lot about the faith from her friends and from attending Bahá'í events. To her own surprise, she was able to answer many of the questions. She was even able to add her own commentary, insights, and experiences to the discussion.

During that very discussion the young woman realized that she was a Bahá'í. She realized that she understood what she was sharing not just in passing, but deep in her heart. She realized that she actually believed what she was saying. In the end, she recognized that the Bahá'í Faith had seeped into her bones without her even knowing it. But it was not until it came out of her mouth in the form of sharing her understanding of it with others that she finally understood what it meant to believe these things. They were now her explanations and her understandings, and they contained wisdom that she used as a guide in her own life. After that experience, signing the card to join the Bahá'í Faith was just a formality.

ANALOGY OF DOCTORS AND SPIRITUAL HEALING

When we go to a doctor with an ailment, we go with symptoms that the doctor uses to diagnose our problem and then prescribe a solution. The doctor needs to learn to listen not just to what we say, but to how we say it. He needs to learn to tune into his patients' subtle messages. He needs to follow his instincts and ask the right questions. He cannot put words in the patients' mouths. He cannot force one solution or another on patients who are not able to bear a diagnosis or solution. Sometimes he needs to work them up to it. Sometimes he needs to run more tests, consult another doctor, or wait to see how things play out before he is confident in prescribing medicine to help the patient.

The teacher of spiritual truth must do the same. He must listen to the needs of his spiritual audience. He needs to be in tune with the seeker's cares, worries, hopes, and dreams. The teacher should not blindly offer the same medicine to every soul who crosses his path. He needs a wide variety of solutions at his disposal. He should not force one solution or another on anyone.

Like a doctor who perfects his practice throughout his lifetime, the teacher needs to constantly be adapting, learning, and growing in his teaching work. He still needs to test new methods and explanations, prove they work, and then refine and adjust them over time to fit the needs of each audience. His job is never done in bettering his teaching abilities. In this way, the spiritual seeker works for an entire lifetime, and is constantly learning how to teach more effectively.

PART III: VISION

CHAPTER 22:

REALIZING THE VISION OF BAHÁ'U'LLÁH

"Let your vision be world-embracing, rather than confined to your own self."

—Bahá'u'lláh, *Gleanings from the Writings of Bahá'u'lláh*, no. 43.5

THE NEED FOR A UNIFYING VISION

The spiritual seeker is not content to look backwards. He does not want to be defined by the past. He wants to be defined by what he is contributing to, what he is building, and what he is creating in this world. He wants to be part of something bigger than himself. He wants to find something that offers a hopeful vision for all of mankind to work for.

When he looks at the world, the spiritual seeker sees unfinished work. He sees a world in crisis. He sees too many people in poverty. He sees too much injustice. He sees too much immorality and degradation. He sees people throwing their lives away in fruitless pursuits of materialistic goals. He sees people finding new ways to divide themselves from their fellowman. He sees too many people living in ignorance, blaming their problems on others, not accepting responsibility for their lives, and unwilling to sacrifice for the greater good.

On the other hand, the spiritual seeker also recognizes that the world today has tremendous capacity to do good works. He recognizes that humanity has the technology to feed everyone, to house everyone, and to provide everyone a fair chance to make a better life for themselves. He sees that we can travel to any point in the world in a matter of days. We have more knowledge available at our fingertips than ever before in human history. Any question we have, we can put into a modern search engine and be presented with a near infinite array of answers. Even people in the most remote areas of the world have access to more information, more connections, and more capacity than ever before.

Truly we live in a remarkable age, yet we largely fail to take advantage of it. Instead of using our technology to unite us, too often we use it to divide us, to separate us, to spy on each other, to make weapons of war, to manipulate others, to pillage the earth's resources, to exploit the vulnerable, to feed insatiable greed, and to play to the darkest and basest instincts of our lower natures. Instead of spreading cures for diseases, we spend more money to spread drugs and alcohol to numb our senses. Instead of spreading inspirational messages of hope and peace, we spend more time spreading messages that glorify crime, violence, materialism, idolatry, and pornography. We have the tools to remake our world into a peaceful, moral, and spiritual place for every single human being on the planet, and yet we do not use these tools to accomplish this goal.

The spiritual seeker feels that something is missing that all of humanity can rally around. It is not enough to know what the right thing is. We need to have a reason to change. We need something to build, to create, and to believe in. The spiritual seeker feels that the world needs a vision to unite around. That is, the world needs goals to work for. The world needs a model to bring our countries together. The world needs a foundation to help us overcome barriers of race, religion, class, and nation. The world needs a basic moral standard to live up to that helps people overcome their lower natures and discover the noble nature that we all inherently possess. The world needs a role for every soul to fill toward making our planet a better place. When the world has a vision, then humanity can use its technologies, capacities, talents, and knowledge to implement this vision, make it a reality, and build a new world civilization.

The spiritual seeker is looking for a cause he can join that looks forward and that offers such a vision. He knows that the only force that has the power to unite people across every barrier, every tradition, and every philosophy is the power of a spiritual cause, a world religion. He is looking for a spiritual cause that is not obsessed with the past, and that is not focused on mindless adherence to traditions, endless debates over theological arguments, and pointless disputes over metaphysical details that do not matter for the future wellbeing of mankind. He is looking for a community that is not hindered by ancient sectarianisms, nationalism, different languages, and different customs. He is looking for an ideology that is not at odds with the modern world and that is willing to embrace the tools we have, the knowledge we have gained, and the capacity we have unleashed in the human experience. He is looking for a cause focused on binding every heart together in one common effort, which is the cause of making the world a better place for every single person on the planet.

INTRODUCING THE VISION OF BAHÁ'U'LLÁH

For the spiritual seeker, the vision of Bahá'u'lláh offers such a cause. The Bahá'í beliefs offer the spiritual seeker clear, logical, and compelling understandings for the nature of God, religion, and faith. These beliefs help him understand why he exists and where he is going after he dies. In addition, the practices of the Bahá'í Faith help him find happiness and detachment, refine his character, discover the benefits of prayer and meditation, raise his family, succeed in his work, and become the kind of person he wants to become.

But when it comes down to it, it is the vision of Bahá'u'lláh that truly spells out why the spiritual seeker becomes a Bahá'í. It is the world that Bahá'u'lláh offers that inspires him to join the cause. The spiritual seeker recognizes that every religion has beliefs and practices. They all want to help us become better people and be of service to others. Therefore, it is the vision of Bahá'u'lláh that truly separates the Bahá'í Faith from the rest of the religions and causes of the world.

The vision of Bahá'u'lláh is different from the causes of the world because of its comprehensiveness. It offers a path to unite humanity in a way never before seen in this world's long and divided history. As the Bahá'í writings state, "That which the Lord hath ordained as the sovereign remedy and mightiest instrument for the healing of all the world is the union of all its peoples in one universal Cause, one common Faith. This can in no wise be achieved except through the power of a skilled, an all-powerful and inspired Physician." (Bahá'u'lláh, *Gleanings from the Writings of Bahá'u'lláh,* no. 120.3).

This vision is not just a happy place to wish for. It is something we can actually create. This vision provides the tools needed to get us there. These tools include a new concept of oneness, a new kind of community to build, a new method of consultation to help us get along, a new story of connection to bind us together, a new system to order and administer the affairs of mankind, and a new idea of citizenship to help us overcome the divisions of nationalism. Together, these tools provide the mechanisms for unifying mankind into a new kind of people and creating a better world for all.

The vision of Bahá'u'lláh is guided by a number of fundamental principles. These principles include:

- The unity of all religions. This means accepting the common core tenants at the heart of all faiths, and not letting the temporal, minor, and often superficial differences distract us from the things that unite us.
- The power of unity in diversity. This means accepting that the differences between humanity in race, gender, and culture are not hindrances to our unity, but essential elements that will be fused and balanced together into a more complete and truly global civilization.
- The commitment to sustainable growth. This means seeing the world and its resources as a sacred trust to be delicately cared for, managed in a sustainable manner, and responsibly harnessed for the betterment of everyone.
- The objective of universal education. This means believing that we will only reach our full potential when every human mind is tapped for its creativity and wisdom. This can only be accomplished when every soul in the world receives a proper material and spiritual education.
- The standard of international peace and justice. This means collectively outlawing all war while unconditionally standing up for certain universal human rights across every national and cultural boundary.
- The goal of an end to extremes of poverty. This means offering a fair chance for everyone to contribute their talents and capacities in the world and never abandoning anyone to the ravages of hunger, preventable diseases, and isolation from the rest of mankind.

Most reasonable people can agree that these principles are good in themselves. Each principle is not new. Many religions have preached their merit. Many nongovernmental organizations work for one principle or another. Many people have written of their benefits, explored their implications, and sacrificed for their realization. What all these efforts miss is a spiritual renewal of all mankind. Without that, the spiritual seeker believes that none of these principles can truly be upheld on a global scale.

This spiritual renewal of mankind is at the core of what it means to be a Bahá'í. The spiritual renewal means that all the manmade baggage, divisions, ideologies, superstitions, and attachments that people have added to religions and movements in the world need to be swept away by a fresh infusion of divine power. Bahá'ís believe that without this wholesale cleansing of the various organizations of the past, humanity cannot move forward. There are too many entrenched interests, too many ingrained prejudices, too many established power structures, and too many generational divides to be able to salvage any of the movements of the past. Humanity needs something entirely new.

Therefore, the core of the spiritual renewal of mankind is ultimately mystical in nature. As stated, it must come from a fresh infusion of divine power in the world. Spiritual renewal is something we cannot capture or measure. It is beyond our comprehension, but it is real. It is what unites all the practices and beliefs of the Bahá'í Faith. Spiritual renewal is the fusing power within them. It starts with the individual reconnecting with his source, awakening to a greater meaning for reality, becoming inspired by a common purpose for his life, and finding a hopeful place in this unfolding story. It is fulfilled when the majority of humankind goes through the process of spiritual renewal, and we arise together as a new race of men and women capable of unifying on material, mental, and spiritual levels.

United, we can then set out to build a better world for everyone. This is what it ultimately means to realize the vision of Bahá'u'lláh. 'Abdu'l-Bahá states, "My hope is that through the zeal and ardour of the pure of heart, the darkness of hatred and difference will be entirely abolished, and the light of love and unity shall shine; this world shall become a new world; things material shall become the mirror of the divine; human hearts shall meet and embrace each other; the whole world become as a man's native country and the different races be counted as one race." ('Abdu'l-Bahá, *'Abdu'l-Bahá in London,* p. 38).

OVERCOMING DIVISIONS OF THE PAST

The spiritual seeker recognizes that humanity is growing, changing, and evolving. Throughout our collective history, human social development has moved outwardly from the family, to the village, to the city-state, to the nation-state, into today's regional blocks, to some rough (albeit imperfect) attempts at global governance. The fact is, if one believes that all people were truly created equal, then no matter what passport they hold or what language they speak, all people deserve some universal human rights. The spiritual seeker sees the next logical step of the evolution of humankind to be the step of becoming a truly global civilization.

Of course, the barriers to such a reality are huge. No one government could ever realistically take over the entire world and make such a thing happen. Seemingly no confederation, alliance, or union of independent nation states, each with its own interests, could ever truly bring about world unity and overcome the ancient religious, cultural, and nationalistic barriers we have erected between us. We need something new. We need a new system of organizing people, resources, and capabilities that is above country and culture. We need to have the capability to overcome the most rigid barriers mankind has created. We need to offer something better for everyone, not just a few.

In addition to political and governance issues to overcome, there are also cultural issues at work. The morals of the world's peoples have degraded to a new low, and they continue to degrade day by day. Too many people have lost their sense of right and wrong. Common decency is increasingly unfamiliar. Social standards are breaking down and being replaced by a materialistic ideology that says, "If it feels good, do it. If you crave it, buy it. If you want it, take it. If you get there first, own it. If you think you deserve it, grab it." Religious values are seen as out-of-date and backward. Cultural values are seen as old and confining. Spiritual values are seen as distracting and superstitious. The materialistic age sees people as objects who exist merely to consume, instead of noble and spiritual creatures who are meant to aspire to something more in this world.

This materialistic mentality is also a symptom of humanity's collective evolution. Whereas in the past we went through collective stages of childhood, today we are going through our collective adolescence. Like a teenager coming of age, we are filled with new powers and capabilities. But with those capacities comes the need to learn restraint, responsibility, and accountability. Most people are simply not there yet. They need to learn the value of restraining themselves from every carnal urge so that they can harness their powers to achieve great things. They need to learn the value of taking responsibility for their actions so that they can make more of themselves. And they need to hold themselves and their society to account for its actions so that together they can overcome the past and make a better tomorrow. As stated above, the world needs a spiritual, as well as a material, reboot. We need a new spiritual vision for who we are and why we exist.

As the spiritual seeker has discovered, Bahá'u'lláh offers a new vision for a new world where humanity has reached maturity and the people of the world are ready for a truly global civilization. Bahá'ís believe that reaching this stage of maturity has been the underlying purpose of all religions and civilizations of the past, and that this is the time of fulfillment—the New Jerusalem and the Day of Judgment that the Bible prophesied. Our collective task, then, is to work together and learn how to use our capacities for good, channel our energies for the betterment of all, and restrain our lower nature for the nobility of our species.

Bahá'ís believe that this time of fulfillment is bringing a twofold process into the world. On the one hand, forces of disintegration are at work in the world. On the other hand, forces of integration are equally emerging. Both processes are happening at the same time, yet both are reinforcing each other.

The process of disintegration is happening as the old world collapses around us. That is, the old ways of doing things have proven deficient. Many of the economic, cultural, social, and governmental institutions we have set up are showing their weaknesses and strain under the pressure of a changing world. Corruption, both moral and political, have seeped into these institutions' foundations and are rotting them to the core. Many of them are paralyzed by partisan gridlock, special interests, prejudice, racism, greed, selfishness, and class warfare.

On the other side of the process of disintegration is the process of integration. This is the process of fusing together the hearts, minds, and spirits of the people of the world into a new reality that is free of the baggage of the past. The same forces that are tearing apart the corrupt regimes of the past are also building up a new world reality that is driven to bring humanity together in peace, progress, and justice for all. It is driven by innovations in technology, communications, and infrastructure that teach us about our essential unity. It is inspired by realizations in the realms of science, medicine, and the natural world that teach us more about our essential oneness. And it is moved forward by a universal need in the human spirit to realize one's own potential and to contribute to the betterment of the condition of all mankind in the process.

At the heart of this process of integration around the world is the Message of the Manifestation of God for this Age, Bahá'u'lláh. He has given us a new way to see ourselves as one family of man, a new way to live with practices and laws perfectly attuned to the needs of this age, and a renewed appreciation for the role of religion in humanity's experience. In addition, we have been given a whole new way to organize ourselves and channel our efforts for the betterment of humanity in the form of the Bahá'í Faith. As the processes of integration and disintegration continues, this world faith provides the galvanizing force for inspiring, unifying, and empowering mankind to come together and build a new world civilization.

As we develop and mature, we will together develop new capacities that will help us deal with this new age, and we will become a new race of men in the process. As the Bahá'í writings state, "All men have been created to carry forward an ever-advancing civilization." (Bahá'u'lláh, *Gleanings from the Writings of Bahá'u'lláh,* no. 109.2).

HOW WE PARTICIPATE IN THIS PROCESS

While all these redefining processes are at work in the world, the spiritual seeker wants to know what his role is. How will he contribute to a better world? How will he mitigate the effects of a declining old world order? How will he serve the new world community? And what will be his legacy at the end of it all? These are the questions he asks himself on a continuing basis, ever-mindful that the answers he finds will define the most critical part of his life.

As he contributes to a cause like the Bahá'í Faith, the spiritual seeker discovers a lot about himself. Building a new world civilization is exciting and also challenging. This is because through service to the Bahá'í Faith, he puts himself in new situations and faces tests, difficulties, and opportunities that he could never find in any other pursuit. Sometimes he feels the support of his community, sometimes he does not. Sometimes he receives encouragement, other times he offers it. Sometimes he feels more spiritually connected, other times he does not.

Therefore, as he observes the collapsing world around him, the spiritual seeker must find his own way to cope with the changes affecting mankind. His first step is to accept that no one is completely immune to the tests and difficulties that humanity is enduring. Even the most spiritual person will be affected in one way or another by the suffering, temptations, illusions, and delusions of our Age.

The goal of the spiritual seeker is not to remove himself from mankind during its time of need, but rather to engage with it. His role is to work in the world, serve mankind, and offer people a better path. He helps calm those who are upset by the chaos. He offers hope to those who are disheartened. He brings love and encouragement to those who are lonely and lost. Overall, he is compassionate, not judgmental. He is supportive, not aloof. He is inspiring, not negative. He sees a better way forward and he makes that possibility clear to all who cross his path.

On the other hand, the spiritual seeker recognizes that those who work to build a new world based on the vision of Bahá'u'lláh are not saints. Bahá'ís are just as imperfect, prone to temptation, and full of personal failings as anyone else. Individual Bahá'ís have to learn to understand that each of us is in a different stage of spiritual development, and that we are all solely responsible for our own selves. We cannot hold others up to the same standards that we hold our own selves up to. Each of us is on a different path to God. Therefore, we must treat others as we wish to be treated: with patience, love, and compassion no matter how imperfect they may be. The spiritual seeker understands that some of the hardest tests in such a cause will come from the other believers in that cause. He knows that Bahá'ís often have high expectations for one another, and that these expectations need to be balanced with the reality that we are all fallible human beings trying to figure this out in our own way.

Finally, as the spiritual seeker evaluates his contribution, he keeps in mind his own legacy to promote this new vision for the world. The spiritual seeker wants to leave the world a little better then he found it. He realizes that the processes of disintegration and integration could go on for a long time. And thus he accepts that the speed of the arrival of that new world envisioned by Bahá'u'lláh is partly determined by how much progress he makes in his own life. He can have an effect, but only if he works at it.

Therefore, he can only bring that new world just a little faster through his own personal efforts. He can work to refine his character, expand his beliefs, and inspire others to the work of the Bahá'í cause in some way every day. And through those efforts his place in building the new world will be assured, his sacrifices for something bigger than himself will be validated, and his efforts will endure. In the end, for the spiritual seeker, no other legacy could ever compare. As the Bahá'í writings state, "... they who are the people of God must, with fixed resolve and perfect confidence, keep their eyes directed towards the Dayspring of Glory, and be busied in whatever may be conducive to the betterment of the world and the education of its peoples." (Bahá'u'lláh, *Gleanings from the Writings of Bahá'u'lláh,* no. 126.1).

THE YOUTH WHO LEARNED WHAT THE VISION OF BAHÁ'U'LLÁH MEANT THROUGH SERVICE

There was a youth who grew up in a Bahá'í family. His family was not perfect. They had endured many hardships, sicknesses, and tests from disunity over the years. But the Bahá'í Faith had been an integral part of their lives. The faith had provided values, standards, and consistent goals for their family throughout all the difficulties.

At a personal level, the youth thought that he would continue to be a Bahá'í when he grew up, but he was not sure what that meant. While the youth did understand many of the practices and beliefs, he did not know much about the vision of Bahá'u'lláh. He appreciated the goals of world peace, universal education, equality and such, but he did not see how the Bahá'ís were going to get there. He did not really understand where the Bahá'í Faith was headed, what it was building, and how it planned to change the world.

When the youth was old enough, he decided to go on a year of service. Many young Bahá'ís dedicate a year of their life in service to the Bahá'í Faith. They usually do this before their higher education or vocational training. This service can take many forms including working at a Bahá'í school, volunteering overseas at an international socioeconomic development project, or supporting any number of local, regional, or international projects. Youth are not paid for this work, and most often have to find a sponsor (or save their own money) to make it happen.

For his year of service, the young man spent a year volunteering at a children's school in Africa. There he served the local members of the community teaching children English and basic virtues. He was not there to "save" anyone. He was only there to render service, love unconditionally, learn from the people, and grow spiritually.

During his year of service, the young man gained a new appreciation for the beliefs of the Bahá'í Faith. Sharing a foundational understanding of why we exist, what our purpose in life is, and how we are all united in a divine spiritual reality with people from another culture in another country was a profound experience for the youth. As soon as he arrived in their country, the local Bahá'ís acted as his spiritual brothers and sisters, even though he had never met them before. He then understood how the beliefs of a faith can unite humanity like no other force in the world. He felt an instant connection to these people that he did not expect to have.

The youth also learned the value of the teachings and standards of the Bahá'í Faith. During his year of service he had many tests and difficulties, and he relied on prayer and meditation to keep him focused and strong throughout them all. The country was also in a very bad situation from corruption, crime, and immorality. He realized how important it was to have a moral standard to live up to by seeing how civilized life can fall apart without such standards. He had a new appreciation for the laws provided by Bahá'u'lláh, even if he still struggled to perfectly follow them in his own life.

Finally, more than anything, the young man realized more about what the vision of Bahá'u'lláh was. More than just a collection of beliefs and teachings, the Bahá'í Faith provided a unifying direction for all of mankind to move toward. The Bahá'ís had a framework to build that was provided by Bahá'u'lláh's world order. In the process the youth realized that the vision of Bahá'u'lláh was about building a new and better world for all of mankind to come home to. To him, this was the most inspiring part of what he learned from his year of service because it meant that all his sacrifices and victories were offered for something bigger than himself. He was contributing to something lasting and important for the world, and that was what it was all about.

ANALOGY OF THE EGG

The analogy of the development of an egg is useful for understanding the changes that today's world is going through. That is, after an egg is fertilized it begins the incubation process. Through this process, the yolk at the core of the egg provides the nutrients for the embryo to grow and develop. But outside the yolk, the outer membrane of the egg begins to thin itself and rot away. This continues until the baby bird inside the egg is strong enough to break out of the shell and hatch.

The world's twin processes of integration and disintegration are the same. The world's broken and outdated modes of operation and divisions between people are rotting away around us. Its institutions are paralyzed by partisanship and distrust, and increasingly unable to provide for the basic needs of society in a fundamentally fair and just way. Its religions are hopelessly deadlocked and unable to overcome their differences and unite in true spiritual harmony. And its culture is decaying and breaking down every moral standard of decency and nobility. As this process accelerates, the shell of human society begins to thin and crack, preparing for the emergence of something new in the world.

Inside the egg of the world the Bahá'í Faith has been conceived and is consuming the spiritual guidance and sustenance provided by the beliefs, practices, and vision outlined in Bahá'u'lláh writings. As the process continues, the tiny Bahá'í community is developing its organs, perfecting its senses, and growing its capacity to function and serve humanity. In the future this small embryo will grow into a baby bird that is ready to break forth from the shell of our old ways of thinking and allow the human spirit to take flight into a new stage of collective spiritual development for all of humanity.

CHAPTER 23:

HEALING YOUR HEART IN THE BAHÁ'Í COMMUNITY

"Now is the time to cheer and refresh the down-cast through the invigorating breeze of love and fellowship, and the living waters of friendliness and charity."

—Bahá'u'lláh, *Gleanings from the Writings of Bahá'u'lláh,* no. 5.1

WE ARE SOCIAL CREATURES

Human beings are social creatures. That is, we interact socially from the minute we open our eyes and see the warm and loving faces of parents who have been anticipating our arrival for months. Of course, our needs change over time. In the beginning we need other people to do everything for us including feeding us, changing our diapers, providing for our education. As we grow older, our needs change, but the reality is still the same. We need other people to interact with, engage, learn from, be challenged by, find inspiration from, and love and be loved by.

The spiritual seeker believes that a key element on the path to spiritual awareness is learning how to prosper in our relationships with others. So much of our growth as human beings comes from learning from one another—it is how we manifest most of the qualities of God that are available to us. That is, without other people how could we show kindness, love, and compassion? How could we express forgiveness, mercy, and benevolence? How could we practice wisdom, patience, and moderation? It is through our relationships that we discover our latent capacities. It is through interacting with people that we test one another's limits, push one another to the boundaries of our capabilities, and ultimately manifest our own spiritual capacity.

Therefore, in our quest for completeness as spiritual beings we have to be a part of a community that brings these spiritual qualities out of us. In the process, we have to get to know one another, we have to serve alongside one another, we have to care for one another, and we have to sacrifice for one another. Only when we have learned to do all this will we find ourselves reaching spiritual maturity and becoming the noble beings we were meant to become.

The social aspect of life is an essential part of the lifelong spiritual journey. Like anything else in life, this aspect of life has its ups and downs, victories and setbacks, challenges and opportunities. The fact is, as we serve a spiritual community we know that it will be made up of people just like us. That is, the spiritual community will be full of people who are also full of imperfections, weaknesses, and inadequacies. We all bring our own spiritual deficiencies and baggage to be worked on. We can take the time to care for one another, however, and learn how to listen, to love, and to serve. In the process, we learn to be patient with one another and to see one another as spiritual beings on unique and wondrous paths toward spiritual development.

Of course, sustained healing from the most challenging ailments in society requires medicine. But as we know, medicine is not always easy to administer, especially when the disease is deeply engrained in our bodies. To that end, the prescription for the healing of today's ailments also present a challenge to people. In this day and age, it is impossible to heal ourselves in isolation. We need a spiritual community to help us. This does not mean that it is the burden of the community to actively heal our spiritual sicknesses. In fact, the opposite could be seen as true. The community is not there for our needs. Instead, we are there for its needs. The community does not exist to solve our problems. Instead, we solve many of our problems by focusing on the community's needs (and not our own). When we stop seeing ourselves as the center of the universe, we realize the purpose for which we were created was to love, create, care for, and forgive. As we turn outward, all our problems, issues, weaknesses, attachments, and failures in life begin to fade in importance when we see the bigger picture, when we contribute to something bigger then ourselves, and when we begin to manifest our own potential through service to mankind.

From a Bahá'í perspective, the medicine we take to help us grow and develop in our community comes in the form of the Bahá'í holy writings. The writings are seen as a guide to right and wrong, as the arbiter when disputes arise, as the consoler of the lonely or disappointed or the lost. They are also seen as the inspirer to action and the re-energizer of the weary soul. The Bahá'í writings teach us to overlook the faults of others. They teach us to see each other as spiritual beings to be preferred over our own selves. They teach us to get over our own weaknesses and frailties and harness the power of the Holy Spirit. They teach us to never give up trying to create the kind of community that uplifts, empowers, inspires, encourages, and heals the hearts of all of humanity.

Everyone in a Bahá'í community is responsible for making the community friendly, open, and welcoming. And everyone is responsible for listening to each other, offering words of support, and challenging one another to advance. As the Bahá'í writings state, "They who are the people of God have no ambition except to revive the world, to ennoble its life, and regenerate its peoples. Truthfulness and good-will have, at all times, marked their relations with all men. Their outward conduct is but a reflection of their inward life, and their inward life a mirror of their outward conduct. No veil hideth or obscureth the verities on which their Faith is established. Before the eyes of all men these verities have been laid bare, and can be unmistakably recognized. Their very acts attest the truth of these words." (Bahá'u'lláh, *Gleanings from the Writings of Bahá'u'lláh,* no. 126.2).

FACING THE CHALLENGES TO UNITY

As we work together to create such spiritual communities, we face a number of challenges and tests that we must learn to overcome. These challenges include diversity, fear, the ego, and our attachments. Each has its unique elements that we need to face openly. If we do not, then these challenges will fester. They can undermine our efforts, impede our progress, and hinder us from reaching our full potential as a community of healing and empowerment.

Diversity is the first challenge. For the spiritual seeker, diversity is a wonderful thing he has learned to appreciate and welcome. But he also recognizes that diversity can bring many challenges. Spending time serving alongside people who are different from us in so many ways can make the work more difficult and time-consuming, it can cause unintended insults, and it can inflict hurt feelings. Diversity is a double-edged sword. While it can bring tremendous benefits when approached with a positive attitude that appreciates the value of a multitude of perspectives and backgrounds, it can also cause conflict when our differences become barriers between us.

Humanity is infinitely diverse in its cultures. People from different cultures have different ways of interacting, different customs, different languages, and different approaches to life and to problem-solving. The spiritual community has to find a way to create a new global culture that blends the good elements from the various cultures it encompasses, while at the same time letting go of the divisive and negative elements that hold us back. For example, some cultures have engrained sexism or racial prejudices, and these must be entirely abolished if we are to harness the full capacity of our community.

Besides culture, race, gender, and such, people are also diverse in their ideas. We all bring different experiences to our communities. These experiences mean we have different ways of seeing the world, different lenses by which we interpret events, and different perspectives on how we see our place in the big scheme of things.

A spiritual community needs to learn how to bring out the good ideas from its members and work on those, while letting go of the ideas that are negative and divisive. For example, some people bring their own ideas about how to run meetings, how to organize events, or how to engage in social interactions. These ideas must be mined for the good elements and balanced with the perspectives of others if we are to find unity in our efforts. Otherwise, if everyone is set in their own way of operating, we will be unable to unify and harness our collective energy to make the changes we need to make.

Another challenge to unity is fear. People are afraid of many things. We are afraid of the unknown. We are afraid of losing control. We are afraid of uncertainty. And we fear chaos and disorder. This fear can cause us to not take risks, to not try new things, to not let new ideas take root, and to not develop as a community. Fear can paralyze us and keep us locked in tradition.

The spiritual community needs to develop collective confidence that comes when we know that whatever happens, we can deal with it. We need to believe that no matter what, we will be there for each other.

This fear can be overcome with trust in ourselves and in each other. Once we have trust we can experiment, explore, and try new things with confidence in the community. A community must constantly be doing things to foster such trust between members in order to achieve sustained victories that, in turn, inspire confidence in our collective abilities.

Another challenge to unity is the selfish ego. If everyone in a community puts themselves first, then there is no community at all. Instead it is just a group of individuals. The selfish ego is what comes between us and the common good. It comes from a desire for power and a need for attention. Those who want to influence others to get their own way all the time are looking to satisfy their selfish ego. And those who crave appreciation and recognition for everything they do are looking to feed their ego.

The spiritual community must constantly avoid the temptation to hold individuals up on pedestals and allow the selfish egos to become tests for people. We need to treat one another with respect and love, but not idolize or blindly follow anyone else's directions. We need to think for our own selves and not set unrealistic expectations for others. To this end, we need to constantly work to remain humble and self-effacing if we are to create the kind of community that fosters spiritual healing and does not put too much burden on some.

Often the best way to do this is to focus on people's positive qualities. 'Abdu'l-Bahá is reported to have said, "If a man has ten good qualities and one bad one, to look at the ten and forget the one; and if a man has ten bad qualities and one good one, to look at the one and forget the ten. Never to allow ourselves to speak one unkind word about another, even though that other be our enemy." ('Abdu'l-Bahá, quoted in *Bahá'u'lláh and the New Era,* p. 82).

TOWARD THE GOAL OF UNITY

For the spiritual seeker, there is no greater test of his faith and his belief than when he inserts himself into the work of a spiritual community. He does not really know what he believes until he has seen his belief tested, refined, and challenged by others. The spiritual seeker needs other people to grow. He needs that constant feedback that comes from interacting with people who are also working to build a better world alongside him. As he contributes, he knows he is helping to build that spiritual community of healing that will attract the rest of humanity.

The reality is, to reach our full potential as a spiritual community, we have to adapt. Adaptation comes from learning. Learning comes from listening, consulting, and acting. As we grow and change as a global community, things do not always work out the way we think they should. Oftentimes the community needs to learn unanticipated lessons. The point is not to become discouraged and lose heart, but rather to be resilient and grateful for the opportunity to grow through this process.

In the Bahá'í community, each individual must recognize that each of us is imperfect. The fact is, we are all still vulnerable to the tests and difficulties, biases and prejudices, and temptations and seductions of a mortal existence. But what must be kept in mind is that each person is in the community for a reason. Our ideas, thoughts, and perspectives are as critical as anyone else's. For many of us, this means we strive to join in the discussions and consultations. We strive to engage in the sharing of ideas. We strive to actively support the efforts of the community. And we strive to offer encouragement and inspiration to all. When we do this, many of us find that we begin to fully learn and adapt as a community.

Throughout all Bahá'í activities there is one overarching goal: to create unity. Of course, this is not a one-size-fits-all kind of unity. It does not demand that everyone act the same, think the same, and live the same. It is more than that. It is a unity that is much more empowering and flexible. It is a unity where everyone has a unique role, where everyone has an important contribution, and where everyone strives to find some way to render service. It is a unity that brings out the best in all of us while compensating for our individual failings and shortcomings. It inspires us at the same time as it challenges us. It is a unity that fuses our individual contributions into something better than we could ever accomplish by ourselves.

Together, even if we start out as a small community of like-minded individuals, we can achieve great things if we are unified. As the Bahá'í writings state, "Look ye not upon the fewness of thy numbers, rather, seek ye out hearts that are pure. One consecrated soul is preferable to a thousand other souls. If a small number of people gather lovingly together, with absolute purity and sanctity, with their hearts free of the world, experiencing the emotions of the Kingdom and the powerful magnetic forces of the Divine, and being at one in their happy fellowship, that gathering will exert its influence over all the earth. The nature of that band of people, the words they speak, the deeds they do, will unleash the bestowals of Heaven, and provide a foretaste of eternal bliss. The hosts of the Company on high will defend them, and the angels of the Abhá Paradise, in continuous succession, will come down to their aid." ('Abdu'l-Bahá, *Selections from the Writings of 'Abdu'l-Bahá*, no. 39.2).

THE WOMAN WHO LEARNED TO HEAL HERSELF

There was a woman who had lived a hard life. She had faced tests, challenges, setbacks, and prejudice throughout her life. She liked to think that that these trials and tribulations did not bother her, but she knew that they did. She felt resentment about how she was treated. She was angry about the lack of opportunities that she had in her life. But she made the best with what she had. She worked hard and earned an education. She overcame hardship and became a stronger person through the experience.

In the process of overcoming her pain, the woman became involved in efforts to fight racism and bring about equal rights. She wanted to see that others did not face the suffering that she faced. She supported civil rights organizations and political groups that seemed aligned with her ideals. She wanted to make a difference.

Despite all of her activism, however, there were also times when the woman still felt discouraged. She felt that all these efforts were superficial. In the end, she felt in her heart that there was a divide between people that could not be crossed with laws, policies, and politics. It would take something more to bring humanity together. She knew a lot of people talked about racism, but they never really did anything about it. A lot of people talked about class-based prejudice, but nobody ever really changed their lives to work on it. A lot of people talked about all the divisions that separated people and that caused injustice, pain, and suffering, but few ever really did anything productive or lasting about it. The woman found this very frustrating.

One day she met an interesting new African American man in her workplace. This man was friendly and open and hopeful for the future of America and the world. She could not understand where this man's optimism came from. One day while they were sitting in the lunchroom, the woman asked him what was up. Why was he so hopeful?

The man answered that he was a Bahá'í, and the Bahá'í Faith offered the world a better path forward. The woman was intrigued. She wanted to learn more. And so she attended a few firesides with the man and got to know some more Bahá'ís in the community. To her surprise, the Bahá'ís were a very diverse group of people. There were African Americans, whites, Persians, Native Americans, and Asians among them. Their children played, studied their faith, and grew up together as spiritual brothers and sisters. The adults all worked together to build up their community, resolve difficulties, and face challenging issues with courage.

Of course, the Bahá'ís were not perfect either. There were still some Bahá'ís who had strange ideas or who had lingering prejudices and class issues. But the difference for this woman was that this community was being forced to deal with these issues. Instead of dividing people up by racial or ethnic grounds, they were uniting around spiritual principles and working toward a common goal. They were being forced to work together because they had a mandate to change the world. They knew that if they did not unite, overcome their differences, and transform their own community into a place of healing and hope, they could never hope to unite the world.

As the woman learned more about the Bahá'í Faith, she saw how its beliefs provided a common foundation for people from all backgrounds to unite as equals. She saw how the laws and standards of the faith gave everyone a common objective to strive for in their personal lives. And she saw how the global vision for a new world civilization focused on justice, education, equality, sustainability, and spirituality worked to galvanize people from every conceivable racial and cultural background into one community. She could see that this process was not always easy. She could see there were setbacks and people who were resistant, even in the Bahá'í Faith, to the changes that needed to happen. But again, she appreciated that the Bahá'ís were even working on this. This was the critical difference to her.

The woman realized that truly eliminating racism and prejudice was not going to happen with a new law, a political power change, or some kind of mass media campaign. Truly eliminating racism and prejudice could only happen when people came together through the love of God. This love for God is the only force that can transcend every national, cultural, ethnic, and religious barrier. Therefore, healing mankind of its deep wounds of racism, sexism, and cultural bigotry would only happen when hearts opened, spirits united, and everyone joined together in a common cause to work on themselves, their families, and their communities. Only then would a better world truly take shape.

The woman wanted to be a part of this effort. She joined the Bahá'í Faith and never looked back. She worked to let go of her fear, resentment, and anger and replaced it with openness, love, and hope for a better world.

ANALOGY OF THE WORKSHOP

A healthy spiritual community is like a craftsman's workshop. It is not a trophy room where we go only when we think we are perfect. Instead, it is a place for working on our own selves. It is a place for learning, developing, and improving ourselves. It is a place to render service and make sacrifices for something bigger than ourselves.

In that workshop we are given a set of tools. Those tools are meant to be used. Each has a unique purpose and requires practice and patience to develop skill in using.

In the Bahá'í Faith there are beliefs and practices that serve as tools to help us in our spiritual workshop. These are the tools provided to us to help expand our understandings, refine our characters, and inspire our spirits. These tools include prayer, meditation, laws, high standards, and spiritual principles to follow.

In a workshop environment, people bring their imperfect blocks of wood or marble to be worked on in the same way that we can bring our imperfect spiritual condition into the spiritual workshop to be continuously worked on, shaped, and refined throughout our lives.

CHAPTER 24:

BUILDING A NEW WORLD ORDER WITH THE BAHÁ'Í ADMINISTRATION

"The world's equilibrium hath been upset through the vibrating influence of this most great, this new World Order. Mankind's ordered life hath been revolutionized through the agency of this unique, this wondrous System—the like of which mortal eyes have never witnessed."

—Bahá'u'lláh, *Gleanings from the Writings of Bahá'u'lláh,* no. 70.1

LOOKING FOR A NEW SYSTEM

The spiritual seeker believes that in order for change to last, it needs to be organized. He has seen that the greatest leaders of history did not achieve lasting influence by acting alone. Instead, these leaders founded causes that were bigger than one person. In fact, most of the great advances in human society were the result of social movements. For example, in the United States, the most important movements for social change included the abolitionists who organized to end slavery, the men and women who worked for women's suffrage, and the countless groups from all backgrounds who united in pursuit of civil rights.

We need organization to be effective. Without organization there is no effective collection and redistribution of resources, no specialization of skills and abilities, no collective learning, and no systematic adaptation and improvement. Without organization there is no fusion of ideas into better ones, no pushback and questioning of individual perspectives, and no checks and balances on our own personal agendas that keep us honest with ourselves and accountable to a greater community. Finally, without a movement we do not leave a legacy. There is no one to pick up where we left off. There is no lasting imprint of our deeds, no community to carry on our efforts, and no place to entrust our experience and pass it on to the next generation.

Therefore, the spiritual seeker believes that the spiritualization of humankind is the most important task in the world. It is the beginning of everything. Without it, efforts will fade. With it, all efforts can become inspired by a foundational spirit of unity and brotherly love that reorients humanity along transcendent realities. But the spiritual seeker believes that the spiritualization of mankind will not happen overnight. It will require sacrifice and systematic efforts on a massive scale. It will require that we live true to our values at all levels of society. We have to be protected from division, sectarianism, partisanship, and misinformation while not crushing individual initiative. It has to inspire people to take ownership over their spiritual lives.

In the end, spiritualization has to empower people to make a difference. And to be effective as a spiritual community, we have to organize the empowered people. We need a system to channel our efforts toward common aims, set objectives that inspire people to sacrifice and push the limits, and distribute our resources effectively. This spiritualization has to be led by the people from the ground up because it must be born in the hearts of men, not imposed on them. It must be fair, open, and transparent. If we can create a system that channels our better natures while compensating for our weaknesses, then we can build a new world civilization that gives every human being the opportunity to reach his or her potential.

INTRODUCING THE BAHÁ'Í ADMINISTRATIVE ORDER

In order to organize the Bahá'í community, there is a system of volunteer-based councils that are elected from the ground up. Each city, town, or locality where nine or more Bahá'ís live can form a Local Spiritual Assembly, also known as an LSA. The LSA is a council of believers that is elected to run the material and spiritual affairs of the community. When a country has enough LSA's to reach a critical mass, it can then elect a National Spiritual Assembly for the entire nation (also known as an NSA). In turn, all the members of that NSA then vote with all the other NSAs of the world for the governing council of the Bahá'ís of the entire world, known as the Universal House of Justice. This election takes places once every five years, while NSAs and LSAs are elected annually.

As the Bahá'í writings state, "The men of God's House of Justice have been charged with the affairs of the people. They, in truth, are the Trustees of God among His servants and the daysprings of authority in His countries." (Bahá'u'lláh, *Tablets of Bahá'u'lláh,* pp. 26–27).

This system is remarkably simple and consistent across the entire Bahá'í world. There is no professional class of Bahá'í administrators. It is entirely volunteer-based at every level of the Administrative Order. A Bahá'í council is responsible for setting the direction of the collective efforts of the community, caring for the spiritual and material needs of the community, and deciding how best to use donated resources for the good of the community. Of course, some councils must hire a staff to run administrative functions or carry out functional tasks in larger communities, but the council members themselves are never paid, except in the infrequent cases in which their service as a member of an elected body (perhaps as an elected officer) requires full-time work.

In addition, all Bahá'í elections are entirely free of electioneering and campaigning. No one ever "runs" for election or "stands" for office. People are not nominated, chosen, or selected for council membership at any level. Instead, membership on councils is meant to be fluid, organic, and entirely free of partisan politicking. Bahá'í elections consist of prayers, open and frank consultation with all the members of the community, and a silent (and secret) voting process. The ballots are then privately counted by tellers who are appointed by the group, and the nine people with the most votes are considered elected.

Those voting in Bahá'í elections are responsible to pick the best people for the job regardless of race, class, gender, education, culture, language, age, or personal agendas. Therefore, in order to make informed decisions, Bahá'ís are asked to stay constantly engaged in the community. All are encouraged to engage in consultation at local, national, and international levels so ideas can be exchanged, different points of view heard, and understandings developed. In this way individuals expand the number of Bahá'ís they know and thus the number of people who they can potentially vote for. In addition, people better understand the needs of the community and can thus make a more informed choice about who would be a good fit for a particular time.

Once elected to an institution, no individual's personal or outside agendas are allowed to take precedence over the fundamental needs of the community. Bahá'ís serving on councils are responsible to God alone in their deliberations. They have to make the right decision based on their conscience, experience, and knowledge. They are not representing one constituency over another. They are representing all mankind all the time. Therefore, they do not make deals and water down their agendas in order to "pass something." They make the best decision they can every time they consult. They look into issues, gather facts, ask questions, and make their best effort to make an informed decision. No decision of a Bahá'í institution is ever associated with individual members of that institution, but rather, conveyed to the community as a decision of the institution.

Finally, the Bahá'í Administrative Order is responsible for providing a source of justice in a community. These institutions must therefore look into every matter fairly and comprehensively. Each council of people decides things based on the merits of each case. They are not swayed by high-priced attorneys and are not subject to the whims of politically appointed individuals. There are no political parties or ideologies to fall back on. And once a decision is made, those decisions of the Local, National, and International councils are binding on the Bahá'ís. Although any Bahá'í is free to appeal any decision to a higher body if they feel they have been unjustly treated.

A COMMUNITY OF LEARNING

Bahá'í institutions also need to keep constantly aware of the times in which they operate, and understand the cultural and social forces at work in their communities. To that end, they need to be constantly learning, adapting, and growing as institutions so that they can stay relevant to the life of the community. The importance of gathering, filtering, and sharing knowledge is critical. Turning that information into wisdom that the worldwide Bahá'í community can act on is also an important role of the Bahá'í Administrative Order.

To fill that need, the Bahá'ís have an entire arm of the Administrative Order devoted to gathering knowledge and information. This arm is called the Institution of the Counselors. Counselors are Bahá'ís who are appointed by the Universal House of Justice to serve as conduits of wisdom throughout the Bahá'ís world. In fact, there are Counselors to cover every region of the Bahá'í world.

Counselors have two main duties: propagation and protection. Propagation includes anything that helps promote, advance, develop, grow, or consolidate the Bahá'í community. Protection includes anything that helps protect the community from external attacks, internal schism, and general disunity. Bahá'ís know that there are many in the world who are resistant to the vision of Bahá'u'lláh including those who represent vested and entrenched interests who may not want a world of equality and justice. In addition, there are occasionally even those among the Bahá'í community who have become deluded enough to want to split the community into schisms and break its unity (and effectiveness). The Counselors are there to keep an eye on things, gather information, and take action in defending and protecting the community from those who may have nefarious intentions.

To fulfill their duties, the Counselors travel widely gathering and sharing knowledge, encouraging people, and offering practical direction that communities can turn into action. Counselors do not have any individual authority to tell Bahá'ís what to do or how to act. Rather they are guides and collaborators who bring an invaluable fountain of wisdom and experience into communities.

Each Counselor cannot possibly accomplish all the tasks needed in their assigned regions, which can often cover multiple countries of the world. Therefore, they appoint individuals known as Auxiliary Board members, who operate on more localized levels, and who may then appoint their own aids to help them in their work of gathering and sharing knowledge and helping the Bahá'ís achieve goals in growth, unity, and development of their communities.

BUILDING A MODEL FOR THE FUTURE

Together, all these elements of the Bahá'í Administrative Order provide a framework for realizing the vision of Bahá'u'lláh in the world. Founded on core values that guide, inspired by a hopeful future that empowers, enabled by a unique system that minimizes weaknesses and maximizes strengths, the Bahá'í Administrative Order provides an adaptive model for changing the world, built from the ground up.

Like a starfish that re-grows its limbs when it loses them, the Bahá'í Administrative Order is resilient. And, crucially, it is not dependent on personalities. It is a flexible system outlined in the Bahá'í writings. It adapts to new situations. It does not need any one individual to function. For Bahá'ís, it is a sacred privilege to be a part of it, and all are encouraged to strive to remember that at all times.

As stated, the foundation of the Bahá'í system is built on strong core values. When an organization has core values, all the decisions it makes then have a context and a framework for being made. In the Bahá'í Faith, the core values center on justice, balance, spirituality, efficiency, and all the other qualities of God. Core values can be turned to whenever there are difficult decisions to make. In this way, people are not beholden to special interests or personal desires.

In addition, the Bahá'í system is inspired by hope. It is a hope for the future that provides a unifying force that brings all together in a common cause. This hope represents the world Bahá'ís are building, the reality they are manifesting, and the work they are doing toward ending most of mankind's self-inflicted suffering. This hope helps the community keep moving even in the face of difficulties. Bahá'ís wake up in the morning with a zest to build this new world. They hunger for it with all their souls. Whenever they encounter the endless stream of suffering humanity inflicts on the weak, helpless, and powerless peoples of our world, Bahá'ís are comforted by the fact that they are contributing, in some small way, to a solution.

Lastly, the Bahá'ís are enabled by a system that supports a highly efficient community. The fact is, the Bahá'í system helps to minimize our weaknesses and maximize our strengths. It provides a way for the people to take control of their destinies in ways that are not corrupted by partisan politics or paralyzed by the selfish egos of individuals. In light of the political power-struggles so prevalent in our modern world, it's not hard to appreciate a system that protects the people from the type of charismatic individuals who have wrought so much harm in the world throughout human history. And all can surely see the value in the idea of joining together as equals, relying on one another, supporting one another, forgiving one another, and working with one another to build this wondrous new system.

Such an adaptive model for changing the world is an evolving reality. The Bahá'í Administrative Order today is still very much in its infancy. Even the most developed LSAs and NSAs currently manage just a sliver of the aspects of the needs of their communities. In the future, Bahá'ís believe that these institutions will be turned to by the masses who are looking for a just, fair, and uncorrupted arbiter and guide for building a better world. But that reality will have to be earned. The Bahá'í global community will have to prove that it can manage its own affairs and improve the spiritual and material condition of its own communities before the rest of the world will turn to it for such assistance.

Therefore, Bahá'ís recognize that there is a lot of work to do. The world has never seen a system such as the Bahá'í system. And this is part of what makes the Bahá'í Faith so important for humanity. As the Bahá'í writings state, "This Administrative Order, unlike the systems evolved after the death of the Founders of the various religions, is divine in origin, rests securely on the laws, the precepts, the ordinances and institutions which the Founder of the faith has Himself specifically laid down and unequivocally established, and functions in strict accordance with the interpretations of the authorized Interpreters of its holy scriptures. Though fiercely assailed, ever since its inception, it has by virtue of its character, unique in the annals of the world's religious history, succeeded in maintaining unity of the diversified and far-flung body of its supporters, and enabled them to launch, unitedly and systematically, enterprises in both Hemispheres, designed to extend its limits and consolidate its administrative institutions." (Shoghi Effendi, "Summary Statement—1947, Special UN Committee on Palestine").

The writings go on to state that "The Faith which this order serves, safeguards and promotes, is, it should be noted in this connection, essentially supernatural, supranational, entirely non-political, non-partisan, and diametrically opposed to any policy or school of thought that seeks to exalt any particular race, class or nation. It is free from any form of ecclesiasticism, has neither priesthood nor rituals, and is supported exclusively by voluntary contributions made by its avowed adherents. Though loyal to their respective governments, though imbued with the love of their own country, and anxious to promote, at all times, its best interests, the followers of the Bahá'í Faith, nevertheless, viewing mankind as one entity, and profoundly attached to its vital interests, will not hesitate to subordinate every particular interest, be it personal, regional or national, to the over-riding interests of the generality of mankind, knowing full well that in a world of interdependent peoples and nations the advantage of the part is best to be reached by the advantage of the whole, and that no lasting result can be achieved by any of the component parts if the general interests of the entity itself are neglected." (Shoghi Effendi, "Summary Statement –1947, Special UN Committee on Palestine").

A NEW BAHÁ'Í RECEIVES A CRASH-COURSE IN THE BAHÁ'Í ADMINISTRATIVE ORDER

There was a man who joined a community of Bahá'ís in a small town. To his surprise, the man happened to be the ninth member of the community. This meant that the community could at last have its first Local Spiritual Assembly (LSA).

The man did not know a lot about the Bahá'í Administrative Order when he joined. He became a Bahá'í because he liked the teachings and the vision of the Bahá'u'lláh, but he did not know much more than the basics. To his surprise, his ignorance did not matter. The community formed an LSA, and whether he was ready or not, he was going to be on it.

The man was a good sport about it. The more he learned about the LSA model, the more he liked it. It was all about transparency and collective responsibility for the Bahá'í community. There were no priests, ministers, gurus, or mullahs in the Bahá'í Faith. As individuals no one had authority over another. He found that the members of such institutions should be united in efforts to learn, grow, and develop—much like a living organism.

Luckily for the man, the Bahá'ís could turn to guidance on how to run an LSA in the Bahá'í writings. By studying the writings, the man quickly learned how an LSA should operate, what kinds of issues it should listen to, and how it should lead the community. He learned that an LSA was responsible for taking care of the community's operations and logistics. It was also responsible for taking care of the spiritual needs of the community. This included ensuring that all the children received a moral education. It also included working to make sure that all the adults had access to the encouragement, guidance, and inspiration that they needed to carry on in their efforts to refine their character, nurture their families, teach the Bahá'í Faith, and serve mankind through work and service.

Later in life, the man traveled to other countries and met with other Bahá'ís. To his surprise, he realized that all the LSAs around the world functioned in pretty much the same way. He realized that this grassroots organization represented one of the most important elements of the Bahá'í Faith because it provided the global network for creating a new race of men.

ANALOGY OF THE HUMAN BODY

One useful analogy when thinking about the Bahá'í community might be to compare it to a human body. In a human body, the bones hold our frames together and absorb the shocks that life throws at us. These bones are essential in keeping us from becoming a mass of useless flesh with no organization. The bloodstream moves resources around the body, ensuring valuable nutrients are delivered to organs. The muscles of the body give us strength and energy to move and effect change. Lastly, the soul gives us life, consciousness, and wisdom. The soul makes us alive, and it inspires us to move forward in life. Without the soul's connection to the body, everything begins to break down and decay.

In the Bahá'í community, the administrative structure is like a spiritual skeleton to the body of the Bahá'í world. As stated, this structure must be incredibly strong and resilient in order to withstand the tests of life. This structure is strong because it is established by Bahá'u'lláh Himself in His writings. No one who honestly reads the writings of Bahá'u'lláh can argue with the authority He has put in His World Order. It is, however, also resilient. When a bone is broken, it can heal. And the same is true in our spiritual communities. No matter what happens in our world, our communities have the freedom to adapt, grow, and change to meet the needs of the age.

The blood of this spiritual community is the Bahá'í Fund. The fact is, only Bahá'ís can contribute to the Bahá'í Fund. This ensures that the blood of the faith is never tainted by outside influences. Like the blood in a body, these financial resources pump dearly needed resources throughout the rest of the body of the community to help it function and achieve its goals.

The flesh and muscle of the body of the Bahá'í Faith are made up of the Bahá'ís themselves. They are what make this community move. They provide the motion and action, and energize it to accomplish its objectives. The ability of the community to affect real change in the world is dependent on its strength, commitment, and resilience. Like strengthening our physical muscles, building our collective strength takes practice, exercise, and consistent challenges. If we ever become relaxed or sit back, we will grow weaker and less effective as a force for good in the world. Therefore, we must be constantly pushing ourselves to achieve greater and greater goals.

And finally, the spirit that animates the Bahá'í community's body is the Word of God. The Word of God sustains us, guides us, inspires us, and provides the living force that drives us on to build an ever-more advanced world civilization. Like in the body, if for any minute our soul is detached from the body, the body will wither and die. The same is true for the worldwide Bahá'í community. If for any minute the community were to sever itself from the Word of God, it would no doubt wither and die.

CHAPTER 25:

HARNESSING THE POWER OF BAHÁ'Í CONSULTATION

"Take ye counsel together in all matters, inasmuch as consultation is the lamp of guidance which leadeth the way, and is the bestower of understanding."

—Bahá'u'lláh, *Tablets of Bahá'u'lláh,* p. 168

TRUE GREATNESS IS ALWAYS A COLLECTIVE ENDEAVOR

Throughout history humanity has reached heights of achievement and accomplishment only when it comes together to become more than the sum of its parts. Greatness seems to come from a combination of talent, practice, focus, openness, challenge, enthusiasm, dedication, excellence, and all the rest of the performance-related qualities that the spiritual seeker aspires to master in life.

For example, looking at history, many of the world's greatest civilizations reached their peaks of power, influence, and greatness when they were the most open, free, and just. They reached their heights when trade and commerce was fair, when minorities were protected, when knowledge was systematically gathered and exchanged, and when people could travel freely to interact. The Roman Empire reached its height of power as it brought a system of commerce, civility, and order to vast stretches of barbaric lands. The Moors of Spain reached their height of greatness in science, knowledge, and the arts when they became one of the most tolerant, fair, and just societies of their time. And the United States of America reached one of its highest points of global influence after the Second World War when its people were confident and thriving, its government was educating its lower and middle class, and its minorities began to demand equality and stand up for it.

These heights of civilizations were not always peaceful or easy, and they did not always last. In fact, they were often very challenging times. But they were times when the people united to solve problems, challenged themselves and each other to do better, and worked hard to create a more just society

There have also been periods in the histories of philosophy, art, music, sports, and technology when people have come together to create intensely creative and energetic pockets of achievement that have gone on to lead the world forward. A study of these periods can also help us appreciate the power of collective action.

In philosophy, we see distinct periods in human history when mankind has made advancements in the understanding of the role of reason, logic, argumentation, and of knowledge itself. In ancient Athens, Plato and Socrates reached the pinnacle of their influence in one of the first truly democratic societies of recorded history. Later, during the Enlightenment, the free flow of ideas, the increasing capacity to print and distribute books, the ability to travel widely and expose people to different cultures and perspectives all helped to inspire a complete revolution in the way people thought. It was an age of tolerance, exploration, and a commitment to reason and logic over superstitions and idolatry. In the end, this age led to explosive change in scientific, intellectual, and cultural life that was unprecedented in human history.

In art, we see the greatest achievements made in communities where artists were challenged by each others' talents and capabilities, and where practice, sharing, and performance were a way of life. For example, during the Italian Renaissance, a new age of artistic achievement flooded Europe. From Michelangelo to Leonardo da Vinci, what they created during that age has endured as a testament to the wondrous capacities latent in mankind. Later, different artistic movements would rise in various places of the world as artists would come together to collaborate, challenge, and inspire one another in new and compelling ways. From impressionism to modernism, from surrealism to expressionism, from Gothic to abstract, nearly all of the great artistic movements of history had their geneses in distinct communities where people came together to achieve more than they could on their own.

This is true for music as well. The great musicians of Europe's classical period congregated in Vienna where the best gathered to be educated, appreciated, challenged, and inspired. From Mozart to Haydn, the great composers from this time collaborated and encouraged one another to become more then they could have become working in isolation. This happened again with the Romantic musical period with Beethoven, Schubert, Liszt, and Chopin who arose in post-Napoleonic Europe to inspire and challenge one another. Even in modern times, musicians have congregated in certain areas to feed off one another's talents. For example , country music in Nashville, blues in Chicago and the deep South, the jazz of New Orleans, alternative rock in Seattle, hip hop in Los Angeles, and indie rock in Austin, and much more.

Today, it is true even in technology. The greatest achievements in technology are being made in regions of the globe where talented minds come to collaborate and challenge one another. From Silicon Valley in California, to Research Triangle in North Carolina, to Cambridge in Massachusetts, there are places where people of capacity, enthusiasm, and resources come together to build the next big advancement. It is not always a pretty process. There are many failures for every victory. But through the process of invention and reinvention, creation and recreation, new ideas are born and old ideas are recycled for new purposes.

Truly, from philosophy to art to music to science, humanity's most enduring achievements are always a result of the fusion of capacity. No man is an island. We need one another. We need to be challenged. We need to be inspired. We need to be tested. Greatness comes to us when we build on each others' ideas, accomplishments, and discoveries.

In the spiritual world, the same principle applies. We reach our full spiritual potential when we work together with others to solve problems, discover truths, and manifest our potential as members of a unified community focused on making the world a better place. Those who can bring the best out of themselves (and others) are the ones who learn to manifest the spiritual qualities required for effective collaboration.

Of course, this is not something people inherently know how to do. Socializing, communicating, adapting, and cooperating in spiritual endeavors must be learned. Just as when we first went to school, one of the first things we learned was how to get along on the playground, how to share and be considerate, and how to achieve what we wanted in life in a healthy and positive way. We have to learn how to cultivate and develop skills in working together on spiritual matters as well.

INTRODUCING THE CONCEPT OF BAHÁ'Í CONSULTATION

The spiritual seeker is looking for tools to help people get along and accomplish more in their lives. For example, in the Bahá'í Faith, the spiritual seeker learns to harness the full capacity of our community through the power of consultation. Bahá'í consultation is a term used to describe a model for discussion, interaction, and action. Bahá'ís are encouraged to use consultation in all aspects of life.

As the Bahá'í writings state, "In all things it is necessary to consult. This matter should be forcibly stressed by thee, so that consultation may be observed by all. The intent of what hath been revealed from the Pen of the Most High is that consultation may be fully carried out among the friends, inasmuch as it is and will always be a cause of awareness and of awakening and a source of good and well-being." (Bahá'u'lláh, in *Compilation of Compilations vol. I,* p. 93).

But before describing what consultation is, it is important to describe what consultation is not. Bahá'í consultation is not about giving up our individuality. It is not about just doing whatever the majority wants. It is not about hiding behind a group and shirking our own responsibilities. It is not about deferring to others when things get tough. And it is not about giving up our duty to create, build, and innovate as individual members of our community.

So what is Bahá'í consultation? Consultation is a way of discussing, analyzing, and resolving issues. It is an approach to interactions that often includes many of the following guidelines: Consultation requires humility, inclusiveness in the process, detachment from personal ideas, complete openness and frankness, and whole-hearted acceptance of the results. Bahá'ís are encouraged to study the topic of consultation, which is mentioned often in the faith's writings. It is a deep and rich subject that many spend a lifetime learning to perfect. In fact, it is often referred to as practicing the "art of consultation." And like any artistic endeavor, it is endlessly improvable and requires us to commit to continually refining our own abilities throughout our entire lives.

To that end, Bahá'í consultation is an interactive, dynamic, and energizing tool for adaptation and development in a community. It is interactive because all are encouraged to participate by both listening and sharing. It is dynamic because it is always changing to meet the needs of the community. And it is energizing because it harnesses the enthusiasm and passions of everyone to achieve objectives. Consultation is the lubricant that flows between the spiritual community's engine parts to keep it working. It fuses people together, drives innovation, and forces change and adaptation.

Bahá'ís use consultation in all aspects of collective and individual life. For example, Bahá'í communities consult as a group regularly at Nineteen-Day Feasts. During a community consultation Bahá'ís are encouraged to bring up new ideas, share suggestions, offer insights, and challenge the rest of the community to solve problems. Community consultation should be vibrant and engaging for everyone.

Bahá'í institutions use consultation regularly as an important tool as well. Local, regional, and national councils, as well as the international governing council, the Universal House of Justice, all use the principles of consultation to guide discussions, come to decisions, and take collective action. But consultation can be used for learning and understanding as much as making decisions. Institutions also use consultation to resolve differences, explore alternatives, and understand issues. They often invite experts and people with relevant experience or insight to join in their consultations. But when it comes time to make decisions those decisions are left to the institutions.

In Bahá'í families, consultation is used to build and maintain unity. Marriages and families today are under tremendous pressure from internal and external forces. Therefore, consultation can be a useful tool for helping people in families adapt to a changing world. For example, in marriages consultation helps us air our grievances, discover alternatives, and make compromises in ways that are respectful. Consultation provides a way to resolve problems between family members in a peaceful manner. It also offers a way to detach ourselves from emotions and find a mature solution to our issues. And lastly, consultation helps us ensure that everyone's voice is heard. Obviously, decisions are not always made by a majority in a family. Sometimes the parents need to make the final decisions on matters. But consultation provides a channel for communication, and it ensures that everyone has a chance to contribute in a healthy and productive dialog.

In workplaces and personal lives Bahá'ís also use consultation to help make big decisions, resolve difficult challenges, and come up with innovative solutions. The fact is, many of our problems in life can be solved if we use the power of consultation. Oftentimes consulting with friends and coworkers can help us put situations into the proper perspective. For example, in consultation our friends and coworkers can offer their insights, experiences, and wisdom in a way that is non-threatening and supportive. And together they can suggest alternatives and help us plan out ways to reach solutions.

Through such consultation, the big decisions in our lives can become less stressful, more informed, and easier to make. As the Bahá'í writings state, "No welfare and no well-being can be attained except through consultation." (Bahá'u'lláh, in *Consultation: A Compilation,* p. 3).

THE PRINCIPLES OF BAHÁ'Í CONSULTATION

The principles of Bahá'í consultation include many fundamental spiritual concepts including the need for full participation, a commitment to results, detachment and humility, and a sense of spiritual responsibility. These are the divine qualifications that help make Bahá'í consultation effective at bringing out the best in people while minimizing our individual weaknesses.

Full participation by everyone involved is one of the keys to successful consultation. To that end, Bahá'ís go to great lengths to ensure that everyone's voice is heard in deliberations. This is very much in line with the faith's emphasis on unity in diversity. This diversity could refer to that of age, race, gender, perspective, and life experience. Without diversity, we only attain a limited perspective, a limited analysis, and a limited result. Bahá'ís believe that all ideas should be brought out in the open for analysis, constructive criticism, and improvement, and that through a healthy and open dialog with others. This means that people should speak up when they disagree. They should bring up other points that have not been considered. They should feel compelled to contribute, *especially* when they question things. As the Bahá'í writings state, "The shining spark of truth cometh forth only after the clash of differing opinions." ('Abdu'l-Bahá, *Selections from the Writings of 'Abdu'l-Bahá*, no. 44.1).

Another principle of Bahá'í consultation is commitment to results. Bahá'ís are called to take personal emotions and individual agendas out of the process, and instead focus on the facts. Toward this end, there are no factions, political parties, or ideological schools in the Bahá'í Faith. All are encouraged to look at situations rationally and logically. Often the goal is to analyze and diagnose a problem, focus on the details, identify some alternatives, assess the potential impact of those alternatives, take collective action, and then reflect to make any necessary adjustments over time. While it is best to have uniform agreement on a matter, there is the option of taking a vote on matters as well. Once a decision is made, all are required to wholeheartedly support it regardless of the views individuals may have expressed during the consultation. In this way, it will become apparent most readily if the decision needs to be revised, and a protest mentality that could impede progress and be divisive will be avoided.

Another important principle for successful consultation is detachment. In Bahá'í consultation, once an idea is offered to the group, that idea belongs to the group. It is no longer associated with the individual who offered it. This principle is designed to take the personal ego out of the equation. Detachment in this process means not holding onto personal ideas regardless of whether they are ultimately rejected or embraced by the group.

Humility is also essential in this process, and plays a significant role in enabling individuals to remain detached from their own ideas. Before entering a consultation, all members are required to strive to be open-minded and willing to be convinced of the truth no matter where it takes them. No one is supposed to enter a consultation with an agenda of their own or with preconceived notions about the intelligence or capacity of others in the group. Inspiration often comes from the most unexpected of sources.

Bahá'í consultation also requires a sense of spiritual responsibility. Bahá'ís in consultation are responsible only to God. They are not beholden to a particular constituency that elected them. They do not work only for one region. When elected, they all represent the entire human family. They all answer only to God. They should have no ambition but to enlighten the entire world, regardless of nationality, state, city, or other locality.

Along with the spiritual responsibility in consultation comes the need for full transparency and trust. To achieve transparency, Bahá'ís strive to be aware of what is going on in their communities. If one is to offer informed advice, one needs to know what is going on. Issues must be investigated fully and completely and all must strive to see every angle, implication, and detail before decisions are made. This requires Bahá'ís to keep an open mind and to ask more questions than they can answer. Lastly, when a Bahá'í institution makes a decision through consultation, that decision becomes binding on the community it represents. When it comes to action, the community acts as one. The system is flexible enough to allow for the appeals of decisions and refinement and adjustments may be made to decisions in the future, however, all are asked to defer to the decisions of the elected institutions and to move forward as a united community under all circumstances.

TAPPING THE BENEFITS OF CONSULTATION

Of course, there is a price to pay by choosing the path of Bahá'í consultation. Many things take longer in a world of consultation. Everything is more involved. Decisions take more effort. Coordination requires patience and humility. And all of our efforts are exposed to criticism. For some who are used to always getting their own way, who truly believe they are smarter and more effective than everyone else, and who would rather not go along with someone else's plan, this price may appear too high.

The spiritual seeker believes the benefits of Bahá'í consultation far outweigh the costs, however. He sees that the benefits include better ideas, better analysis, and better results overall. To the spiritual seeker, these benefits speak for themselves. As the Bahá'í writings state, "Man must consult in all things for this will lead him to the depths of each problem and enable him to find the right solution." ('Abdu'l-Bahá, in *Lights of Guidance,* p. 228).

In terms of better ideas, this can apply to any number of fields including the political, scientific, artistic, and literary. As stated above, consultation allows the free flow of information. It breaks down barriers and inspires universal participation. It brings in a diversity of perspectives, races, genders, and differences in personal lives. Consultation not only helps us become more effective contributors, but it also nullifies our weaknesses, combines our resources, and builds on our capabilities to create something better for all of us.

Another benefit of Bahá'í consultation to consider is its focus on results. Unity is a critical element of the process. As we learn to work together in consultation, we often see the best and worst in people. But as we stick with it, as we show courage, patience, resignation, honesty, transparency, openness, and all the other qualities of God in our deliberations, we begin to see real results. We begin to see projects completed, problems solved, and issues resolved. Through this process we also see people enjoying one another more, using more of their talents and capacities for the betterment of the world, and growing and developing more effectively as a community. And when we see these results, we reinforce our commitment to consultation.

Success with consultation, therefore, builds upon itself. As with many spiritual things in life, sometimes we have to try it to begin to appreciate it. As the Bahá'í writings state, "Settle all things, both great and small, by consultation. Without prior consultation, take no important step in your own personal affairs. Concern yourselves with one another. Help along one another's projects and plans. Grieve over one another. Let none in the whole country go in need. Befriend one another until ye become as a single body, one and all ..." ('Abdu'l-Bahá, in *Lights of Guidance,* p. 178).

THE WISE MAN WHO USED CONSULTATION AT EVERY STAGE OF HIS LIFE

There was a boy who grew up in a strong Bahá'í family. The family used consultation extensively in all aspects of their lives. Whenever there was a dispute that could not be resolved between two members, the entire family would call a consultation and everyone would have a chance to offer insight, advice, and help to resolve the differences. Whenever there was a big family decision such as where they would go for a vacation, what kind of car they would buy, who would do what chores, and what types of service the family would render together, they would consult together. In fact, the family had a regular weekly consultation every Monday night after dinner. At family consultations all issues were brought up and discussed openly, fairly, and honestly. Consultation was a safe place to talk about difficult things, and it helped the family overcome hardship, maintain unity, and grow together. As the boy grew older and had to make decisions about friendships, studies, and his future, the family consultation helped him to think through those decisions more thoughtfully.

The boy also took the principles of consultation up with some of his friends in school. He formed a small council of friends that he met with every week at lunch. This little group of friends would help each other with issues, concerns, and challenges. They stayed together as a council throughout their education, even when they stopped hanging around each other as friends. That is, some of them became involved in sports, others in music, and others in technology and computers, but they all still met regularly to listen, counsel, and advise one another about questions and challenges they were facing.

When the boy grew up and became a young man, he went off to college. At his university he had to form a new friend council with some college students. He found a few friends whom he trusted and felt would take the counsel seriously. They agreed to join it and the council helped each of them deal with the pressures, tests, and challenges of life in college. They would meet every Thursday night at a coffee shop, sometimes for hours. It became a support group for all the members of the group, and it ensured that they always had a place to go when they felt overwhelmed or burdened by their experiences of becoming adults.

When the young man married and started his own family, again he formed a new council of dads that he relied on for advice on dealing with all the challenges of fatherhood and marriage. This helped him deal with the pressures of providing for a family, maintaining a healthy marriage, balancing his career, and finding time for service to the community. They would meet every Saturday morning, early before the rest of their families would wake up and their fatherly responsibilities would begin. The council of dads provided the man with an invaluable source of encouragement, inspiration, and ideas on how to be a successful father, husband, and professional.

Throughout his life, the man became very good at bringing people together to form councils for making smarter decisions and for dealing with challenges. He instituted a family council of his own with his children. He also encouraged his children to form their own council with their friends. He formed councils wherever he worked with coworkers from across the organizations. And he formed councils in his community to deal with issues in their neighborhoods or regions.

In all of these councils, the man would never restrict membership to any particular religion, gender, or background. On the contrary, he went out of his way to invite people from a diversity of cultures, experiences, and interests. He felt that by bringing together people with a variety of perspectives, they would create the best advice in whatever they did. As long as it was someone who would take the responsibility seriously, who could follow the principles of consultation, and who was willing to commit to seeing it through, he or she was invited to join.

All this experience with consultation made this man a huge asset to the Bahá'í communities. He was adept at seeking out opinions and ideas, making others feel comfortable to bring up opposing viewpoints, and finding solutions that everyone could feel good about.

By creating councils that he could rely on at every stage of his life, the man was never alone in his decisions. He always felt supported, guided, and inspired. He felt more confident and more focused in his efforts. In fact, the man attributed much of his success in life to the councils that had helped him along the way. And he counted the people who joined him as some of his closest and dearest friends.

ANALOGY OF A WELL-BUILT HOUSE

Two men built very different houses. The first man built a big house with one strong beam going through the middle. All the weight of the house's structure rested on that beam. The second man built a house built with a variety of beams, supports, and structures.

A storm came and knocked out the first man's strong beam, and the rest of the house came crashing down around him. The other man's house lost a few support beams, but it did not come crashing down. The other man's house had many other supports that worked together to compensate for those beams that had fallen down in the storm.

The spiritual seeker believes in the value of having a rich support structure across all aspects of life. He knows the danger that comes from relying too heavily on one person to make all decisions. When a storm in life comes and knocks out that one person, or when his knowledge fails, or when he loses his strength, he has no one to turn to for help. It is better to build a robust, adaptable, and smoothly functioning team that can withstand the storms of life and offset the weaknesses of any one of us. Bahá'í consultation provides the tool to bring people together at every stage of life to help us make better decisions, unify our efforts, and work together to make a better world.

CHAPTER 26:

CONNECTING WITH THE STORY OF THE BAHÁ'Í FAITH

"The Ancient Beauty hath consented to be bound with chains that mankind may be released from its bondage, and hath accepted to be made a prisoner within this most mighty Stronghold that the whole world may attain unto true liberty. He hath drained to its dregs the cup of sorrow, that all the peoples of the earth may attain unto abiding joy, and be filled with gladness."

—Bahá'u'lláh, *Gleanings from the Writings of Bahá'u'lláh,* no. 45.1

INTRODUCING A NEW APPROACH TO HISTORY

The Bahá'í approach to history is more than just a collection of facts, dates, and stories. It is more than just an interesting background. To Bahá'ís, history offers an explanation and a vision that looks backwards and forwards. It is founded on an understanding of who we are, why we exist, and what we are here to accomplish as individuals and as a global community. It unites all mankind including people from all religions, countries, races, and cultures together in a single story where each narrative has a critical part to play.

This approach to history offers a lens on the past. From a Bahá'í perspective, a divine force is actively involved in shaping the course of history. This force is what Bahá'ís call God. It desires to be known, and therefore It brings all of creation into existence. This creation is not the linear model often interpreted by limited minds. It is not a world with a starting point and an endpoint. No, this creation is bigger, more encompassing, more mysterious, and more wondrous than anything we can possibly imagine. This creation is infinite, everlasting, and eternally being renewed throughout endless worlds and limitless cycles.

Man, in this story, is the discoverer, the explorer, the wonderer, the questioner, the comprehender, the lover, and the server of creation. The Bahá'í model proposes that humanity is on a path of collective advancement that never ends—that we are growing together, maturing together, and discovering our capacities together. We are going through stages of development as a global community just as a human goes through infanthood, childhood, adolescence, adulthood, and maturity.

Bahá'ís believe that religion is progressive. That is, each religion brings knowledge and understanding to the people. And the knowledge of each religion then combines with, and builds upon, the knowledge and understanding of the past. Each religion offers wisdom and guidance for how to live, how to think, and how to serve. And each religion provides the systems and methods needed to organize, channel, and cultivate the capacities of people to reach their full potential. And yet they are all connected along fundamental truths. Newer religions reference those of the past. And those of the past reinforce and offer justification for the newer faiths. From this perspective, there is essentially one religion of God, which is progressively advanced over time with the coming of the various Messengers or Prophets.

For instance, the Zoroastrian Faith taught basic concepts of right and wrong with important teachings on good vs. evil. All other religions include this concept. The Hindu Faith brought teachings about cycles of change and transformation in the universe, and the importance of fulfilling our potential in each level of awareness. Many other religions include this idea. The Buddhist Faith brought teachings of contentment through detachment by offering paths to end suffering. Many other faiths follow these basic teachings. The Jewish Faith taught justice with the concept of an "eye for an eye" and civil society. Many communities and religions have incorporated this concept in their civil codes. The Christian Faith taught peace and forgiveness with the mandate to "turn the other cheek" and to love the poor. Many people have used the example of Jesus Christ to inspire countless acts of service and charity. The Islamic Faith taught concepts of universal tolerance for all "people of the Book." Many people were awakened to the idea of equality of all men through this faith. And the Bahá'í Faith today teaches the unity of all mankind through the concept of world citizenship, and many nations and peoples of the world are turning to this concept in order to find ways to make the world a more peaceful place.

In reality, these are just simplistic examples of what each faith teaches. The fact is, every faith brings an infinite variety of teachings and understandings that add to the tapestry of spirituality and awareness in this world, and it is necessary to appreciate each one if we are to truly understand the human experience.

Besides spiritual teachings, other elements of this world are progressive including governments, society, technology, and culture. They all go through stages of growth and development. For example, throughout human history, the concept of governance has evolved from the tribe, to the city, to the state, to the nation, and today to continental or regional blocks. In the future, Bahá'í s believe, it will extend to the entire world.

Societies have also progressed throughout history. Social progress has proven most effective when people are given the opportunity to choose their own destinies in all aspects of life. The fact is, most of the successful societies functioning at the peak of material and mental progress were also the most open, just, and free.

Technology has also progressed. Technological changes have brought humanity closer together than ever before. Today a person can travel to any point of the globe in a matter of days. He can communicate instantly with anyone in the world. With so much capacity to transmit information, people are more informed and aware of the conditions of all mankind than ever before in human history. Technology, biology, medicine, and chemistry are all working together to enable people to live longer, healthier, and more leisurely lives than ever before.

And there is incredible cultural change also taking place in the world. A new global culture has emerged in the past fifty years unlike anything in history. It is tapping into what it means to be young, and what it means to be old. It is harnessing the creativity, energy, and enthusiasm of entire generations to make this world a more interesting and entertaining place. It is hopeful, idealistic, tolerant, and united like no other movement in history.

The Bahá'í approach to history explores the impacts of all of these trends in religion, governance, society, technology, and culture, and it implies that all of this change is happening for a reason. It all has purpose, and that purpose is to see mankind reach maturity and fulfill its noble destiny. That is, humanity is being pushed to unite as world citizens whether we are aware of it or not. Humankind is coming together through culture, technology, governance, and society whether we want to or not. We are becoming one people whether we are ready or not. There is no going back. The Bahá'í student of history understands that idea, welcomes that awareness, and builds upon this reality as a foundational concept.

THE STORY OF THE BAHÁ'Í FAITH

Bahá'ís break the story of their faith into three ages: (1) the Heroic Age, (2) the Formative Age, and (3) the Golden Age. The Heroic Age of the Bahá'í Faith has passed. As a consequence, today we are living in the Formative Age. In the future, Bahá'ís believe there will be a Golden Age that will see the entire globe living with peace and justice.

The Heroic Age of the Bahá'í Faith took place between 1844 and 1921. It encompassed the ministries of the Báb, Bahá'u'lláh, and 'Abdu'l-Bahá. The Heroic Age started from the moment the Báb declared that He was the Promised One. He claimed to be the One Who had been foretold by the Messengers of the Past. His first disciple found Him in 1844. He started a religion called the Bábí Faith, and many thousands of people in Persia accepted His Cause. The Bab's mission was short-lived and dramatic. His purpose was to prepare the way for the coming of a greater Prophet Who would be the Promised One alluded to in all the religious scriptures of the past. The Heroic Age continued through the life of Bahá'u'lláh Himself, who declared that He was the Promised One foretold by the Báb. For over forty years Bahá'u'lláh wrote, taught, and ministered to His followers, and created a strong and vibrant community. This period ended with the death of His son and appointed successor, 'Abdu'l-Bahá. It is known as the Heroic Age because of the incredible sacrifices made by the Bahá'ís during this period. The lives sacrificed and blood shed by tens of thousands of martyrs of the Bábi and Bahá'í revelations made this religion real. This period set the standard for sacrifice. It showed how important it was to bring this message of peace, unity, and justice to the world. The example of the Bahá'ís and Bábis of this Age will be remembered, honored, and praised for thousands of years to come.

The Formative Age of the Bahá'í Faith started in 1921 when 'Abdu'l-Bahá appointed His Grandson Shoghi Effendi to be the Guardian of the Bahá'í Faith. Shoghi Effendi ran the administrative and spiritual affairs of the Bahá'í world until he passed away in 1957. During this time he worked tirelessly to build the worldwide Bahá'í community into a unified force for spiritual change in the world. He inspired countless Bahá'ís to pioneer to remote places in the world and help spread the teachings of Bahá'u'lláh to every corner of the globe. He also appointed individuals to be the Hands of the Cause of God. These Hands of the Cause traveled the world teaching, educating, training, inspiring, and empowering the Bahá'ís in their work. And Shoghi Effendi, as the authorized interpreter of the word of God, furthered the important work of translating the holy writings into other languages, which brought the words of Bahá'u'lláh to an ever-expanding audience. Lastly, Shoghi Effendi wrote many letters, messages, and books to help Bahá'ís understand the full impact of the Bahá'í Faith. He also explained the Administrative Order and its importance for the future of mankind.

After the passing of the Guardian of the Bahá'í Faith, the affairs of the Bahá'í Faith came under the guidance of the Universal House of Justice, which today is the supreme governing council of the Bahá'ís of the world. All Bahá'ís follow the guidance of the Universal House of Justice. This institution continues to help fulfill the promise of the Formative Age of the Bahá'í Faith. The Universal House of Justice appointed Counselors to fill the role of the Hands of Cause of God to educate, empower, and protect the Bahá'í community as it manifested the vision of Bahá'u'lláh. Today the Universal of Justice decides on matters of Bahá'í law and manages the affairs of the Bahá'í world, providing the global community with plans to implement, guidance to follow, and inspiration to sustain it. This institution is a precious gift to the Bahá'í world designated by the pen of Bahá'u'lláh Himself.

When this Formative Age completes its work, Bahá'ís look forward to the Golden Age of mankind. When the Golden Age arrives, the reality of the Bahá'í revelation will be fully realized in the world. This is what all Bahá'ís essentially work and strive to create. The details of this Age can be scarcely imagined today, but Bahá'ís fully expect to create a global society that is just, fair, free, unified, and spiritualized. It will be a tolerant society focused on harnessing the capacities of all people. It will offer a new perspective on life, work, and family. It will be centered on the children of the world, where every single child is guaranteed an education, love, encouragement, and an opportunity to manifest his or her potential in this world. It will bring about a new global system that is resistant to corruption, free of political intrigue and partisan bickering, and dedicated to maintaining peace and security of all people. This Golden Age of the Bahá'í Faith is the fulfillment of Bahá'u'lláh's vision for mankind, and it is the reason so many Bahá'ís give their time, energy, resources, and even their very lives to make it happen. For a Bahá'í, there is no greater Cause, no greater purpose, and no greater meaning in life than to work to make the Golden Age of the Bahá'í revelation into a reality.

STUDYING THE HISTORY OF THE BAHÁ'Í FAITH

There are many books one can turn to in order to gain a better understanding of Bahá'í history. Many Bahá'ís start with the famous trilogy of books written by H. M. Balyuzi, published by George Ronald (http://www.grbooks.com/). He wrote three books entitled:

- *The Báb, The Herald to the Day of Days*
- *Bahá'u'lláh, King of Glory*
- *'Abdu'l-Bahá, the Centre of the Covenant of Bahá'u'lláh*

Each book introduce us to the lives and times of the great figures of the Bahá'í Faith. They are wonderful ways to begin to gain a deeper understanding of the central figures of the Bahá'í revelation and to appreciate the sacrifices made during the Heroic Age of the Bahá'í Faith. There is also a very popular four volume set of books by Adib Taherzadeh entitled *The Revelation of Bahá'u'lláh,* also published by George Ronald.

Those who are ready to read about the Formative Age of the Bahá'í Faith can read about the life of Shoghi Effendi in *The Priceless Pearl*, written by his wife, Ruhiyyih Rabbani and published by the Bahá'í Publishing Trust UK (http://www.bahaibooks.org.uk/). This book talks about the work of building the foundation of Bahá'u'lláh's World Order and the sacrifices, inspiration, and wisdom that Shoghi Effendi provided to the Bahá'í world during his lifetime.

Students of Bahá'í history can also read some of the many stories about the Hands of the Cause of God, those individuals appointed by Shoghi Effendi to help carry out the work of building this new world system.

The Hands of the Cause include Martha Root, (1872–1939), who was a schoolteacher and newspaper reporter from Ohio, and one of the most dedicated and widely traveled of the faith's early teachers. They can read about how she traveled around the globe meeting people from every background, including many heads of state. She even taught the Bahá'í Faith to Queen Marie of Romania, who was the first monarch to accept the Bahá'í Faith.

They can read about George Townsend (1876–1957), who before he became a Bahá'í was the Canon of St. Patrick's Cathedral, which is a prestigious position in the Anglican Church. He joined the Bahá'í Faith and became one of its foremost scholars. He wrote about the relationship between Christianity and the Bahá'í Faith with a famous trilogy of books.

They can read about Louis Gregory (1874–1951), a lawyer who in 1922 was a the first African American elected to the National Spiritual Assembly of the Bahá'ís of the United States. He travelled throughout the United States promoting race unity and spiritual justice at a time of deep segregation and prejudice in American history.

They can read about Rahmatu'llah Muhajir (1923–1979), who was a fourth-generation Bahá'í from Iran. As a medical doctor he spent many years pioneering in the remote Mentawai Islands of Indonesia teaching the natives. After he was appointed a Hand of the Cause, he then tirelessly traveled the world inspiring the Bahá'ís for the rest of his life.

They can read about Enoch Olinga (1926–1979), an African believer from Uganda who was an author and a civil servant and who pioneered to Cameroon for the Bahá'í Faith. He also traveled around Africa and the world in service to the faith.

And they can read about William Sears (1911–1992), a radio and television personality in Chicago, who wrote several wonderful

Bahá'í books including *Thief in the Night* and *God Loves Laughter*. He pioneered to Africa with his family and spent much of his life traveling and serving the Bahá'ís of the world.

Learning about these important figures in Bahá'í history, along with many more who gave so much for the Bahá'í Faith, can be inspiring and empowering to any Bahá'í. What can be learned from this history is how each person who serves the Bahá'í Faith has something unique and wonderful to offer. Every soul has a contribution to make. Learning how others found a way to make their mark can inspire us to find our own way.

THE NEW BELIEVER WHO FOUND DEEPER FAITH THROUGH STUDYING THE HISTORY OF THE BAHÁ'Í FAITH

There was a woman who discovered the Bahá'í Faith and believed in its teachings, beliefs, and vision for the future. She joined the religion soon after hearing about it. As a Bahá'í, the woman strove to practice its teachings and follow its practices. She used prayer and meditation on a daily basis. She worked hard to live up to its high standards. She joined the community and worked to be of service. In the process, she felt she had been changed and had grown into a more hopeful and positive person.

But as she followed the practices and became more involved in the community, she did not really feel a deep connection with Bahá'u'lláh. Being a Bahá'í was very intellectual to her. She did not yet feel a deep connection in her heart. That is, until one night when she went to a special prayer session. This prayer session was devoted to remembering the martyrs of the Bahá'í Faith. At this special event, she heard stories from Bahá'ís, often of Persian descent, who told of family members who had been martyred or suffered great hardships for the faith. She also heard many stories read from the history books of Bahá'í Faith of those who had given their lives in dramatic and selfless ways.

As she heard these stories, she realized that the Bahá'í Faith was more than just an intellectual endeavor. For someone to give their life for such a cause there had to be more than just some good ideas in it. She realized that what these people had was a connection of the heart that was so deep, so profound, and so powerful that it inspired people to willingly make the greatest sacrifice.

These stories inspired the woman to ask herself if she was ready to make that leap of giving her heart over to Bahá'u'lláh. She wondered what that meant. She wondered what she would have to give up if she gave her heart in this way. She wondered if she was strong enough, if she would be disappointed, and if she could sustain it.

She wanted to obtain every ounce of benefit out of life as a Bahá'í, and feeling this emotional and spiritual bond seemed to be one of the most powerful forces in life. She decided it was worth trying for.

And so the woman started to offer her heart to this cause in the only place she could think to begin with, and that was in her prayers. She began to let the words of the prayers sink deeper into her heart. She let the feelings and emotions pour into her being and flood her soul. She thought of those martyrs who had given everything for this cause, and she let herself imagine what it must have taken to do such a thing. She imagined the incredible trust in God it must have demanded. She imagined the incredible longing for a connection to our source that it must have inspired. And she imagined the incredible selflessness it must have manifested in their hearts.

As she began to actively open her heart to all these feelings, she began to feel her own personal faith strengthened. She felt her convictions solidify and her confidence increase. After a time, the woman realized that this level of love and devotion was the core of all religious belief. Creating this feeling in people was what all the practices, beliefs, and vision were all about. When she opened herself to this reality, she felt her spirit grow to a whole new level of awareness and empowerment. With this feeling in her heart, nothing was impossible. With this new connection, she took her existence to a whole new reality and grew as a spiritual being in ways she could have scarcely imagined before.

In truth, through this process the woman learned what the history of spirit really meant in all religions. She felt connected to all people of faith who had sacrificed for something bigger than themselves. She was one with them across time and space.

ANALOGY OF A MAP AND THE STUDY OF HISTORY

The spiritual approach to the study of history is like getting a map for the human experience. A map gives us context. It shows us where we are in relation to other places. It shows us the possibilities, the limits, and the borders of our world. It gives us a sense for where we fit in the big scheme of things.

Studying Bahá'í history does the same thing for us. It helps place us into the big scheme of things. It explains how we got here. It helps us appreciate the levels of sacrifice and dedication required to do our job effectively. It provides an example to follow and to be inspired by, and it offers us a path forward based on those who have gone before us.

CHAPTER 27:

LIVING THE CONCEPT OF WORLD CITIZENSHIP

"The earth is but one country, and mankind its citizens."

—Bahá'u'lláh, *Gleanings from the Writings of Bahá'u'lláh,* no. 117.1

ONE PLANET, ONE PEOPLE

Many enlightened thinkers throughout history have realized one essential truth, whether it was a teaching from religion, a realization from philosophy, a conclusion from scientific evidence, or just an observation from traveling the world and getting to know people. That truth is this: We are all one. We are one people. We are one family.

The spiritual seeker sees the history of mankind as a long journey to this realization. It is a journey full of victories and setbacks, with triumphs and tragedies, sometimes with two steps forward and one step backward. It is a journey of mankind discovering the various stages of unity, starting from the family and uniting to the tribe, to the city, to the nation, to regional and cultural blocks, and eventually toward that final state: the unity of the entire world. At each stage in our collective development we have learned something new about ourselves and about our world, and at each stage we became more than we were before.

Yet, each stage required us to adapt and change. In each stage we have had to revive the concept of who we think we are and how we fit into the bigger scheme of things. We have had to adapt to a wider sense of identity. We have had to adopt larger and larger groups of people as our own. Sometimes it went smoothly as the unity made economic and political sense. Sometimes these unities were forged by the fire of various threats that brought people together. And sometimes people came together through shared values, shared institutions, and a shared vision of the future in spite of nay-sayers and cynics. Whatever the cause of this growth from age to age, the result was an ever-increasing loyalty to a wider community.

Today we find the entire world facing these same forces bringing us together. Global trade and commerce are uniting humanity and forcing new levels of economic cooperation, coordinated policy-making, and the development of international systems of justice. In addition, threats from weapons of mass destruction, religious fanaticism, and organized crime are forcing humanity to unite to protect itself through regional military alliances, multinational antiterrorism networks, and international policing institutions. And the spread of a global media, commercialism, and development of a world culture are forcing humanity to recognize shared values, appreciate the diversity of cultures, and build a new sense of common identity that crosses borders.

The spiritual seeker recognizes that the world needs a new sense of global identity to help it cope with all the changes in the world today. He sees the potential for wondrous good in the world available to us, if we could just learn how to get along and see each other as true brothers and sisters. If we could expand our loyalty to all mankind, no matter what passport we carry, no matter what language we speak, no matter what culture we are raised in, no matter what religion we follow, then we could become so much more as a human race. The spiritual seeker sees the world racing toward a decision point. Either we learn how to unite as one people, or we will destroy ourselves.

The dangers are very real to the spiritual seeker. The dangers come from the very forces that are uniting us. For example, in trade and commerce, either we learn how to regulate the global economy, or we continue toward total financial and economic collapse. Either we learn how to control and use our technical abilities to unite us and foster development, safety, and progress for all people, or we can use those same powers to oppress, pollute, and ravage the world's resources. Either we learn how to communicate in a positive and enlightened manner, or we can use our communications to spread anger, distrust, and fear amongst people. Either we can learn how to train and empower all people to lift themselves out of poverty, or we can use education to increasingly separate the haves from the have-nots and widen the gap between rich and poor. And finally, in our media and culture, either we can learn to celebrate our differences and create a noble and inspired world community, or we can choose to focus on the lowest common denominators, become slaves to our lower natures, and reduce life to a pointless pursuit of materialistic and soulless pleasures.

INTRODUCING WORLD CITIZENSHIP

The spiritual seeker sees the need for the concept of world citizenship at the core of many of our international problems. In order to address this, the concept of world citizenship has been offered as a fundamental teaching of the Bahá'í Faith. From one perspective, it can be broken down into four key components: the oneness of humanity, unity in diversity, social justice, and economic justice. Each component is related to the other, and Bahá'ís teach that they can all be brought into reality when we all, as human beings, accept our highest loyalty as citizens of the world. As the Bahá'í writings state, "Let your vision be world-embracing, rather than confined to your own self." (Bahá'u'lláh, *Tablets of Bahá'u'lláh,* p. 86).

World citizenship starts when we recognize the power of the oneness of humanity to open the hearts of all mankind. The oneness of humanity means that we think of ourselves beyond nation, race, culture, and religion. It means we find common cause to spiritualize our world one heart at a time.

World citizenship is empowered by the idea of unity in diversity. Unity in diversity is a state in which all people potentially have a voice, and our differences are celebrated. In a unified and diverse environment the various talents, faculties, traits, and capacities of all people can bring about a richer human experience across all facets of life. It requires us to let go of the things that divide us, degrade us, or hinder us from collective advancement including our prejudices, fears of our differences, ancient grudges and long-standing sources of distrust. It requires us to give everyone a chance to teach us something, to share experiences with us, and to enjoy the wonders of this world alongside us.

World citizenship is driven by the promise of social justice to bring peace in the world. Social justice means we stand up for everyone's right to think and believe for themselves. It means everyone has the right to reach their full potential as spiritual and material beings. It means men and women are given equal rights and equal opportunities to succeed. It means that differences of race and class do not give certain people special rights or selective opportunities in this world. It means we set standards for how we behave, how we treat one another, and how we serve mankind.

And world citizenship is realized when we harness the power of economic justice to remake the globe into a healthy and balanced world of opportunity for all. Economic justice is realized when all men and women have the chance to reach their full potential and make a unique contribution in the world. It requires that all people reach for greatness in whatever they choose to do. It means we are all affected when one of us experiences poverty. It means everyone works to ensure that we all have a fair shot in life including an education, basic health, and an equal chance to make a difference. It is not about a forced redistribution of wealth. Instead, it is about an inspired and willing sharing of our collective resources with all people in a spirit of service. In addition, effecting a spiritual transformation of our economy includes cultivating a new relationship between employers and employees founded on the principles of the oneness of mankind, developing a more just system of resource allocation based on fairness and capacity, building a renewed foundation of trustworthiness at all levels of society, and practicing a new consultative approach for solving problems and overcoming our challenges with a spirit of true unity.

HOW DO WE CULTIVATE WORLD CITIZENSHIP?

The spiritual seeker recognizes that becoming a world citizen is not something that happens overnight. It is something we have to work at. It requires changing our attitudes, acquiring knowledge and understanding, opening our hearts, and simply being willing to imagine a better world. This is work that the Bahá'ís are very familiar with.

As stated above, changing our attitudes is the first step to becoming a world citizen. We change our attitudes by changing the way we feel about people. We put away suspicion and fear and we learn to assume good intentions in others. We learn to overlook the faults and weaknesses of others and learn to focus on strengths and capacities. We learn to let go of ancient hatreds and cultural prejudices and together grab hold of a new cause that clears away the past and creates a new future for all of us. For Bahá'ís, this new cause is found in working to manifest the vision of Bahá'u'lláh in the world. Through this work, there are no divisions among men. We are all equal, we are all important, and we are all required to add our distinctiveness to the effort.

Bahá'í communities are generally made up of an incredible diversity of race, class, education, and experience. Just working alongside such a diverse group of people gives community members a new appreciation for the power of unity in diversity. Exposure to diversity means that many of us are more willing to read and study about different cultures, peoples, and geographies. We are more confident to travel and even live overseas not just to sightsee, but to experience the variety of the human experience firsthand. For many, being a Bahá'í is a constant cultural, intellectual, and spiritual adventure.

If we open ourselves up to the possibility of brotherhood with all peoples, we discover that all have the same capacity to love one another, to care for one another, to forgive those who have oppressed us, to inspire and encourage those who need to be uplifted, and to manifest their own potential in this world of diversity. As Bahá'is, we learn to truly love and serve humanity as spiritual beings. That is, Bahá'ís learn not just to see people who are different from us as interesting, but to see them as potentially unique, wondrous, and luminous reflections of God's qualities in the world. In this way, we learn to prefer other people before ourselves. We learn to sacrifice for the betterment of all mankind. And we learn that there is no greater cause than the cause of increasing love in the world. When we recognize all this, our hearts open up to the needs of every soul on this planet as if they were our closest and dearest companions.

Finally, world citizenship requires that we develop a sense of vision for our lives that encompasses the entire human race. We need something to work for, something to live for, and even something to die for if we are to make a difference in the world. The fact is, it can be very challenging to become a world citizen. It can be a struggle to let go of our hatreds, fears, and prejudices. The fact is, a world citizen may be asked to make great sacrifices for other people, and he or she needs a reason to do so that comes from a more inclusive understanding for what it means to be a human being.

For example, a world citizen is committed to the safety and security of all people. This may mean that we need to stand up and courageously defend the innocent against an aggressor, no matter who they are, where they live, or what passport they carry. We may even need to put our own lives on the line for people we do not know and do not really understand. In addition, we may need to sacrifice some of our comfort so that all people can have a descent standard of living or to heal some of the environmental damage our technological advancement may inflict. We may need to care for the orphans, love the neglected, educate the ignorant, free the oppressed, heal the abused, and provide opportunity for the unlucky. Oftentimes it takes a goal to strive for to keep us continuing in this important work. We want to know our efforts will not be in vain.

For Bahá'ís, that unifying goal is found through working to manifest the vision of Bahá'u'lláh for a better world—through working to create a world where no price is too high and no sacrifice is too great for the goal of seeing all of humanity united, empowered, peaceful, educated, spiritual, and enlightened. These are the tangible goals of the Bahá'í Faith, and by extension they are the goals of the spiritual seeker who accepts that faith.

As the Bahá'í writings state, "The Great Being saith: Blessed and happy is he that ariseth to promote the best interests of the peoples and kindreds of the earth. In another passage He hath proclaimed: It is not for him to pride himself who loveth his own country, but rather for him who loveth the whole world. The earth is but one country, and mankind its citizens." (Bahá'u'lláh, *Gleanings from the Writings of Bahá'u'lláh,* no. 117.1).

THE SCHOOLTEACHER WHO TAUGHT HER STUDENTS TO BECOME WORLD CITIZENS

There was a schoolteacher who loved history. She loved to teach children about the past and how it directly affected everything we are today. She enjoyed telling the stories and sharing the facts that opened the minds of young people to endless possibilities. She felt that studying history was important for young people to understand who they were, why there were here, and where they were going in life.

Unfortunately, the teacher struggled to transfer her enthusiasm for history to her students. Generally speaking, her students seemed uninterested in history. They were more interested in cell phones and videogames, schoolyard gossip and relationships, pop culture and major league sports. She became very depressed over the years. Her failure to inspire them began to make her question herself and her abilities.

At one point, the teacher did have a student who seemed to care about the world. This young student called herself a world citizen, and she was always writing papers about world peace, world governance, and world unity. The student seemed to have access to a vision that brought new energy and a new perspective to history. One day, the teacher asked her student where she got all these ideas. The young student said that the ideas were from the Bahá'í Faith. Intrigued, the teacher began to study this new religion. She soon realized that she agreed with many of the teachings and practices it stood for. After a short time, the teacher joined the Bahá'í Faith.

As a Bahá'í, the teacher began to think of new ways to inspire her students. Instead of trying to cram them full of information and data, she decided to inspire in them a sense of world citizenship. She thought that if she could make them feel ownership over history and a duty to learn from its lessons and apply them to the world, then maybe she could get the students more excited about the subject in general.

So she started to teach the children more than just knowledge about the world. She began work on the students' attitudes, feelings, and imaginations. She helped change their attitudes by encouraging an openness and enthusiasm for diversity. She invited speakers from various cultures and backgrounds to share wisdom, food, and stories from their lands. She encouraged students to empathize with people in history, to act out their lives, to put themselves in their historical shoes, and to feel emotions through role-playing. She began to help them imagine a better world. She asked them to write papers, articles, and profiles of the world they wanted to create for the future, and how they thought we could get there using the lessons of history.

All this work helped put the study of history into a bigger context for the students. The students felt more engaged with the topic. This engagement then translated into better scores on their exams, the retention of more information, and the ability to interpret events in a wider context. These results helped the teacher feel as though she was actually accomplishing something valuable in her work. In the end, the woman taught her students to become world citizens whether they realized it or not. It was a lesson they would take with them throughout the rest of their lives, and to her, this was the most important legacy she could give to them as a teacher.

ANALOGY OF THE SYMPHONY

Humanity and its different cultures and experiences can be seen as analogous to a collection of instruments and musicians in a symphony. Each instrument brings its own distinct sound to the performance, each instrument is delicately crafted and perfected, and each musician has years of training and practice. When this all comes together it makes for a magical sound that inspires the spirits of an audience.

When people become world citizens, they cease to see their own country's instruments as more important than any other instrument, and they begin to hear the full harmony of all the cultures and peoples of the world playing together in unity. Any sound that shrieks or breaks the melody—the world citizen knows—is not going to last. Therefore, any cultural elements that lead people to division and isolation from the rest, or that inspire injustice or abuse of anyone, will be washed away by the cleansing power of world citizenship as together we meld into the unified symphony of humankind.

CONCLUSION

CHAPTER 28:

FACING DOUBTS WITH COURAGE

"Only when the lamp of search, of earnest striving, of longing desire, of passionate devotion, of fervid love, of rapture, and ecstasy, is kindled within the seeker's heart, and the breeze of His loving-kindness is wafted upon his soul, will the darkness of error be dispelled, the mists of doubts and misgivings be dissipated, and the lights of knowledge and certitude envelop his being."

—Bahá'u'lláh, *The Kitáb-i-Íqán*, p. 195

THE ROLE OF DOUBT IN SPIRITUAL GROWTH

The spiritual seeker has faced many doubts in his life. In fact, it is his initial doubts about what he had been taught about faith and religion growing up that led him to his own spiritual search. He is not afraid of doubt. He is not ashamed to say that he doubts his faith, his ideas, and his convictions from time to time. Doubt is not a sign of weakness to the spiritual seeker. Instead, it is a sign of self-awareness. It is a way we overcome our past and find new and better ways to live. Doubt causes innovators to create new solutions, build new technologies, and make new discoveries. Doubt has led mankind to question its prejudices, seek answers to longstanding problems, and take a fresh look at the impossible.

For the seeker, much of his time in meditation is spent in questioning himself, his life, his beliefs, and his actions. This isn't because he is weak in his belief. It is because he is strong and he wants to stay that way. The spiritual seeker feels that the best way to keep that faith strong is to constantly examine it, probe it, explore it, and expand it as he grows and develops as a spiritual being. A doubt, from this perspective, is a question. It is a moment of reflection that ensures we are on the right path, that we have accepted the right message for this age, and that the life we live is aligned with something good and true. As the Bible says, we must continually "try the spirits whether they are of God...." (1 John 4:1). And we know they are of God by their fruits (Matthew 7:16).

As he lives out his life, the spiritual seeker recognizes that he is not perfect. He recognizes that he will fall from grace from time to time. He accepts that he will not understand the wisdom of some teachings or the full implications of his choices. And so he uses his own doubts to fuel his constant discovery, and reflection, and to make adjustments in his life. He constantly makes sure he has the strength and the courage to be different, to be honest with his faith, and to face whatever response the world might give him. He knows that if he is not willing to question his own faith, then he will not be ready when the world questions him. Therefore, channeling his doubts into study, meditation, and prayer is an important aspect of his spiritual development.

Having doubts about our faith is not a sign of confusion, it is a sign that we are thinking. It means we have taken ownership over our spiritual path and that we are seeking answers. Doubts, in this context, are spiritual questions about what we believe, what is true, and how should we live. Without such questions in our lives, we would have no spiritual destinations to strive to reach. We would have no mountains to climb, no oceans to cross, and no foundations to lay in our spiritual lives. The reality is, once we resolve these doubts, once we conquer these challenges, once we overcome our fears, we are stronger then we were before.

There is a fine line, however, between legitimate questions about deep and profound spiritual matters, and mere excuses we create to justify something we want to do. A doubt is legitimate when we are honestly seeking an answer. It is legitimate when we are willing to consider alternatives, when we put away prejudices and preconceived notions, and when we are open to wherever our spiritual search will take us. On the other hand, an excuse is often used when we seek to justify something we have already decided to do. If we have already made up our mind and we just want to find reasons to legitimize that decision, then perhaps it is an excuse. No one can tell us whether we are facing doubts or making excuses. We have to answer this question for ourselves.

RESOLVING DOUBTS

In the spiritual path, resolving doubts requires courage, humility, and openness. It takes courage to study an issue and think about it in a way that may upset one's preconceived notions or long-established worldviews. It takes humility to open our heart and mind to ideas that may imply we were wrong about something. And it takes openness to the whole story to see the bigger picture rather than focus on just one issue that we might be obsessed with.

To elaborate, courage is an essential quality to develop in overcoming our doubts because it means we have to move out of our comfort zones and expose our ideas, our thoughts, and our beliefs to the light of questioning and examination. Some people do not want to do this. They are perfectly happy to live in a bubble where they can believe whatever they want and never face rejection or criticism. Some people do not want to take the time to read things that may prove difficult to comprehend or upsetting to their own personal worldviews.

The spiritual seeker has found the courage to lay out his beliefs in this way. He reads books, studies scripture, and constantly challenges his own understandings. He finds the prospect of overturning his own understandings with some new epiphany as one of the most exciting things he could imagine in his spiritual life. As a Bahá'í, he goes to deepening classes and brings himself fully engaged to the consultative approach to study. He is never afraid to lay out his ideas for others to challenge and analyze from an open-minded perspective.

In personal meditation and prayer, humility is an important part of overcoming doubts. When we approach our quiet moments with a heart that is willing to admit that we might be wrong, that we might be limited in our understandings, that we may not have all the information, and that we may not see the big picture, then we enter the process with a humble spirit. That is, when we are humble in our spiritual search, and we are open to any ideas or conclusions that may come through the investigation process, then humility helps fertilize our souls for inspiration that can bring us whole new understandings about life and our place in the universe.

Lastly, openness is a critical element of overcoming doubts. We need to be open to inspiration wherever it may come from. As a Bahá'í, the spiritual seeker may come across several teachings, laws, and practices that he struggles to understand. He remains open to resolving these questions. He does not close the door on all the bounties that can come from being a Bahá'í, living the Bahá'í life, and contributing to realizing the vision of Bahá'u'lláh because he cannot resolve a few questions.

For the spiritual seeker this is different from blindly trusting the interpretation of another person. It is not blind faith; it is more a question of trust. The spiritual seeker believes that the Bahá'í Faith has earned his trust through the fact that its teachings, beliefs, and practices are generally logical and reasonable. That is, the Bahá'í Faith has earned his trust because the vision of Bahá'u'lláh is focused on doing something that is fundamentally good in the world. The goal is to open our hearts and our minds to truth wherever it is found. As the Bahá'í writings state, "It behooveth every man to blot out the trace of every idle word from the tablet of his heart, and to gaze, with an open and unbiased mind, on the signs of His Revelation, the proofs of His Mission, and the tokens of His glory." (Bahá'u'lláh, *Gleanings from the Writings of Bahá'u'lláh,* no. 7.1).

ADDRESSING SOME COMMON DOUBTS

There are, of course, some very common doubts that people wrestle with in the Bahá'í Faith or in any religion for that matter. The explanations offered in the Bahá'í writings may not resolve them completely for us. We may need to grow, mature, and develop before we can see the wisdom of everything. But the first step to resolving them is to explore those explanations in our minds and let their wisdom work in our hearts.

Many spiritual seekers, for example, question the existence of God, even after they become Bahá'ís. This may sound surprising to some, but it actually makes a lot of sense. If Bahá'ís believe in God as an unknowable essence, then it is only natural that we will never really feel as though we can "know" God. In fact, some of God's names include the Unsearchable, the Unknowable, the Unfathomable. Therefore, belief in God is something every honest seeker might question from time to time. It is certainly normal that we test our belief throughout our lives in order to make sure it is the right one.

In addition, some may doubt the spiritual aspects of their faith. The fact is, some people may never really feel a spiritual connection that others seem to feel. Belief may be more a matter of trust and confidence than any kind of transcendental or mystical experience. Because they do not have tangible realities to cling to, they may wonder if God really exists, or if religion is all nonsense, or if anything really happens after they die?

Even the spiritual seeker has faced this doubt from time to time. One answer that has brought him peace is that even if nothing happens after you die, he still wants to live a spiritual life of adding value to something bigger than himself. That is, even if it is just an empty void of darkness and there is no afterlife, it is not as if he is going to be embarrassed about believing in God all his life. He will not exist, so it will not matter either way. But what will matter is how having belief could have helped him in his life. If religion taught him self-discipline, offered him peace of mind, and inspired him to do great things for mankind, then his life was richer for it. If religion and faith gave him a standard to live up to that made him a more capable, aware, and complete human being, then he lived a healthier and more bountiful life for it. If it encouraged individual thought, reason, and logic in the spiritual path, then he lived a more intellectually complete life for it. If it freed him from superstitions and liberated him to decide truth for his own self, then what is the harm in that? For some spiritual seekers, these reasons alone would be enough to investigate a cause such as the Bahá'í Faith. Once this door is opened to investigating it, people begin discovering that there are profound and life-changing possibilities that come from accepting the Manifestation of God for the age and learning to live in alignment with His teachings. But getting to this latter stage takes time. Cultivating a deeper understanding and appreciation for the Message of the day can be something people engage in over a lifetime of service, study, and worship.

Of course, for others, the conclusion that following such a religion at least doesn't cause people harm – is not enough. There are some who will not believe in God unless a white-bearded figure of their imaginations floats down on a cloud into their living room and commands them to believe in him. Such people are waiting for a figment of their own imagination to appear in order to believe. They want some kind of metaphysical experience in order to be convinced.

But the spiritual seeker recognizes that metaphysical experiences are not reliable. He has seen how many throughout history have claimed to be inspired by dreams, visions, and unexplainable experiences and then gone on to plant bombs in subways or take up a sword and declare a holy war to "liberate" a far off city they have never seen. Even the miracles of Jesus did not convert everyone who saw them. The miracles of Moses did not convert the Egyptians. The miracles of Muhammad did not convince the people of Arabia. The miracles of the Buddha did not convince the people of India. The fact is, miracles and metaphysical signs from God are not enough.

As the Bahá'í writings state, "But these narratives are not decisive proofs and evidences to all; the hearer might perhaps say that this account may not be in accordance with what occurred, for it is known that other sects recount miracles performed by their founders. For instance, the followers of Brahmanism relate miracles. From what evidence may we know that those are false and that these are true? If these are fables, the others also are fables; if these are generally accepted, so also the others are generally accepted. Consequently, these accounts are not satisfactory proofs. Yes, miracles are proofs for the eyewitness only, and even he may regard them not as a miracle but as an enchantment. Extraordinary feats have also been related of some conjurors." ('Abdu'l-Baha, *Some Answered Questions,* p. 37).

For the spiritual seeker, belief in God is additive. It is not a matter of a single miracle or epiphany that leads us to discover all the answers to all of our questions about life. Belief in God often starts small and proves itself over time. When planting a seed in the ground, the farmer is trusting that a plant will grow there. But it is also his job to feed and care for that plant by providing water, sunlight, and fertile soil. It is his job to protect the plant from the elements and animals who would otherwise devour his harvest. So the spiritual seeker must plant the seed of belief in his heart and protect it, feed it, and nurture it if he wants to see it grow into a fruitful tree in this world.

People who become Bahá'ís may also have doubts that linger about which religion is actually right or wrong. Oftentimes they may have been told that leaving their specific religious community (or denomination) would mean they were going to hell for eternal damnation. Someone telling a person this with conviction can cause a deep-seated angst in even the most spiritually aware person. Therefore, some might still have a question in their heart about whether they are joining a cult, following a false prophet, or obeying the antichrist if they have been raised to fear such things.

The spiritual seeker has several responses to these doubts. First of all, he is detached from what other people tell him. He studies issues with an open mind for himself, and comes to his own conclusions. In addition, the spiritual seeker studies the actual scripture on perplexing matters, instead of just listening to people's individual interpretations. Once he studies these questions of the Bible in the light of the Bahá'í Faith, for example, he learns that the Bahá'ís have examined this issue in detail and have come to very different conclusions about what these prophesies refer to. For example, the Bible says that the antichrist must deny that Jesus is the Christ (1 John 2:22), that false prophets arise from the Christian community (2 Peter 2:1), that the devil can have no truth in him (John 8:44). Then he learns that Bahá'u'lláh upheld that Jesus was the Christ, that Bahá'u'lláh came from the Muslim community, and that Bahá'u'lláh teaches the value of love, peace, unity, and the divine inspiration behind Christianity. Therefore by the Bible's standard, Bahá'u'lláh cannot be a false prophet or the antichrist.

Secondly, the spiritual seeker can just look at what this kind of belief says about the religion you believe in. The Bahá'í Faith is a tolerant, intelligent, mature, and thoughtful faith focused on making the world a better place. If this is not good, then what is? If God is really so unjust, unfair, childish, small-minded, and jealous as to condemn a person to hell for not accepting one sect of one religion, then what kind of God is that? Any All-Powerful Being that sends people to eternal torment for such a reason is not worth worship. It is not love. It is not just. It is not right. It is not God. The spiritual seeker believes that this kind of religious supremacy-thinking is not healthy for anyone, no matter what religion they come from. In fact, the darkest histories of all faiths have come from such a mentality. It is an interpretation created to instill fear in the followers and keep them in line, and often used to oppress, resent, and eventually destroy cultures and communities that are different. Therefore, such doubts spring from a vision of the world that is not an empowering, inspiring, and spiritualizing message.

Finally on this matter, the spiritual seeker does not put a lot of stock in what religious leaders tell him because of his study of history. He has seen the poor track record of religious leaders throughout time when it comes to accepting a new religion. The fact is, religious leaders have the most to lose when a new religion comes, so they are often the ones who work the hardest to undermine and destroy it. It was religious leaders who persecuted Jesus and convinced the Roman governor that He was a threat. It was religious leaders who convinced Pharaoh to persecute Moses and His people. It was the religious leaders who led the people to rise up against Muhammad and His followers and drove them out of Mecca in the dead of night. In the process, too many of the religious leaders have failed the test of wisdom when it comes to honestly evaluating new religions. Therefore the spiritual seeker takes what they say with a grain of salt.

Another doubt that many spiritual seekers have is whether or not they can live up to the Bahá'í standards. Some seekers find the laws against drinking alcohol, avoiding sexual relations outside of marriage, and not backbiting, to be unfamiliar, inhibiting, and difficult to understand. But the spiritual seeker believes that we do not have to understand the wisdom of every law in order to accept the cause of Bahá'u'lláh.

But even if he is not perfect, the spiritual seeker still sees the vision of Bahá'u'lláh as important to work for. He knows that his sins are between him and God. The spiritual seeker believes that if he does his part to live up to the standards of the faith as much as he can in his life, then maybe the next generation will do better than he did. Maybe that next generation will be more aligned then he was. It is not an all-or-nothing equation. Instead, it is a step-by-step, day-by-day, process of growing, developing, and improving throughout the course of life.

Lastly, many spiritual seekers struggle with doubts about whether they can deal with the tests that come from being among the first of a new spiritual community. The fact is, it can be hard to be the first Bahá'í in your family, in your neighborhood, in your workplace, or even in your city. The reality is that in the early days of this religion, there are not a lot of amenities to rely on. There are few material and social support activities that people might find in more established communities. The spiritual seeker appreciates the desire for these things, but he is not worried about not having them. He knows that we will get there. And when we do have them, the Bahá'í amenities will be open to people of all faiths to enjoy. Therefore, when people join the Bahá'í Faith they are likely not joining for the social or the material benefits. They are rather doing so because they believe it is true. They are doing so because the vision of Bahá'u'lláh is something that they want to realize.

We also need to realize that there are advantages to being the first of a new community. As early believers, we have the opportunity to make a bigger impact and contribute a more lasting legacy to this new faith community. As the first Bahá'ís we have the opportunity to build things the way we think they should be from the ground up. This kind of attitude can help becoming a Bahá'ís feel exciting and inspiring.

Of course, being among the first to accept a new religion takes incredible courage and fortitude. The fact is, being the first Bahá'í often means facing misunderstanding, rejection, prejudice, mischaracterization, and even persecution and intolerance. These tests can be difficult to overcome. It takes perseverance in order to stick with it over the years, through good times and bad. In many ways, staying in the Bahá'í Faith is like staying in a marriage. We often join it with rose-colored glasses, but we soon realize that we are just imperfect people trying to figure this thing out. The next step is to find a way to make it work, to add value, and to grow in a way that keeps us aligned. If we do not then we risk drifting away from each other and breaking the unity in the relationship. But if we do find a way to make it work, then we become stronger, more faithful, and more capable people in the world.

Of course, the spiritual seeker understands that mankind often resists new religions, and that this is just part of the price we pay for being among the first to accept a renewed truth. It is the same price paid by the early followers of Moses who wandered homeless in the desert with Him for years. It is the same price paid by the early Christians who were forced to meet in secret caves outside Rome in order to hide from the authorities. It is the same price paid by those first followers who fled with Muhammad to Medina in the dark of night. It is the same price paid by the early followers of Bahá'u'lláh who continue to this day to be denied basic human rights in Iran, the land of the faith's birth.

The list of people who have given everything for causes of faith, truth, and social justice throughout human history is long. Human beings are capable of amazing acts of nobility when called to it.

'Abdu'l-Bahá states, "Let your ambition be the achievement on earth of a Heavenly civilization! I ask for you the supreme blessing, that you may be so filled with the vitality of the Heavenly Spirit that you may be the cause of life to the world." ('Abdu'l-Bahá, *Paris Talks*, no. 31.10).

THE WOMAN WHO CREATED HER OWN UNIQUE FAITH

There was a woman who had spent a lot of time thinking about the type of religion she wanted for herself. She had analyzed the world's faiths and found the teachings she liked in them. In the process, she disregarded the teachings that she did not like. She had also analyzed many of the causes and social movements around the world and adopted many of their goals and objectives into her personal ideology. Throughout this process of personal discovery, the woman spent a lot of time creating a detailed and elaborate framework for understanding her world and realizing meaning within it. She was willing to question every assumption and open any dialog in order to refine and evolve her personal ideology.

In the end she felt she had developed a fusion of all the world's religious teachings that was adapted to the values of today's world, and she was very excited about it. The woman then dedicated much of her life to sharing her ideology with people. She wrote a book and started giving talks to people across the country in coffee shops, churches, on college campuses, and in libraries.

Yet after many years, the woman tired of promoting her book and living on the lecture circuit. Sometimes she felt as though she was working uphill against the entire human race. She was teaching about the unity of all religions when all of mankind seemed to be ever more divided by religion. She was teaching about the unity of all mankind, when all of mankind seemed ever more divided by nationalism and ethnocentrism. She was teaching about spiritual awareness when all of mankind seemed ever more enslaved by materialism. Her book was just one small drop of water trying to move an ocean of intransigence. She became discouraged and doubted that she could ever make a difference.

One day, the woman came across a very inquisitive attendee in one of her lectures. The attendee was very polite but asked a lot of questions. These questions were very profound and offered the woman a chance to expound on some of the most intricate aspects of her ideology. At the end of the talk the woman invited the inquisitive attendee to join her for dinner and continue their discussion.

Over dinner, the woman learned that this attendee was a Bahá'í. The woman had heard a little about the Bahá'í Faith, but did not know much. As she learned more about the Bahá'í Faith from her new friend, the woman discovered that it was founded on many of the same principles that she had put into her own ideology. The woman was very intrigued and wanted to learn more.

As the woman learned more, she realized that beyond the principles that she agreed with, there were many things that she did not agree with. There were some teachings about personal morality that she did not think fit with a modern life. And there were was some rules that she did not think made sense. Still, she kept investigating the Bahá'í Faith because she felt that this cause was working for the same goals and ideals that she believed in.

As she studied, prayed, and meditated about the Bahá'í Faith, the woman began to realize that this cause was much bigger than just a set of beliefs that she partly agreed with. It was a movement. In fact, there were millions of people working together from nearly every corner of the globe who shared in the same beliefs, held themselves to the same standard, and worked to realize the same vision for a better world.

The woman realized that she was holding herself back from joining this cause because she had attachments to her own understandings of a few teachings and rules. Since the Bahá'í Faith seemed immensely practical and logical on so many fronts, the woman began to wonder if the Bahá'í reasoning behind the items that she did not agree with might be practical and logical too. She began to wonder if she might be wrong about a few of her assumptions. She wondered if she was being held captive by her own ego from fully appreciating the wisdom of these laws.

Eventually the woman did become a Bahá'í because so much in the faith's teachings aligned with what she wanted for the world. As she grew, developed, and matured as a spiritual being within the Bahá'í Faith, the woman did come to resolutions on most her questions, but not all of them. When it came to some issues, the woman just trusted in God that the reasons were sound and that she might not understand them until she reached the next world.

ANALOGY OF SWIMMING

Overcoming our doubts is very similar to the first time we learn how to swim. No matter how much someone explains it to us, there is no way we can really know what the act of swimming feels like. No matter how much we hear it described, we can never really know what it feels like to float and move about in water until we actually jump in and experience it for ourselves. Many have their doubts about whether they can swim or not even after they have jumped in. This is because we cannot learn to tread water and swim until we get in and start practicing. Therefore, sometimes we have to trust in our ability to learn in order to have the courage to even get into the water.

The same thing is true with joining the Bahá'í Faith. A spiritual seeker can have every question answered, every concern addressed, every idea explained over and over until their ears bleed, but until they jump in and join in the work of making Bahá'u'lláh's vision a reality, they may never really get it. They may never really understand what it means to be a Bahá'í until they join it, practice it, and live it.

CHAPTER 29:

TAKING THE NEXT STEPS

"Through the Teachings of this Daystar of Truth every man will advance and develop until he attaineth the station at which he can manifest all the potential forces with which his inmost true self hath been endowed."

—Bahá'u'lláh, *Gleanings from the Writings of Bahá'u'lláh,* no. 27.5

WELCOME TO A NEVER-ENDING JOURNEY

This book has looked at three main components of Bahá'í life. We have examined the beliefs that animate the spirit of the Bahá'í Faith. These beliefs can help us understand our world, comprehend our nature, and discover our capacity.

We have also explored the practices that channel the energy of the Bahá'í Faith. These practices include prayer, fasting, and teaching. These practices help us refine our characters, improve our capabilities, and empower our spirits.

And we have presented the vision of Bahá'u'lláh, which inspires the Bahá'í Faith. The vision of Bahá'u'lláh includes building a global community to unite humanity, creating an adaptive administrative order to channel our efforts, and cultivating the concept of world citizenship in order to inspire a collective sense of responsibility. The vision of Bahá'u'lláh provides a path to fulfillment for mankind that is practical, hopeful, and engaging.

As we have explored the various elements of the Bahá'í Faith, we have been accompanied by the spiritual seeker. The spiritual seeker has offered us a view into a heart that is discovering its true potential in life. We have seen how he approaches every aspect of the spiritual journey with an open mind, a detached heart, and a willing spirit. His open mind is manifested in his willingness to explore new explanations and entertain new interpretations. His detached heart is manifested in his ability to let go of his materialistic and egotistical attachments and find spiritual goals to strive for. And his willing spirit is manifested in his capacity to try to live the life, practice the teachings, and follow the guidance of Bahá'u'lláh.

Throughout all of it, the spiritual seeker has shown us what it means to take ownership of our own search. He understands that no one can ever save our souls for us. Instead, we must heal our own spirits from the darkness of selfishness, isolation, numbness, resentment, fear, and self-absorption. We alone should decide what to believe, how to serve, and how to live. While we may consult with people from time to time, we cannot rely on anyone else to tell us what to do when it comes to our own personal spiritual search. We must rely on our own spirits to guide us throughout the entire process.

MAKING A CHOICE

As the spiritual seeker explores the Bahá'í Faith, he discovers various options for moving forward. Bahá'ís believe that everyone needs to follow their own individual investigation of truth. The fact is, all aspects of the Bahá'í Faith are available to all people. You do not have to be a Bahá'í to agree with the Faith's beliefs. You do not need to sign a card to practice its teachings. And you do not need to be a Bahá'í to want to manifest the vision of Bahá'u'lláh in the world. Bahá'ís invite everyone to study their Faith and take what they want from its vast wealth of ideas, concepts, practices, and vision for the world. Therefore the seeker might choose one of many paths in his investigation. For example, if he is not ready to accept the faith, he can live as a friend of the Bahá'ís, perhaps serving alongside them and mutually learning from their shared experiences. If he is curious to learn more and see if this faith is right for him, he can become an active seeker of the Bahá'í Faith. Lastly, if he finds that he truly believes this faith to be from God, he can become a member of the worldwide Bahá'í community and commit himself to continuing his spiritual journey using the toolkit provided by this Faith for the advancement of his spirit and the development of a whole new world civilization.

The first option, to become a friend of the Bahá'í Faith, is a starting-point for many people who encounter this vast faith. The point here is to realize that Bahá'ís want to work with all people from all backgrounds. They want to serve alongside those whose causes, issues, and movements align with the teachings and vision of the faith for the world.

Another option is to actively investigate the Bahá'í Faith. Spiritual seekers who look at this faith might be intrigued by one aspect or another of this faith, and want to know more about it. Bahá'ís invite seekers to learn more about the community and its teachings, practices, and vision. The fact is, the Bahá'í Faith is a community for learning and development. Therefore everyone's questions and concerns are welcome. All are invited to challenge the Bahá'í beliefs and viewpoints in a spirit of honest discovery and exploration of the truth.

The last option is to actually join the Bahá'í Faith. For some, this is an easy choice. They have been looking for a religion like this all their life. For others it takes some time. Bahá'ís believe that no one should feel compelled to join the Bahá'í Faith. Bahá'ís believe that individuals should *want* to become Bahá'ís. They should want to accept the beliefs, live the practices, and embrace the vision of Bahá'u'lláh because they want something better in the world, not because anyone told them they had to.

In the end, the goal is that each person decide for themselves, and that each investigates the truth in their own way. When we use wisdom in our spiritual search, we are open to wherever that journey takes us. Wisdom demands patience, open-mindedness, and commitment to seeing the search through to the end. It is an essential condition for discovering reality. But it must be actively practiced. We cannot rely on others to tell us what to believe in this process. As the Bahá'í writings state, "Be ye guided by wisdom in all your doings, and cleave ye tenaciously unto it." (Bahá'u'lláh, *Gleanings from the Writings of Bahá'u'lláh*, no. 96.4).

ABOUT THE AUTHOR

Nathan Thomas is the author of several books about the Bahá'í Faith. With over a decade of experience in technology and media, he is the founder of Greysands Media, LLC, and the creator of the WhyUnite Project. Nathan grew up in an active Bahá'í family and in his youth traveled widely serving Bahá'í communities in many capacities. Today, he works as a product leader, consultant, and writer on various topics. He also spends his free time enjoying skiing, hiking, and other outdoors activities with his wife and children. Nathan holds a graduate degree from Georgetown University and an undergraduate degree from the University of Washington.

WhyUnite?
because your journey
matters to the world.

Made in the USA
Coppell, TX
11 October 2021